Praise for

The Age of the Strongman

"In telling us about strongmen who dominate politics around the world, Gideon Rachman paints a picture that is at turns illuminating and terrifying. A must-read."

—Peter Frankopan, author of *The Silk Roads:*
A New History of the World

"Drawing on a wide range of sources, and providing a truly global perspective, Rachman illuminates the common instincts, tactics, and behavior that link leaders as diverse as Trump, Putin, Xi, and Modi."

—Anne Applebaum, author of *Twilight of Democracy*

"To understand the chilling stakes of the global Great Game defining this century—the battle between autocracies and democracies—you need only turn to Rachman's magisterial and deftly written book."

—Catherine Belton, author of *Putin's People: How the KGB*
Took Back Russia and Then Took On the West

"It was not long ago that most commentators thought globalization had triumphed over nationalism and the world was heading towards some version of liberal democracy. Today, we are in the midst of a vigorous resurgence of nationalism led by authoritarian strongmen. This is partly because many people have failed to benefit from economic growth, and their aspirations have been dashed. But it is also because there is now a supply of powerful authoritarian, nationalist ideas. This readable book does an admirable job of providing the lay of the land and highlighting the importance of the battle of ideas for the future of our institutions and norms."

—Daron Acemoglu, coauthor of *Why Nations Fail*
and *The Narrow Corridor*

"When it comes to making sense of today's world, Gideon Rachman is in a league of his own. He is sharp, original, and unsentimental. Where others see a new clash between democracy and authoritarianism, he describes the rise of strongman politics as a defining feature of both authoritarian regimes and many of the world's largest democracies. And the bad news is that the global revolt against the separation of powers and liberal constitutionalism has good chances of succeeding."
—Ivan Krastev, coauthor of *The Light that Failed*

"A superb and scintillating portrait of leaders who have upended the smug consensus of globalization."
—Shruti Kapila, author of *Violent Fraternity: Indian Political Thought in the Global Age*

"An illuminating blend of dark warnings about the present and optimism that strongman rule can never prevail in the long term."
—*Kirkus Reviews*

The Age of the Strongman

Also by Gideon Rachman

*Easternization: Asia's Rise and America's Decline
from Obama to Trump and Beyond*

Zero-Sum Future: American Power in an Age of Anxiety

The Age of the Strongman

HOW THE CULT OF THE LEADER THREATENS DEMOCRACY AROUND THE WORLD

Gideon Rachman

Other Press
New York

First published in 2022 by Bodley Head, an imprint of Vintage.
Vintage is part of the Penguin Random House group of companies.

Production editor: Yvonne E. Cárdenas
This book was set in 11.5 / 14pt Dante MT Std
by Jouve UK Ltd, Milton Keynes.

10 9 8 7 6 5 4 3 2 1

Library of Congress Cataloging-in-Publication Data
Names: Rachman, Gideon, author.
Title: The age of the strongman : how the cult of the leader threatens
democracy around the world / Gideon Rachman.
Description: New York : Other Press, 2022. | Originally published:
London : The Bodley Head, 2021.
Identifiers: LCCN 2021052765 (print) | LCCN 2021052766 (ebook) |
ISBN 9781635422801 (hardcover) | ISBN 9781635422818 (ebook)
Subjects: LCSH: Authoritarianism. | Heads of state—Biography. | Charisma
(Personality trait)—Political aspects. | World politics—21st century.
Classification: LCC JC480 .R34 2022 (print) | LCC JC480 (ebook) |
DDC 320.53—dc23 / eng / 20211210
LC record available at https:/ / lccn.loc.gov / 2021052765
LC ebook record available at https:/ / lccn.loc.gov / 2021052766

In memory of Jack Rachman (1938–2021)

Contents

Introduction

In the spring of 2018, the White House was preparing for a summit between Donald Trump and Kim Jong-un. In the Old Executive Office Building, where the US president's national security staff work, one of Trump's aides remarked to me, with a slightly sheepish smile: "The president enjoys dealing face-to-face with authoritarian leaders."

It was clear that Trump's fondness for dictators made even some of his senior staff squirm. The unspoken thought, left hanging in the White House air, was that Trump himself had introduced some of the habits of a dictatorship into the heart of the world's greatest democracy. The president's wild rhetoric, his fondness for military parades, his tolerance for conflicts of interest and intolerance for journalists and judges are all features of the "strongman style" in politics – a style that, until recently, was thought to be alien to the mature democracies of the West.

But Trump was in tune with his times. Since 2000 the rise of the strongman leader has become a central feature of global politics. In capitals as diverse as Moscow, Beijing, Delhi, Ankara, Budapest, Warsaw, Manila, Riyadh and Brasilia, self-styled "strongmen" (and, so far, they are all men) have risen to power.

Typically, these leaders are nationalists and cultural conservatives, with little tolerance for minorities, dissent or the interests of foreigners. At home, they claim to be standing up for the common man against the "globalist" elites. Overseas, they posture as the embodiment of their nations. And, everywhere they go, they encourage a cult of personality.

The Age of the Strongman began long before Trump won the White House. It will continue to be a central theme of world politics in the post-Trump era. The two emerging superpowers of the twenty-first century, China and India, have both fallen prey to strongman politics.

Although they operate in very different political systems, Xi Jinping and Narendra Modi have led their countries towards a more personalized style of leadership that embraces nationalism, a rhetoric of strength and a fierce hostility to liberalism. The two most important powers on the eastern borders of the European Union, Russia and Turkey, are run by strongman leaders. Both Vladimir Putin and Recep Tayyip Erdoğan have now been in power for the best part of twenty years. The strongman style has entered the EU itself through Hungary's Viktor Orbán and Poland's Jaroslaw Kaczynski. Even Britain's Boris Johnson has flirted with this style of politics – in his attitudes to law, diplomacy and dissent within his own party. Latin America's two largest countries, Brazil and Mexico, are currently led by Jair Bolsonaro and Andrés Manuel López Obrador (popularly known as Amlo). Bolsonaro is on the far right; Amlo is on the populist left. But both leaders fit the strongman template, encouraging a cult of personality and contempt for state institutions.

This international pattern underlines a central theme of this book: the strongman style is not confined to authoritarian systems. It is now also common among elected politicians in democracies. A strongman leader operating in a democracy, such as Donald Trump, faces institutional constraints that do not inhibit the likes of Xi Jinping or Vladimir Putin. But the instincts of a Trump, a Duterte or a Bolsonaro are disconcertingly similar to strongman leaders in China and Russia.

The rise of strongman leaders across the world has fundamentally changed world politics. We are now in the midst of the most sustained global assault on liberal democratic values since the 1930s. From the wreckage of the Second World War, political freedom advanced around the world for roughly sixty years. The progress was unsteady, and definitions of democracy are imprecise, but the overall direction of travel was clear. In 1945, there were just twelve democracies in the world. In the year 2002, that figure had risen to ninety-two, exceeding the number of autocracies for the first time ever.[1]

Since then, the group of countries formally defined as democracies has stayed just ahead of autocratic regimes. But a process of democratic erosion has set in. Freedom House, which reports annually on political liberty around the world, pointed out that 2020 was the fifteenth consecutive year of declines in global freedom. After the post-Cold War surge in civil and political liberties, the tide turned in 2005. In every year since then, the number of countries where freedom has diminished has been larger than those experiencing an increase in political and civil liberties. As Freedom House put it, "The long democratic recession is deepening."[2] The rise of strongman leaders has been central to this process. That is because the political style of the strongman puts the leader's instincts above the law and institutions.

Today's strongman leaders are operating in a global political environment that is very different from that of the dictators of the 1930s. Wars between great powers are no longer common. Globalization has transformed the world economy. The spread of international law has created new expectations about how international leaders behave. But the technologies of the twenty-first century are also handing strongman leaders new ways of communicating directly with the masses, as well as dangerous new tools of social control – in particular the ability to monitor the movements and behavior of citizens. As these tools are deployed, they could strengthen the twenty-first century's authoritarian turn.

Joe Biden has made the global promotion of democracy a central goal of his presidency. But he has come to power in the midst of the Age of the Strongman. Populist and authoritarian leaders are now shaping the direction of world politics. They are riding a tide of resurgent nationalism and cultural and territorial conflict that may be too powerful to be turned back by Biden's reassertion of liberal values and American leadership.

Even in the US itself, Biden's victory has not definitively turned the page on strongman politics. Donald Trump did well enough in the 2020 presidential election to spark immediate talk of him running for the presidency again in 2024. Even if Trump himself pulls back from frontline politics, future Republican contenders are likely to embrace the political formula he has identified.

Chinese nationalists frequently portray Biden as an old, weak leader, presiding over an America that is facing irreversible decline. By contrast, China portrays itself as a resurgent power, under a strong and vigorous leader. In the emerging world order, the president of China may soon contest the title routinely bestowed on the president of the United States – the "most powerful man in the world."

The central challenge for Biden as president will be to demonstrate the vitality of liberal democracy both at home and abroad. If he fails, the Biden presidency may prove to be just an interlude in the Age of the Strongman.

If political liberals are to win the battle with strongman politics, they need to understand what they are dealing with. This book will attempt to answer three central questions about the Age of the Strongman. When did the strongman tendency take hold? What are its main characteristics? And why did it happen?

On December 31, 1999, Vladimir Putin came to power in Russia. He was to become an important symbol and even an inspiration for a new generation of would-be authoritarians who admire his nationalism, his daring, his willingness to use violence and his contempt for "political correctness."

But in his early years in power, Putin was keen to be seen as a reliable partner in an established world order. When Bill Clinton met him at the Kremlin in June 2000, the US president declared his Russian counterpart "fully capable of building a prosperous, strong Russia, while preserving freedom and pluralism and the rule of law."[3] At his first meeting with George W. Bush in 2001, Putin impressed the US president, who remarked: "We had a very good dialogue. I got a sense of his soul."

Putin only truly emerged as a foe of the US-led order with a speech denouncing America in Munich in 2007, followed by Russia's military assault on neighboring Georgia in 2008. From then on, Putin's bombastic and aggressive political style seemed anomalous set alongside the cautious pragmatism of the other key world leaders of the time: Barack Obama in the US, Angela Merkel in Germany and Hu Jintao in China. Merkel dismissed Putin as a leader using nineteenth-century means to solve twenty-first-century problems.[4] But rather than being an anachronism, Putin was a harbinger of things to come. Symbolically, he had taken power at the dawn of the twenty-first century.

In 2003, three years after Putin took power in Russia, Recep Tayyip Erdoğan became prime minister of Turkey. As with Putin, Erdoğan's embrace of the strongman style took a while to emerge. Initially widely hailed in the West as a liberal reformer, Erdoğan has become increasingly autocratic over two decades in power – imprisoning journalists and political rivals, purging the army, the courts and the civil service, building himself a massive palace in Ankara, and embracing a paranoid and conspiratorial world view.

Russia and Turkey are both big countries with economies large enough to qualify for membership of the G20. But they are no longer superpowers. So the moment at which the Age of the Strongman became truly entrenched as a global phenomenon is best pinpointed to 2012: the year that Xi Jinping took power in China.

In the decades that followed the death of Mao Zedong in 1976, the Chinese Communist Party had carefully moved towards a more collective style of leadership. But although China is now an unrecognizably richer and more sophisticated country than it was in Mao's era, President Xi is clearly nostalgic for some of the Maoist themes of his youth. Under his leadership, the party propaganda machine began to create a cult of personality around "Xi Dada" (Uncle Xi). The move towards strongman leadership was cemented when presidential term limits were abolished in 2018 – potentially allowing Xi to rule for life.

Asia's other emerging superpower, India, followed a similar path in 2014 with the election of Narendra Modi, leader of the Hindu nationalist BJP. As an opposition leader, Modi had been sufficiently controversial to be banned from entering the US because of concerns about his role in an anti-Muslim pogrom in his home state of Gujarat in 2002. As India's leader, he positioned himself as the man who would stand up to the nation's enemies at home and abroad. His willingness to bomb alleged terrorist bases in Pakistan in 2019 thrilled many Indians and set the stage for a successful re-election campaign, in which Modi assured voters: "When you vote for the Lotus [his party's symbol], you are not pushing a button but pressing a trigger to shoot terrorists in the head."

In 2015, the strongman style also made an important breakthrough inside the European Union, which styles itself as a club of liberal democracies. That year Viktor Orbán, Hungary's increasingly authoritarian prime minister, became a hero for the populist right in the West by leading the campaign to stop the arrival of refugees and migrants from the Middle East. In that same year, Law and Justice, a populist right-wing party led by Jaroslaw Kaczynski, won both presidential and parliamentary elections in Poland.

Europe's migration crisis also served as the backdrop to Britain's Brexit referendum in June 2016. The Leave campaign led by Boris Johnson capitalized on fear of Muslim immigration, claiming falsely that

Turkey was poised to join the EU and would swamp Britain with new migrants. Vote Leave's chosen slogan "Take Back Control" was a potent vote winner powering the campaign to a surprise victory. Steve Bannon, Trump's campaign manager in 2016, later claimed that the moment he knew Trump would win the presidency was when Britain voted for Brexit.

So when Trump did indeed win the White House in November 2016 he was – in some ways – just part of an established global trend. But the unique economic and cultural power of the US meant that Trump's ascent changed the atmosphere of global politics, strengthening and legitimizing the strongman style, and giving rise to a wave of emulators.

Trump's first overseas visit as president was to Saudi Arabia in May 2017. In that same year Crown Prince Mohammed bin Salman became the de facto leader of that country – the richest and most powerful Arab nation. The new leader swiftly built a global profile of a sort that was unprecedented among the secretive and introverted Saudi royal family. MBS, as he became known, was hailed by some in the West as just the kind of authoritarian reformist that Saudi Arabia needed – until the murder and dismemberment of Jamal Khashoggi, a dissident journalist, shocked the crown prince's Western fans. When MBS was embraced by a laughing Vladimir Putin at the next G20 summit, the image seemed to sum up the lawlessness and impunity of the Age of the Strongman.

Brazil, the largest country in Latin America, fell to the lure of strongman politics in 2018 with the election of Jair Bolsonaro as president. The "Trump of the tropics" emerged from a career spent on the obscure fringes of right-wing politics to win the presidential election, after adopting many of the themes and slogans of Trumpism – denouncing "political correctness," "globalism," the "fake-news media" and environmental NGOs, while embracing gun owners, evangelicals, ranchers and the state of Israel.

Africa in 2018 seemed to offer some relief from the onward march of strongman politics. Abiy Ahmed, the new leader of Ethiopia – the second most populous country on the continent – gained international attention by releasing political prisoners and ending a long war with Eritrea. He was rewarded with the Nobel Peace Prize in 2019. But the following year, the Ethiopian leader launched a military campaign against rebels in Tigray province, which led to thousands of deaths and allegations of war crimes. Abiy's about-face raised fears that he would be the latest world leader to be hailed in the West as a liberal reformer only to turn into a strongman autocrat.

This tendency for Western commentators to initially mistake strongman leaders for liberal reformers is something of a pattern. When Erdoğan first came to power in Turkey, he was described in the *New York Times* as "an Islamic politician who favors democratic pluralism."[5] In a similar vein, Nicholas Kristof, a *New York Times* columnist, predicted in 2013 that Xi "would spur a resurgence of economic reform and probably some political easing as well." He expressed the hope that under Xi "Mao's body will be hauled out of Tiananmen Square."[6] Two years later, Thomas Friedman, another influential *New York Times* columnist, portrayed Crown Prince Mohammed bin Salman as a reforming whirlwind, "on a mission to transform how Saudi Arabia has been governed."[7] In 2017, as complaints about MBS's human-rights record mounted, Friedman appeared to wave away these objections, writing that "Perfect is not on the menu here. Someone had to do this job – wrench Saudi Arabia into the twenty-first century."[8]

And then there was the British columnist who welcomed Narendra Modi's rise to power in 2014 with an article headlined: "India needs a jolt and Modi is a risk worth taking." Who was that? Me, actually. I also described the Indian leader's rise from humble tea seller to the leader of the country as "thrilling."[9] Today, having witnessed Modi's cavalier attitude to civil rights, I would choose a different word.

Looking back at this catalogue of naive predictions and dashed hopes, it is interesting to ask why Western commentators kept getting it wrong. In retrospect, I think it was a mixture of overconfidence in the power of liberal political and economic ideas born from "victory" in the Cold War and wishful thinking. As a result, Western opinion-formers were slow to grasp that the global tide was turning against liberalism. By 2020, however, a generation after Putin took power, it was hard to miss what was happening. Liberal values such as freedom of speech, independent courts and minority rights were under assault all over the world.[10]

This bleak trend leads on to two further questions: what is strongman politics and why is it on the rise?

★

The argument that we are now living in an Age of the Strongman is open to an obvious objection: is it really possible to compare democratically elected leaders such as Trump or Modi with unelected autocrats like Xi or MBS?

Such comparisons need to be handled with care and a sense of proportion, but I believe they are valid – and, indeed, vital. The strongman leaders discussed in this book are part of a continuum. At one end, there are unchallenged autocrats such as the leaders of China and Saudi Arabia. Then there are figures in the middle like Putin and Erdoğan. They are subject to some of the constraints of a democracy, such as elections and limited press freedom; but they are also able to imprison opponents and to rule for decades. Then there are politicians who operate in democracies but who display contempt for democratic norms and who seem intent on eroding them: Trump, Orbán, Modi and Bolsonaro are at this end of the spectrum.

This book is not intended to be a guide to the world's dictators, however. While I discuss strongman leaders like Donald Trump and Benjamin Netanyahu, I have excluded a tyrant such as Kim Jong-un, and other thuggish leaders, such as Alexander Lukashenko of Belarus or Hun Sen of Cambodia. *Age of the Strongman* describes the rise of a new generation and type of nationalist and populist leader, linked by their contempt for liberalism and their embrace of new methods of authoritarian rule. Since the beginning of the twenty-first century, the strongman phenomenon has taken hold in almost all the world's major power centers: the US, China, Russia, India, the EU and Latin America. By contrast, Hun Sen and Lukashenko control small states and were both in power by the 1990s; the Kim dynasty has run North Korea since 1948. These three leaders all have strongman traits, but they are not central to the change in the climate of global politics over the last twenty years.

Some British readers will raise an eyebrow at the inclusion of Boris Johnson in the roll call of strongman leaders. Supporters of the prime minister and of Brexit may see it as an unwarranted slur. But when Johnson finally achieved his ambition to become prime minister in 2019, he sold himself as a strongman figure: somebody tough enough to get Brexit done by any means necessary. From the backbenches, Johnson had cited Donald Trump's approach to diplomacy as a model for how to deal with the EU. As prime minister, he took measures that his predecessor, Theresa May, had shied away from, such as sacking senior members of his own party and proroguing Parliament, an act that was swiftly ruled illegal. Donald Trump claimed a kinship with Johnson, labelling him "Britain Trump" and Joe Biden agreed, calling Johnson a "physical and emotional clone" of Trump.[11] Brexit, the cause championed by Johnson, was a vital moment in the backlash against globalized liberalism.

One reason for worrying about the democratically elected strongmen is precisely because their behavior and rhetoric overlaps so clearly with the behavior of autocrats. It is striking that people with experience of genuinely autocratic systems were among the first to sound the alarm about Donald Trump. Russian exiles in particular, Garry Kasparov and Masha Gessen, were very clear about the way in which Trump's behavior was reminiscent of Putin.* [12] But the US was not a unique aberration in the democratic world. Other political systems that are meant to be based on institutions, laws and political parties have started to throw up strongman figures such as Modi, Bolsonaro and Duterte.

There has also been a move towards the strongman model within countries that were already authoritarian. China and Saudi Arabia were never democracies but, before Xi and MBS, their leadership was more collective, grouped around the Communist Party and the Saudi royal family. In recent years, however, both nations have moved towards a more personalized style of government.

As a result of this international movement towards personalized politics, it has become harder to maintain a clear line between the authoritarian and democratic worlds. Traditionally, US presidents have drawn a sharp distinction between "the free world" (led by the US) and undemocratic countries. But Donald Trump played down this difference. When it was put to him in 2015 that President Putin (whom he had just praised) had killed journalists and political opponents, Trump replied, "I think our country does plenty of killing also."[13] As president, he mused to Bob Woodward: "I get along very well with Erdoğan . . . The tougher and meaner they are, the better I get along with them."

Rather than defend the free press as an essential part of a free

---

* By contrast, during the Cold War, Soviet dissidents were usually dismissive of Western liberals who claimed to see parallels between the USSR and the US.

society, Trump spent his time denouncing the "fake news media." And rather than lauding America's independent courts and free elections, Trump castigated judges as biased if they ruled against him; and tried to overturn the result of the 2020 presidential election, claiming fraud. Trump's behavior and language were adopted by other leaders of democratic countries. Both Netanyahu in Israel and Bolsonaro in Brazil have complained about "fake news" and a "deep state" working against them. When Netanyahu lost power in 2021, he made Trump-like claims that he had been the victim of "the greatest election fraud . . . in the history of any democracy."

This erasure of a clear line between leadership in democratic and authoritarian systems has been a key goal of the authoritarians for decades. Early in Vladimir Putin's long reign in Russia, I met his spokesman, Dmitry Peskov, in the Kremlin. When I asked him about some of Putin's recent repressive acts, Peskov smilingly replied that "All our systems are imperfect." Trump's discourse seemed to confirm this long-standing Russian and Chinese position. Here was an American president willing to say: we also lie, we also kill, our media is fake, our elections are rigged, our courts are dishonest. As the historian of China Rana Mitter puts it: "The anti-liberal discourse is helpful for China since it makes it easier to suggest that there is no fundamental difference between an authoritarian state and a democratic one . . . that it is a question of degree, not type."[14]

The strongman leaders portrayed in this book are not "all the same." But they are similar. And those similarities are important and enlightening. There are four cross-cutting characteristics that are common to the strongman style: the creation of a cult of personality; contempt for the rule of law; the claim to represent the real people against the elites (otherwise known as populism); and a politics driven by fear and nationalism.

Strongman leaders want to be regarded as indispensable. Their goal is to convince people that they alone can save the nation. "I alone can fix it," Trump told Americans. The distinction between the state and the leader is eroded, making the strongman's replacement with a lesser mortal seem dangerous or inconceivable. Ideally, they will be admired not just for their strength but also for their morality and their intellect.

Once again, this is a characteristic that spans autocracies and democracies. In China, Xi Jinping has gone a long way towards restoring the cult of personality that was last seen under Mao Zedong. "Xi Jinping thought" has been incorporated into the Chinese constitution, a distinction previously only accorded to Mao. Term limits on the Chinese presidency have been abolished, potentially allowing Xi to rule for life. In Shanghai in 2020, I was even shown a street mural of Xi, with the rays of the sun protruding from his head.

This kind of idolatry is easier to insist upon in a dictatorship. But the cult of personality has also entered the semi-democratic and democratic worlds. In India, the BJP's electoral campaigns have centered around Modi and his claims to wisdom, strength and personal morality. As Ramachandra Guha, a leading historian of India, has put it: "Since May 2014, the vast resources of the state have been devoted to making the prime minister the face of every programme, every advertisement, every poster. Modi is India, India is Modi."[15]

In Russia and Turkey, Putin and Erdoğan have also encouraged the idea that they have a unique rapport with ordinary people. In both countries constitutional amendments have been pushed through, allowing both men to remain in power for decades – potentially for life. Elsewhere, nationalist prime ministers like Japan's Shinzo Abe and Israel's Benjamin Netanyahu have set new records for longevity in office. In the US, Donald Trump enjoyed upsetting his opponents by "joking" about extending his term in office beyond eight years. The extent to which the Republican Party had succumbed to a cult of personality was revealed in 2020, when the party's platform for the presidential election was reduced to the simple statement that "The Republican Party has and will continue to enthusiastically support the President's America-first agenda."

Another common aspect of the cult of personality is the merging of the interests of the strongman and of the state. It is quite common for family members of the leader to be appointed to key positions in government. Erdoğan made his son-in-law, Berat Albayrak, his finance minister – before falling out with him. Trump gave Jared Kushner, his own son-in-law, a central role in US diplomacy and domestic politics. In Brazil, Jair Bolsonaro has used his three sons, Flavio, Eduardo and Carlos, as surrogates and spokesmen and nominated Eduardo as Brazil's ambassador to the US. In the Philippines, Duterte's preferred candidate to replace him as president was his own daughter, Sara – with Duterte senior potentially slotting in as vice president. In Britain Boris Johnson appointed his brother Jo to the cabinet and then later to the House of Lords.

Strongman leaders also typically believe that institutions and the law are standing in the way of what needs to be done. Once again, this is a trend that spans both democracies and autocracies – although it plays out differently, depending on the political context. Before Xi Jinping came to power, liberal thinkers in China were pushing to give Chinese courts some independence from the rule of the Communist Party. Xi has rejected this idea and reasserted the dominance of the party led by him, arguing, "We must never follow the path of Western 'constitutionalism,' 'separation of powers' or 'judicial independence.'"[16]

In the West, judicial independence has often been the first target of the new generation of strongman leaders. One of the earliest moves of the Hungarian and Polish governments, led by Viktor Orbán and Jaroslaw Kaczynski, was to change their countries' constitutional arrangements to bring the courts under their control. In the UK, when Britain's Supreme Court ruled against the government on important Brexit-related issues, its judges were denounced in the *Daily Mail* as "Enemies of the People." In the US, Donald Trump claimed, "When somebody is president of the US, the authority is total."[17]

For a strongman leader, the law is not something to be obeyed: it is a political weapon to be used against opponents. Lavrenti Beria, Stalin's secret police chief, put it best when he stated: "Show me the man and I will find the crime." Imprisoning political opponents is standard practice. An early sign that Vladimir Putin's Russia had tipped into autocracy was when the president had the troublesome oligarch Mikhail Khodorkovsky tried and imprisoned in 2005. The pattern has continued, most recently with the imprisonment of the opposition leader Alexei Navalny in 2021. Once in power, Xi swiftly initiated an anti-corruption campaign in China that saw over a million people arrested and imprisoned. His response to opposition in Hong Kong was to have the leaders of the democracy movement put in prison. In the Philippines, Senator Leila de Lima, who had investigated Rodrigo Duterte's involvement with death squads, was arrested and imprisoned on trumped-up drugs charges. In Saudi Arabia, MBS used an anti-corruption drive to terrify and shake down much of the country's elite who (in a rather Saudi touch) were incarcerated in the Ritz-Carlton hotel and forced to sign over some of their wealth. Trump lacked these arbitrary powers but clearly hankered after them. In the 2016 presidential election, he and his surrogates led chants of "Lock her up" aimed at Hillary Clinton.

A long period in power gives strongman leaders the ability to appoint loyalists to the courts, as Trump attempted to do in the US. In the Philippines, Duterte has packed the Supreme Court with sympathetic judges. And in Turkey, more than 4,000 judges and prosecutors were purged, after the declaration of a state of emergency by Erdoğan in 2016.

The courts are the most important institution for a strongman leader to control. But most strongmen are impatient with any independent institutions that can check or challenge their authority. The media are a frequent target. So are state institutions, such as the intelligence services or the central bank. Within months of taking power in 2019, Amlo had fired the heads of many of Mexico's regulatory agencies.

From challenging the courts, it is a relatively short step towards challenging elective democracy itself. The anti-democratic nature of Trump's politics became clear when he attempted to overturn the result of the 2020 presidential election. A rejection of democracy is implicit in the logic of strongman politics. As Erdoğan once put it: "Democracy is like a tram that you ride, until you get to your destination."[18]

Strongman leaders disdain institutions but they love "the people." Typically, they claim to have an intuitive understanding and sympathy for ordinary folk. That is why the strongman phenomenon is closely associated with populism – a style of politics that disdains elites and experts and venerates the wisdom and instincts of the common man.

Populism, in turn, is closely linked to a style of political argument known as "simplism."[19] This is the idea that there are simple solutions for complex problems that are being frustrated by nefarious forces. Sometimes these solutions are so simple that they can be summarized in just three words – "Get Brexit Done," "Build the Wall." Because the solutions to complex problems are supposed to be obvious, those who frustrate these simple solutions are often deemed to be either stupid or evil. And when simple solutions run into difficulties, the strongman promises to crash through legal barriers to make sure the will of the people is obeyed.

Strongmen often claim that the law and state institutions are not just unnecessary obstacles to getting things done: as they see it, legal obfuscation is a deliberate tool used by shadowy elites. It needs a strongman to break through these plots and obstacles and to thwart the conspiracies of this "deep state," which Boris Johnson once characterized as "the people who really run the country." In Johnson's view, the British deep state was conspiring to thwart Brexit.[20] The deep state is a concept that was familiar for decades in Turkey, before it was adopted by Trump, and then by Bolsonaro, Netanyahu and others.

Shadowy foreigners who are deemed to be plotting against the nation are another favorite target. In Xi's China, the media often warn citizens to guard against Western plots to split the country. Outside China, many strongman leaders have chosen the same bogeyman figure as the alleged manipulator, working on behalf of globalist elites against the common people. As we will see, the financier George Soros has had the honor of being denounced by Vladimir Putin, Donald Trump, Recep Tayyip Erdoğan, Viktor Orbán and Jair Bolsonaro. The claim to be fighting on behalf of the common man against the globalist elite is often surprisingly easy to combine with accruing massive wealth. Many of the populist strongmen – including Putin, Orbán and Erdoğan – have used their political power to enrich themselves, or their family members and friends.

The strongmen also typically espouse traditional views on the family, sexuality and gender. They scoff at the "political correctness" of liberal politicians, who often turn out to be women, such as Germany's Angela Merkel or New Zealand's Jacinda Ardern.

The political bases of strongman leaders are often strikingly similar. In country after country, they have campaigned against urban elites and made their pitch to people living in small towns and the countryside. In the US, Trump lost in almost all of America's big cities in both 2016 and 2020. He also split the American electorate on educational lines, losing heavily among college graduates but winning almost 80 percent of the votes of non-college-educated white men. Little wonder that he remarked in 2016: "I love the poorly educated."

This pattern holds outside the US. In the UK, 73 percent of those who had left school without any qualifications voted to leave the EU; 75 percent of people with postgraduate degrees voted Remain. In the

Philippines, Rodrigo Duterte campaigned against "imperial Manila" and its liberal elite. In France, Emmanuel Macron swept central Paris in 2017, while populists thrived in the country's "left-behind" areas. In Hungary and Poland, the drift towards authoritarianism was met with massive anti-government demonstrations in the capital cities of Budapest and Warsaw, while Orbán and Kaczynski could rely on the loyalty of small towns and the countryside.

Looking at these patterns, it is all too easy for urban liberals to conclude that support for populist politics and strongman leadership can be accounted for by a lack of education or even stupidity. But, in the Western economies, the "poorly educated" are most likely to have seen their wages stagnate and their standards of living decline in recent decades. Under those circumstances, it is very tempting to opt for an anti-system candidate. The temptation becomes all the more powerful when a strongman leader promises to bring back the good times and make America (or Russia or Britain) "great again." This brings us to the final element of the strongman style of politics – nostalgic nationalism.

Strongman leaders almost all use local variants of Donald Trump's famous promise. President Xi's talk of a "great rejuvenation of the Chinese people" is, essentially, a promise to make China great again – restoring the nation to its rightful position as the Middle Kingdom. The Chinese and American leaders are not alone in holding out the prospect of a restoration of national greatness. President Putin described the collapse of the Soviet Union as a catastrophe and has made the restoration of Russian global power central to his time in office. Shinzo Abe cited the Meiji restoration of the nineteenth century, which made Japan the leading power in Asia, as his inspiration. In India, Narendra Modi leads a nationalist movement that appeals to Hindu pride in a glorious and sometimes mythologised past, before the British and the Moghul empires. In Hungary, Viktor Orbán has talked of one day regaining the territories that Hungary lost after the First World War. In Turkey, President Erdoğan seeks inspiration from the glories of the Ottoman empire, which collapsed in the early 1920s. And in the UK, Boris Johnson's plan for a "Global Britain" draws upon nostalgia for the period when Britain was the foremost global power – rather than just one of twenty-eight members of a European club.

The recourse to nostalgic nationalism across the world is striking. It is also relatively new. In Britain and the US, until recently, the most successful politicians were forward-looking. Bill Clinton spoke of building a "bridge to the twenty-first century." And David Cameron positioned himself as a modernizer, comfortable with contemporary Britain. Even China and Russia, before the Xi and Putin eras, seemed more interested in forging a new future than looking back to past glories or brooding over past humiliations.

To understand the strongman phenomenon, we need to look more closely at what it is about the modern world that has created a political market for figures like these.

For a brief period in world history, liberal democracy seemed ascendant and unchallenged. After the fall of the Berlin Wall in 1989, the big economic and political questions appeared settled. In economics, the answer was free markets. In politics, the answer was democracy. In geopolitics, America was now the sole superpower. In society, expanding rights for women and minorities was the obvious path forward. With all the big questions settled, government was reduced to "the administration of the inevitable," as Thomas Bagger, a German intellectual and diplomat, put it.[21]

But the unchallenged liberal ascendancy lasted less than twenty years. By 2007 Vladimir Putin had begun to openly reject the political and strategic beliefs that underpinned liberal internationalism. The financial and economic crisis of 2008 undermined the economic assumptions behind the liberal consensus. The word "neoliberalism" began to be used – by both the left and the right – as a critical term to describe the excesses and errors of the dominant economic model.

The financial crisis of 2008, combined with the Iraq war and the continuing rapid rise of China, also punctured the idea that the Western dominance would stretch long into the future. By the time Xi Jinping took power in 2012, it had become clear that the West's geopolitical ascendancy could no longer be taken for granted. The idea that liberal democracy was the best route towards social peace was also under challenge, as social divisions widened in the West amid a bitterly contested "culture war."

The strongmen described in this book are all, in different ways, in revolt against the liberal consensus that reigned supreme after 1989.

Their success is a symptom of the crisis in liberalism. That crisis is multifaceted, but can be broken down into four elements: economic, social, technological and geopolitical.

Standing on a stage in Hong Kong in 2017, Steve Bannon presented his explanation for the rise of Donald Trump and the backlash against globalization. The occasion was replete with ironies. As a former banker with Goldman Sachs, Bannon himself had personally profited from the "globalism" that he was now busy denouncing. Indeed, he was picking up a large fee for lecturing to a group of Asia-based bankers, whose livings depended on the economic cooperation between the US and China that Bannon wanted to dismantle.

Bannon is on the far right of Western politics. But, sitting in the audience, I was struck by how much of his analysis overlapped with the views of the left. His argument was that the roots of the populist revolt that led to Brexit and the election of Donald Trump lay in the financial crisis of 2008. As he saw it, the failure to punish and imprison bankers implicated in the crash – combined with the subsequent stagnation in ordinary people's living standards – had led inevitably to a backlash. Bannon argued that there were right- and left-wing variants of this populism: while Trump and Nigel Farage carried the banner for the right in the US and the UK, Bernie Sanders and Jeremy Corbyn led the charge for the left-wing populists. But in the West, at least, it was the populists on the right who made the political breakthroughs.

In the US and Europe, populists have thrived in left-behind areas with high unemployment, such as northern France, the American Rust Belt, eastern Germany and Britain's depressed coastal towns. But these conditions are not confined to Western Europe and the US. Fiona Hill, a Russia specialist in the Trump White House, who was brought up in the northeast of England, came to believe that the factors that had driven the rise of Putin in Russia were similar to those that had created support for Brexit in Britain and for Trump in the US. The destruction of traditional industries, on which whole regions had depended, created a yearning for a leader who promised to bring back the prosperity and stability of a bygone era.[22] As Hill later wrote, "Putin shared the same political base as Trump in the US with similar grievances – older, more male, less educated than others."[23] But while post-crash economics helps us to understand the appeal of populist strongmen in the West, it does not offer a complete explanation. How, for example, does one explain the rise of populist strongmen in Asia, where living standards have risen sharply in recent years?

In China and India too, economics play a part. While China has experienced a huge increase in national wealth over the last forty years, economic transformation has created losers as well as winners. In the 1990s many loss-making Chinese state enterprises were allowed to go bankrupt – with as many as 30 million workers losing their jobs. Men who had been part of the industrial working-class elite lost their place in society.[24] So in China – as in Russia, the UK and the US – there was a group of older, less educated workers, susceptible to the appeal of a strongman who promised to bring back the good old days.

In both China and India, the dislocating effects of a period of rapid globalization – including mass migration of people and industries – have increased the nostalgic appeal of a more stable, homogeneous and nation-centered past. In addition, the argument that corruption has ensured that the gains from globalization have gone overwhelmingly to a connected elite is very powerful in much of the developing world, leading to demands for a tough guy who can lock up the crooks. As soon as he came into office, Xi Jinping made an anti-corruption drive his major domestic focus. In a similar fashion, Narendra Modi's image as a common man who has risen from humble origins is central to his political appeal, allowing him to claim that he can create new opportunities for the frustrated middle classes and small-town India.

Many of the strongman leaders who have emerged outside the West have capitalized on the frustrations created by weak states that seem to have failed to deal with street crime and high-level corruption. Both Rodrigo Duterte in the Philippines and Jair Bolsonaro in Brazil appealed to those frightened by high murder rates in the cities.[25] Bolsonaro came to power on a wave of public disgust after scandals had revealed pervasive corruption in the highest levels of politics and business.

By labeling an entire elite as corrupt and self-serving and the system as "rigged" against the common man, the populists helped to create a demand for an outsider – a strongman who could take on the crooked, globalist elites and stand up for the ordinary man.

But "strongman politics" is not just about economics. It is when economic grievances are linked to broader fears – such as immigration, crime or national decline – that strongman leaders really come into their own.

Many of this new breed of leaders have stressed migration above all. While the liberal era that followed the Cold War was epitomized by the destruction of the Berlin Wall, the strongman era has been symbolized by the demand for new walls – the "big beautiful wall" that Trump promised along the Mexican border, the wall constructed by Viktor Orbán to keep Syrian refugees from entering Hungary, the wall built by the Netanyahu government to separate Israel from the Palestinian territories.

For the populist strongmen, some migrants are clearly less welcome than others. One of President Trump's first acts as president was the unsuccessful attempt to bar all Muslims from entering the US. Indeed, a strong streak of Islamophobia runs through nationalist populism in both the West and Asia. For the American and European far right, Muslim immigration represents a threat to the survival of "Judeo-Christian" civilization.

Muslim minorities are also a favored target for Asia's strongman leaders. In China, Xi Jinping's government has pioneered an extraordinary and sinister effort to "re-educate" the Muslims of Xinjiang, who are accused of both separatism and sympathy for terrorism. More than a million Muslims have been sent to re-education camps which, some believe, represents the largest mass incarceration since the Second World War. Both the Trump and Biden administrations have gone as far as labeling the treatment of the Uighurs as "genocide."[26]

Anti-Muslim sentiment is central to the political appeal of Narendra Modi as well and underpins some of the Indian prime minister's most controversial acts. In 2019, Modi abolished the special status of the Muslim-majority state of Jammu and Kashmir, an act that was accompanied by mass arrests, a curfew and a shutdown of the internet. The Indian prime minister also threatened to expel or incarcerate hundreds of thousands of Muslims in the state of Assam, who are accused of being illegal immigrants.

Strongman leaders often play upon a deep fear that a dominant majority is about to be displaced, suffering enormous cultural and economic losses in the process. The conspiracy theory that Muslims are planning to take over the West has been promoted by authors such as France's Renaud Camus, whose book *Le Grand Remplacement* (The Great Replacement) has become a favored text for the far right. In Hungary, Viktor Orbán has argued that mass migration poses a threat to the very survival of a Hungarian people. In Israel, Benjamin Netanyahu pushed through legislation defining Israel as a Jewish state, partly in response to a perceived demographic threat from the Arab minority.

The prospect that in the US the present white majority will become a minority by 2045 helped to fuel the social and racial fears that drove the rise of Donald Trump. Social scientists found that anxiety about racial and demographic change was a strong predictor of support for Trump. Some thoughtful observers now even question whether democracy itself can withstand the pressures of racial rivalries and group competition. As Barack Obama put it in 2020: "America is the first real experiment in building a large multiethnic, multicultural democracy. And we don't know yet if that can hold . . ."[27]

The evidence from other large multi-ethnic, multicultural democracies such as Brazil and India is not particularly encouraging. The 2010 census in Brazil revealed that, for the first time, white Brazilians were outnumbered by Black and mixed-raced compatriots. The political discourse of the Brazilian far right is reminiscent of the arguments deployed by Trump supporters in the US. Bolsonaro's supporters often argued that the left had gained power illegitimately by buying the votes of racial minorities through social payments or direct corruption.

The fear of losing majority status seems much less rational for Indian Hindus, who make up close to 80 percent of their country's population. But that has not stopped leading figures in Modi's BJP from campaigning against the so-called "love jihad" – an alleged plot by Muslims to marry Hindu girls and dilute the purity of the nation. Five BJP-run states have enacted or considered laws against "love jihad."[28]

Authoritarianism is no protection against these ethnic fears and tensions. In China some 92 percent of the population is Han Chinese. But the Xi era has been characterized by growing paranoia and intolerance of racial and ethnic minorities. Chen Quanguo, the Communist Party official in charge of repression in Xinjiang, had previously developed his tactics of forced assimilation in Tibet.

The willingness to "get tough" with unpopular groups – foreigners, migrants, Muslims – is integral to the appeal of the strongmen. Their macho posturing also makes them likely to appeal to traditional ideas of male strength and to scorn feminism and LGBT+ rights. At a time when social mores are changing rapidly – and not just in the West – this appeal to traditional social values is a potent and perhaps underestimated weapon in the armory of the new authoritarians. In countries as varied as the US, Russia, Brazil, Italy and India, there is a large group of disgruntled men (and some traditionalist women) who seem to thrill to an old-fashioned strongman.[29]

The extent to which gender is a dividing line between the populist strongmen and their liberal challengers was evident in the 2016 US presidential election. Many in Trump's camp feared that their candidate might be fatally wounded when a tape surfaced of him boasting of grabbing women "by the pussy." But the controversy did not prevent his victory, with men voting disproportionately heavily for Trump rather than Hillary Clinton. Fear of a female president may have been a more powerful factor in the 2016 election than disgust at a "pussy-grabbing" man.

Macho language and posturing is even more pronounced among strongman leaders outside the US. Rodrigo Duterte once notoriously "joked" about his regret that he had not taken part in the gang rape of a murdered missionary. Jair Bolsonaro of Brazil has said that if he ever came across men kissing in the street he would punch them in the face. Matteo Salvini, Italy's would-be strongman, has waved around inflated sex dolls onstage, likening them to his female political opponents. President Putin has also sought to cultivate support among cultural conservatives, in the West as well as Russia, by regularly decrying the follies of "political correctness" in the West, with a particular focus on gay rights and feminism. When I asked Konstantin Malofeev, one of the ideologues of Putinism, what he regarded as the essence of Western liberalism, he replied: "No borders between countries and no distinction between men and women."[30]

The nationalism and the cultural traditionalism of the new authoritarians mean that, in many ways, they are nostalgic, backward-looking leaders. But in one crucial respect the strongmen are very much in tune with their times: with few exceptions, these leaders are very adept users of social media. The rise of new forms of political communication helped to fuel the move towards strongman politics. Donald Trump made Twitter his primary form of communication. In doing so, he established a direct form of communication with voters that allowed him to bypass the "fake news media." A personal connection between a strongman leader and his disciples is crucial for the establishment of a cult of personality and Twitter is the ideal medium for creating this. In Brazil, Bolsonaro's Twitter followers were similarly in thrall to the man they called "the legend." India's BJP are also notably adept on social media, using Facebook and Twitter to inspire support for Modi and to intimidate his opponents.

Facebook and Twitter have been key to undermining the traditional media's role as the arbiter of truth and fiction in news. The presidential campaign of Rodrigo Duterte in 2016 pioneered the use of Facebook to spread made-up stories that favored their candidate. Some Facebook executives later referred to the Philippines as "patient zero." A few months later, the spread of pro-Trump narratives on Facebook were also critical to the rise of America's very own strongman leader. While traditional media are meant to ask whether a story is true or false, Facebook asks its users if they "like" or "dislike" a posting: the appeal is to emotion and loyalty, rather than to reason. Research conducted in Britain during the Covid-19 pandemic revealed that people who get most of their news from social media are far more likely to believe conspiracy theories. Some 45 percent of those who believed that the government was deliberately exaggerating the number of Covid-19 deaths got most of their news from Facebook; of those who rejected this conspiracy theory, just 19 percent relied on Facebook for their news.[31]

In the early days of the internet, liberal optimists believed that the free flow of information would inevitably favor democracy because it would make it harder for authoritarians to censor the news. There is some truth to this. There is a reason that China has blocked Twitter, YouTube and Facebook. In Russia, Alexei Navalny used YouTube to publish highly damaging video investigations of corrupt dealings by Putin and his circle. But optimism about the liberating potential of social media has to be strongly qualified. New social media have also turned out to be ideally suited for the type of political communication favored by the strongman – slogans or unreliable claims, which appeal to the emotions and are likely to be rapidly shared by followers, before they can be fact-checked by the media.

The most recent developments in China's use of the internet are even more politically sinister. With the internet and mobile phones now essential to life in a modern society, the Chinese authorities are able to monitor the activities of their citizens in ways that are truly Orwellian. Every journey, online transaction or posting on social media can be monitored. Citizens suspected of subversive activities can then be punished through a system of "social credit," in which everything from promotion at work to the ability to take out a loan or even buy a train ticket is potentially put at risk for dissidents. China's technological prowess, particularly in the field of artificial intelligence, means that its system of online social control is of interest to authoritarian governments beyond its borders – and potentially available for export to friendly foreign strongmen.

The Age of the Strongman has also been a period of profound geopolitical change. In 2000, American ascendancy was unchallenged. At that time, the Chinese economy was just 12 percent the size of the US. By 2011, three years after the financial crisis, it was 50 percent the size of the American economy. By 2020, just before Covid-19 hit, the Chinese economy was over two-thirds the size of that of America. Measured in purchasing power, China had actually become the largest economy in the world in 2014.

Beyond the realm of abstract statistics, the real-world effects are coming through. China is now the world's largest manufacturer, the largest exporter, the largest market for vehicles and smartphones, and the largest producer of greenhouse gases. It also now has a larger navy than the US. The rise of China and the relative decline of the US is part of a bigger story of the decline of the West's economic and political clout, as wealth and power shift to Asia. The knowledge that America's global pre-eminence is fast eroding underpinned Trump's yearning for a restoration of national greatness.

In rising Asian powers, such as China and India, the global power shift has inspired ambitions to revive the national and cultural greatness that was eclipsed during the age of Western imperialism. Asian nationalism is driven by rising expectations; the West's nationalism is driven by disappointed hopes. But the political outcome is surprisingly similar: a call to make the country "great again."

After the financial crisis of 2008, Chinese leaders became more confident in making the case for their authoritarian model of development in contrast to the economic chaos that Western democracy had allegedly created. Indeed, China's economic success has boosted the prestige of its model, particularly in Africa, where Chinese influence has grown fast over the past decade. The disastrous record of many post-independence African strongman leaders such as Mobutu in Zaire or Mugabe in Zimbabwe had not been a great advert for authoritarianism. In the 1990s, after the end of the Cold War, there was a wave of democratization in Africa. But more recently, the economic success of leaders such as Rwanda's Paul Kagame or Ethiopia's Meles Zenawi has given fresh impetus to the authoritarian model in Africa.

Trump's four years in office have done a great deal of damage to the "soft power" of the United States. A crucial question for the Biden era is whether the new president will be able to restore the prestige of the American liberal democratic model – and so halt the global march of strongman politics. I will return to that question in the epilogue to this book. But to understand how things may develop, it is necessary to go back to the beginning.

1 Putin – the archetype (2000)

Vladimir Putin was annoyed – or maybe just bored. The Russian leader had been patiently fielding questions from a small group of international journalists in the restaurant of a modest hotel in Davos. Then one of the queries seemed to irritate him. He stared back at the questioner, an American, and said slowly, through an interpreter: "I'll answer that question in a minute. But first let me ask you about the extraordinary ring you have on your finger." All heads in the room swiveled. "Why is the stone so large?" A few in the audience began to giggle and the journalist, whose ring was now being scrutinized by everybody in the room, looked uncomfortable. Putin took on a tone of mock sympathy and continued: "You surely don't mind me asking, because you wouldn't be wearing something like that – unless you were deliberately trying to draw attention to yourself?" There was more laughter. By now, the original question had been forgotten. It was a master class in distraction and bullying.

The year was 2009, and Putin had already been in power for almost a decade. But this was my first encounter with the Russian leader in the flesh, during his visit to the World Economic Forum. Putin's ability to radiate menace, without raising his voice, was striking. It was a reminder of his background in the secret service of the Soviet Union, the KGB – formative years, which remain a key to his character, his mystique and his behavior in office. He is, in the words of one of the best books about him, an "Operative in the Kremlin."[1]

In many ways, Putin is both the archetype and the model for the current generation of strongman leaders. It is all too symbolic that he took power on New Year's Eve in 1999, at the dawn of the twenty-first century.

Until Xi Jinping took over in Beijing in 2012, the Russian leader's style looked like a curious anomaly among the leaders of the world's major powers. His macho authoritarianism and encouragement of a cult of personality looked out of place in a technocratic age when the dominant political figures were cool, understated figures, such as China's Hu Jintao, Germany's Angela Merkel or Barack Obama in the White House.

In fact, when Putin first emerged as leader of Russia, it was not obvious that he would last very long in the job – let alone that he would emerge as a new model of authoritarian leadership. As the chaotic Yeltsin era of the 1990s drew to a close, Putin's ascent to the top job was eased by his former colleagues in the KGB. But he was also approved of by Russia's richest and most powerful people, the oligarchs, who saw him as an unthreatening figure: a capable administrator and "safe pair of hands," who would not threaten established interests.

Viewed from the West, Putin looked like a relatively reassuring figure. In his first televised speech from the Kremlin, given on New Year's Eve 1999, just a few hours after taking over from Yeltsin, Putin promised to "protect freedom of speech, freedom of conscience, freedom of the mass media, ownership rights, these fundamental elements of a civilised society."[2] In March 2000, he won his first presidential election and proudly asserted afterwards that "We have proved that Russia is becoming a modern democratic state."[3]

Experienced observers of Russian elections argued that the whole process was carefully stage-managed. Putin himself had hardly bothered to campaign. But it was still significant that he felt the need to assert that Russia was becoming a modern liberal democracy. Twenty years later, still in the Kremlin, Putin would take a very different line, declaring with relish that "The liberal idea has become obsolete." Russia, he now asserted, had nothing to learn from the West. Liberals "cannot simply dictate anything to anyone, just like they have been attempting to do over recent decades."[4]

Yet, while Putin may have initially found it convenient to use the rhetoric of liberal democracy, his early actions as president quickly revealed a tough-guy, authoritarian streak. In his first year in office, he moved immediately to rein in independent sources of power, to assert the central authority of the state and to use warfare to bolster his own personal position – all actions that were to become trademarks of Putinism. The escalation of the war in Chechnya made Putin appear as a nationalist hero, standing up for Russian interests and protecting the ordinary citizen from terrorism. In an early move that alarmed liberals, the new president reinstated the old Soviet national anthem. He also took on some of Russia's richest men. Significantly, the oligarchs that he rounded on first were those who controlled independent media organizations, Vladimir Gusinsky and Boris Berezovsky. Within a year of Putin taking power, both men had fled the country. Berezovsky, who had backed Putin for the presidency, died in suspicious circumstances in Britain in 2013.[5]

Putin's early promise to protect media freedom turned out to be empty. Russia's few independent television networks were swiftly brought under the control of the government. In moving quickly to tighten control of the media, Putin set a template for other strongman leaders around the world.

The speed with which Putin consolidated his power matched the rapidity of his rise up the Russian system. Just ten years before he became head of state, Putin had been a lowly figure in the intelligence services – working as an officer for the KGB in Dresden in East Germany. This was not a glamorous or high-profile position. The main KGB outpost in East Germany was in Berlin; Dresden was a provincial city. Catherine Belton, Putin's biographer, suggests he may have had a more sensitive and nefarious role than his relatively minor position suggests and has presented evidence that he liaised with terrorist groups operating in West Germany. Even so, Putin did not strike colleagues as a particularly forceful character. "He never pushed himself forward. He was never in the front line. He was always very kind," was how one member of the Stasi, the East German secret service, remembered him.[6]

From Dresden, Putin had a close-up view of the collapse of the Soviet empire after the fall of the Berlin Wall in 1989. In a well-known passage in his memoirs, he recalled his sense of hopelessness, as Communist rule collapsed all around him. He had looked to Moscow for instructions – "But Moscow was silent." For a Soviet patriot like Putin, worse was to come. On Christmas Eve 1991, the Soviet Union itself was dissolved, and the hammer-and-sickle flag was lowered for the last time over the Kremlin to be replaced by the colors of Russia.

Unlike many other former and current members of the Russian intelligence services, Putin had not been born into the Soviet Union's ruling class. He grew up in a small flat in a run-down apartment building, with communal facilities, in Russia's grandest city, Leningrad – which has now reverted to its original name, St. Petersburg. Putin's family had been profoundly marked by the city's tragic history – in particular, the Nazi siege that lasted for nine hundred days, in which hundreds of thousands of residents died, either of starvation or in the bombardment of the city. His father, also called Vladimir, served in a commando battalion, linked to the secret police, that fought behind German lines. Putin's older brother Viktor died aged five during the siege.[7]

Vladimir himself was born in 1952 and brought up in an environment shaped by the privations and sacrifices of the "Great Patriotic War." From an early age he displayed a strong devotion to the Soviet system. As a teenager, he visited the local branch of the KGB to ask for advice on what subject to study at university. The answer he got, ironically, was law. Putin graduated in that subject from Leningrad State University in 1975 and immediately joined the KGB.

The drive and self-discipline he had displayed as a young man, as well as his ability to appear unthreatening, served Putin well in the chaos of the 1990s. He was recalled from Dresden to Leningrad in 1990, just as the Soviet system was collapsing. His key contact was Anatoly Sobchak, one of his former law professors, who became St. Petersburg's first democratically elected mayor in 1991. Putin followed Sobchak into government, becoming a deputy mayor and officially leaving the KGB in August 1991, just a few months before the collapse of the USSR. As Sobchak's assistant, Putin developed a reputation as a capable official. But he also seems to have been involved with organized criminals running illegal operations out of the port.[8] When Sobchak lost office in 1996, Putin moved to Moscow to work in the Kremlin.

His first job did not sound particularly important: working in the department that managed presidential property. In reality, however, the Kremlin's property portfolio was a tremendous source of patronage. The following year, he became deputy chief of the presidential administration and his ascent to the summit of power soon accelerated. As Hill and Gaddy point out, "In less than two and a half years . . . Putin was promoted to increasingly lofty positions, from deputy chief of the presidential staff, to head of the FSB, to prime minister, then to acting president."[9] President Yeltsin then stepped aside to allow Putin to take over at the turn of the millennium.

The remarkable speed of Putin's rise has inevitably attracted speculation and conspiracy theories. Putin's ascent was clearly eased by his
former colleagues in the KGB, now renamed the FSB, who shared his
determination to reassert state power and his anger at the extraordinary wealth accumulated by a few oligarchs in the 1990s, as state assets
were sold off on the cheap. But Putin was also careful to reassure some
of those who had become rich – in particular, the Yeltsin family – that
he would protect their interests. Unlike the famously drunken Yeltsin,
he was a teetotaller and he looked like the kind of capable administrator who might be able to restore order to a chaotic situation. As
Valentin Yumashev, Yeltsin's son-in-law and chief of staff, later recalled,
"He always worked brilliantly. He formulated his views exactly."[10] He
was careful to hide any ambition to become a successor to other
strongmen who had once ruled Russia from the Kremlin, such as Peter
the Great or Stalin. On the contrary, Putin frequently insisted that "I
am just the manager" and "I have been hired."[11]

As Putin established himself in office, however, the image-makers got
to work in crafting a strongman persona for the Russian leader. Gleb
Pavlovsky, one of the first spin doctors to polish up Putin's image, later
described the Russian president as a "quick learner" and a "talented
actor." Key images were placed in the Russian media and around the
world: Putin on horseback, Putin practicing judo, Putin arm-wrestling
or strolling bare-chested by the side of a river in Siberia. These images
attracted plenty of mockery from intellectuals and cynics. But the Kremlin's image-makers were deliberately taking a leaf out of Hollywood's
book. As Pavlovsky later put it, the goal was to ensure that "Putin cor-
responds ideally to the Hollywood image of a savior-hero."[12]

By the time he took power, many Russians were ready for a strongman leader. The collapse of the Soviet system had allowed for the
emergence of democracy and freedom of speech. But as the Soviet
economic system atrophied and then fell apart, many Russians experienced a severe drop in living standards and personal security. By 1999,
life expectancy for Russian men had fallen, by four years, to fifty-eight.
A UN report attributed this to a "rise in self-destructive behaviour,"
which it linked to "rising poverty rates, unemployment and financial
insecurity."[13] Under those circumstances, a strong leader who promised to turn back the clock to better days had real appeal.

It generally helps if the image of a leader bears at least some relationship to the underlying political project. The spin doctors' focus on Putin's alleged virility fitted with Putin's personal preoccupation with the restoration of national strength. One of his most famous remarks is his description in 2004 of the collapse of the Soviet Union as "the greatest geopolitical catastrophe of the twentieth century." This comment has sometimes been used to paint the Russian leader as an unrepentant Stalinist. Others see it as a statement of intent: a suggestion that Putin aspired to reassemble the fifteen independent states that were once part of the USSR into a single political entity, once again ruled directly from Moscow. But even though Putin probably feels a genuine nostalgia for the era of Soviet greatness, most of his supporters insist that he knows that the USSR belongs to history. As Vyacheslav Nikonov, a pro-Putin member of the Russian Duma (parliament) and the grandson of Vyacheslav Molotov, the former Soviet foreign minister, put it to me, regretfully, in 2014: "The Soviet Union was like a glass. Once it has been shattered, it cannot be put back together again."[14]

But while Putin probably did not harbor any illusions about sticking the Soviet Union back together again, he was determined to return Russia to the first rank of world powers. Fyodor Lukyanov, an academic who is close to Putin, told me in 2019 that when Putin came to power he believed there was a real risk that, for the first time in centuries, Russia could permanently lose its status as one of the world's great powers.[15] Whereas the post-1945 British establishment more or less reconciled themselves to the idea that their job was "the management of decline" after the end of empire, Putin was determined to rebuild Russia's great-power status.

This determination, and his resentment at what he regarded as American slights and betrayals, set the Russian leader on a collision course with the West. A landmark moment came with a speech that the Russian leader gave at the Munich Security Conference in 2007. The MSC is the foremost gathering of the military and foreign policy elite of the West. Sitting in Putin's audience were the German chancellor, Angela Merkel, the US defense secretary, Robert Gates, and Senator John McCain, who the following year would become the Republican candidate for the US presidency.

The speech that Putin gave was a direct challenge to the West and an expression of cold fury. He accused the United States of an "almost unconstrained hyper use of force – military force – in international relations" and "of plunging the world into an abyss of conflicts." The Putin of 2000, who had expressed pride at Russia's transformation into a modern democracy, had given way to a man who denounced Western talk of freedom and democracy as a hypocritical front for power politics. As the academics Ivan Krastev and Stephen Holmes put it: "It was in Munich that Russia stopped pretending to accept the celebratory storyline that the end of the Cold War represented a joint victory of the Russian people and Western democracies over Communism."[16]

Putin's Munich speech was not just an angry reflection on the past. It also pointed the way to the future. The Russian president had put the West on notice that he intended to fight back against the US-led world order. A lot of what was to come was implicit in his speech: Russia's military intervention in Georgia in 2008, its annexation of Crimea in 2014, its dispatch of troops to Syria in 2015, and its meddling in the US presidential election of 2016. All of these actions burnished Putin's reputation as a nationalist and a strong leader. They also made him an icon for other strongmen throughout the world, who rejected Western leadership and the "liberal international order." So it is vital to understand the sources of Putin's conduct.

The Russians and their allies argue that the case laid out by Putin in Munich, and in many subsequent speeches, was both sincere and well grounded. The story you hear in Moscow is that, from the beginning, the West was determined to destroy Russian power – and that Western leaders repeatedly lied to their Russian counterparts, hypocritically citing rules and laws that they then broke themselves.

But Putin's critics inside and outside Russia respond that this is self-serving nonsense. Putinism has never been about the protection of Russia from the predatory West. Instead, it is a spoils system through which Putin and the Russian elite have enriched themselves. Putin protects those oligarchs who stay out of politics, and, in return, the oligarchs protect Putin and bankroll his circle.

On this view, the nationalism spouted by the Russian leader is simply a cynical means to divert attention from the corruption and criminality at the top. As one Russian liberal put it to me: "Politics in Russia is a contest between the fridge and the television. People look in the fridge and they see there is no food there. But then they turn on the television and they see Putin standing up for Russia – and they feel proud."

So which of these two stories is true? Is Putin an angry nationalist or a cynical manipulator? Although the two narratives sound like they are in direct opposition to each other, both contain elements of truth.

The nationalist indictment of the West, pushed by those around Putin, goes all the way back to the 1990s. It is argued repeatedly in Moscow that the expansion of NATO to take in the countries of the former Soviet empire (including Poland and the Baltic states) was a direct contradiction of promises made to Russia after the end of the Cold War. NATO's intervention in the Kosovo war of 1998–99 is added to the list of grievances, proving, in the Kremlin's eyes, both that NATO is an aggressor and that Western talk of respecting sovereignty and state borders is nothing but hypocrisy. Russians are not reassured by the Western riposte that NATO was acting in response to ethnic cleansing and human-rights abuses by Serbia. Indeed, as one liberal Russian politician put it to me, in a moment of frankness: "We know we have committed human-rights abuses in Chechnya. If NATO can bomb Belgrade for that, why could they not bomb Moscow?"[17]

The Russian polemic goes on to include the Iraq war launched by the US and its allies in 2003, in the wake of 9/11. For Putin, the massive bloodshed in Iraq, after the fall of Saddam Hussein, is proof that the West's self-proclaimed pursuit of "democracy and freedom" only brings instability and suffering in its wake. If you mention the brutal behavior of Russian forces in Chechnya or Syria in Moscow, you will always have the Iraq war thrown back in your face.

Crucially, for Putin the West's promotion of democracy posed a direct threat to his own political and personal survival. In 2004 and 2005, pro-democracy "color revolutions" broke out in many of the states of the former Soviet Union – including Ukraine, Georgia and Kyrgyzstan. If demonstrators in Independence Square in Kiev could bring down an autocratic government in Ukraine, what was to stop the same happening in Red Square? In Russia, many believed that the idea that these were spontaneous uprisings was a "fairy tale." As a former intelligence operative whose whole professional career had involved running "black operations," Putin was particularly inclined to see the CIA as pulling the strings behind the color revolutions. The goal, the Kremlin believed, was to install pro-Western puppet regimes. Russia itself could be next.

The shock of the Iraq war and the color revolutions were the recent experiences that underpinned Putin's Munich speech in 2007. And, as the Kremlin sees it, this pattern of Western misdeeds has continued. Putin has argued that in 2011, the Western powers intervened to overthrow Mu'ammar Gaddhafi, the Libyan dictator, having duplicitously promised the Russians that they would do no such thing. The Libyan intervention is a particularly sore spot for Putin since it took place during the four years from 2008 to 2012 when he was serving in the lesser job of prime minister, having stepped aside, at the end of his first two presidential terms, in favor of his acolyte, Dmitry Medvedev. As Putin's supporters see it, a naive Medvedev was duped by the West into supporting a UN resolution that allowed for a limited intervention and the Western powers had then predictably exceeded their mandate to overthrow and kill Gaddhafi. They have no time for the Western response that the Libyan intervention was indeed made on human-rights grounds, but that events then took on a life of their own, as the Libyan rebellion gained steam.

But Medvedev's alleged naivety also proved useful for Putin: it established the idea that he was indispensable as Russia's leader. Any substitute, even one chosen by Putin himself, would leave the country vulnerable to the scheming and ruthless West. In 2011, Putin announced that he intended to return to the Kremlin as president, after the potential presidential term had recently been extended to two consecutive terms of six years. This announcement provoked rare public demonstrations in Moscow and other cities, which once again fanned Putin's fears about Western schemes to undermine his power. I was in Moscow in January 2012 and witnessed the marches and banners, some of which carried pointed references to the fate of Gaddhafi. It was easy to see why Putin was alarmed. The fact that Hillary Clinton, then America's secretary of state, expressed public support for the demonstrators was deeply resented by Putin and may have justified, in his own mind, Russia's efforts to undermine Clinton's presidential campaign in 2016.

Putin secured his re-election but his sense that the West remained a threat to Russia was further stoked by events in Ukraine in 2014. The prospect that Ukraine would soon sign an association agreement with the European Union was seen as a serious threat in the Kremlin, since it would pull Russia's most important neighbor – once an integral part of the USSR – into the West's sphere of influence. Under pressure from Moscow, the Ukrainian government of President Viktor Yanukovych reversed course. But this provoked another popular uprising in Kiev, forcing Yanukovich to flee. The loss of a compliant ally in Kiev was a major geopolitical setback for the Kremlin. Putin's response was to dramatically raise the stakes, by crossing the line into the use of military force.

In March 2014, Russia invaded and annexed Crimea, a region that was part of Ukraine but that had belonged to Russia until 1954 and was populated largely by Russian speakers. It was also, by agreement with the Ukrainians, the home of Russia's Black Sea fleet. In the West, the annexation of Crimea along with Russian military intervention in eastern Ukraine were seen as flagrant violations of international law that could easily be the prelude to further acts of Russian aggression. But in Russia, the Crimean annexation was widely greeted as a triumph – it was the Russian nation's long-awaited fightback. Putin's approval ratings in independent opinion polls soared to over 80 percent. In the immediate afterglow, Putin came closer to achieving the ultimate goal of strongman ruler – the complete identification of the nation with the leader. Vyacheslav Volodin, the speaker of the Russian parliament, exulted: "If there's Putin, there's Russia. If there's no Putin, there's no Russia."[18]

The West's response to Putin's misdeeds was to slap economic sanctions on Russia. These were further tightened after Russian-backed militias shot down a Malaysian airliner (MH17) over Ukraine in July 2014, killing all 298 people aboard. There were more sanctions, as well as the expulsion of diplomats, after Russian operatives attempted to assassinate the former FSB agent Sergei Skripal on British soil, in Salisbury in 2018.

To the Kremlin, Western sanctions are further proof of the original conviction that a hypocritical and power-hungry West is out to "get" Russia. But to Putin's critics, inside and outside Russia, this long tale of woe is fabrication and distraction. The real story, they argue, is not about a brave Russian leader standing up to Western hypocrisy. It is about a ruthless quasi dictator repeatedly breaking international law and using violence to protect his position in power and those of his cronies.

The argument that the Putin narrative is a big lie is often bolstered by pointing to all the smaller lies that are deployed to support it. Despite the convincing evidence laid out by a detailed Dutch inquiry, the Russian government continues to deny that it had any role in the shooting down of MH17. Involvement in the murder attempt on

Skripal or in the successful killing of another former Russian agent, Alexander Litvinenko, in the UK in 2006, is also denied. The presence of Russian militia and agitators (the so-called "little green men") in Crimea was initially dismissed as Western propaganda, only for Putin later to admit Russia's role, once the annexation was a fait accompli. Meanwhile elections at home are routinely rigged. Political opponents with a real following sometimes end up dead – including Boris Nemtsov, who was shot and killed on a bridge near the Kremlin in 2015.

Others are framed and imprisoned. Mikhail Khodorkovsky, the richest of the 1990s oligarchs, who had helped to fund independent media and opposition causes, was arrested on board his private jet in Siberia in October 2003 and later put on trial and imprisoned for ten years. Alexei Navalny who, in recent years, has been Putin's most prominent and daring political opponent was arrested and imprisoned thirteen times on a variety of trumped-up charges.[19] Then, in the summer of 2020, he was the subject of an assassination attempt and went into a coma after being poisoned on a flight in Siberia. After recovering in hospital in Germany, Navalny flew back to Russia – where he was immediately arrested at the airport, put on trial and imprisoned again.

It was Navalny who came up with a damagingly effective name for Putin's United Russia Party, labeling it the "party of crooks and thieves." Through online campaigning and YouTube videos, he has presented much-watched exposés of corruption at the top of Putin's Russia. It is these charges of greed and graft that Putin seems to find most threatening of all. The publication of the so-called Panama Papers – a trove of documents leaked from the offshore financial center in 2016 – seemed to link Putin and some of his closest associates to $2 billion that had been spirited overseas.[20] The video exposing Putin's palace by the Black Sea, which Navalny released as he returned to Russia to face arrest in 2021, went viral on social media, garnering millions of views within a few days. The normally slick Kremlin media operation was speechless for a while. Eventually Arkady Rotenberg, a billionaire oligarch and childhood friend of Putin, came forward to claim that the palace belonged to him.[21]

Putin, it is sometimes claimed, is "the world's richest man."[22] Whatever the truth (or even the meaning) of a statement like that, there is no doubt that many of the Russian leader's close associates and collaborators have become extremely wealthy. It is not just billionaires like Roman

Abramovich, the owner of Chelsea football club or Oleg Deripaska, the aluminium magnate: Putin's spokesman, Dmitry Peskov, was photographed at his wedding in 2015 wearing a $620,000 watch.

If Putin is both a genuine nationalist and the frontman for a corrupt regime, the link between the two is the deep and corrosive cynicism (which his followers describe as "realism") that runs through the Russian leader's approach to politics and life. The Putin camp genuinely believes that Western governments are out to dominate and humiliate Russia and that their talk of democracy and human rights is hypocrisy and lies. This, for Putin's circle, justifies a weaker Russia to lie and cheat in response. In that sense, the official Russian line about world affairs is simultaneously completely cynical and utterly sincere. The government is in the business of propagating lies about its own behavior and the wider world; but it sincerely believes that these lies are justified as part of a broader campaign against Western dishonesty and aggression.

The same mixture of cynicism and sincerity applies to the personal conduct of officials. One view of Putin and his inner circle is that their motives are purely venal. As one Russian friend put it to me: "The only thing that really upsets them is if you get between them and the cash machine." Yet while corruption runs deep in Russia, that does not mean Putin and his advisers are not also genuine nationalists, who believe that they are strengthening Russia at home and abroad. They argue that by taking control of Russia's assets, they have prevented them falling into foreign hands. And if they have personally reaped the rewards for this – well, that's the way of the world.

For all the problems caused by corruption, sanctions and the oscillation of the oil price, it is true that Russia today is a more prosperous and stable place than it was in the 1990s. The World Cup of 2018 allowed Putin a chance to showcase his country. Visiting Russia for the first time as a tourist, rather than a journalist, I was genuinely surprised by the prosperity and efficiency of central Moscow and St. Petersburg – and even provincial outposts like the city of Kazan. Of course, huge efforts had gone into presenting Russia in as favorable a light as possible. But this was not simply a case of foreigners being taken in by a Potemkin village. The fast train between Moscow and St. Petersburg, the clean, well-run budget hotels and the bustling Moscow cafes were all still there when I visited the country a year later. Parts of the Russian state are also functioning well. The tax authority has attracted international praise for its cutting-edge collection of transaction data, in real time.[23] The central bank is widely admired for its handling of sanctions and management of the ruble.

The World Cup gave Putin center stage. At the opening match – Russia v Saudi Arabia – he sat next to the Saudi leader, Mohammed bin Salman. It was an intriguing pairing because MBS is representative of a new generation of strongman leaders who clearly see Putin as a model and an inspiration. One British adviser to the Saudi prince noted MBS's awestruck admiration for Putin. "He was fascinated by him. He seemed to admire him. He liked what he did."[24] As Putin's long reign in the Kremlin has worn on, so the ranks of his foreign admirers has swelled. Rodrigo Duterte, the president of the Philippines, has said that "my favorite hero is Putin." Rudy Giuliani, President Trump's close adviser and lawyer, has expressed admiration for Putin's annexation of Crimea, remarking, "He makes a decision and he executes it, quickly. And then everybody reacts. That's what you call a leader."[25] Nigel Farage, the former leader of UKIP and the Brexit Party and a friend of Donald Trump, once named Putin as the world leader he most admired, adding, "The way he played the whole Syria thing. Brilliant. Not that I approve of him politically."[26] Matteo Salvini, the leader of the populist right Northern League Party in Italy, flaunted his admiration for the Russian leader by being photographed in a Putin T-shirt in Red Square and in the European Parliament. In 2017, his party even signed a cooperation agreement with Putin's United Russia.[27]

As the praise from figures like Farage and Salvini suggests, admiration for Putin in the West is much more than a question of style: it also has a clear ideological aspect. For right-wing and nationalist politicians spanning the spectrum from cultural conservatives to outspoken racists, Putin has become something of an icon. He is a symbol of defiance of the Western liberal establishment, epitomized by figures such as Hillary Clinton and Angela Merkel, with their encouragement of immigration, gay rights, feminism and multiculturalism. As the author Anne Applebaum noted, an idealized version of Putin's Russia has become an inspiration for "right-wing intellectuals, now deeply critical of their own societies, who have begun paying court to right-wing dictators who dislike America."[28]

In turn, when these Western reactionaries denounce "globalism" or "liberalism," their ideas are picked up and amplified in nationalist circles in Russia. In Moscow in 2019, I met Konstantin Malofeev, a heavily bearded intellectual and billionaire, who made his fortune in investment banking, before becoming an emissary between the Kremlin and the far right in Europe and America. His denunciations of globalism and defense of nations and traditional sexual roles could easily have come from the mouth of Salvini, Farage or Steve Bannon. And indeed Malofeev had helped to arrange a €2 million loan to Jean-Marie Le Pen, the founder of France's National Front, and sponsored conferences that brought together leading figures in the French, Italian, Austrian and Russian far right.[29]

Malofeev was also campaigning for Russia to restore the monarchy and proudly showed me a portrait of his favorite tsar, the deeply reactionary Alexander III. He was duly delighted when, a few months later, it was announced that Russia was intending to change its constitution to allow Putin to run for two more six-year terms in office. That would potentially allow Putin to stay in the Kremlin until 2036, when he would be eighty-four – a stint as Russia's leader that would easily exceed that of Stalin.

When Putin first came to power in 2000, it would have seemed absurd to suggest that he might still be ruling Russia some thirty-five years later. The idea of Putin as the strongman that the country needed was invented initially for domestic consumption. But as the anti-liberal and nationalist tide has gathered force all over the world, so Putin has become an exemplar of a different style of leadership. Dmitry Peskov, Putin's spokesman, was not simply spouting propaganda when he remarked in 2018: "There's a demand in the world for special, sovereign leaders, for decisive ones who do not fit into general frameworks and so on. Putin's Russia was the starting point."[30]

The examples that Peskov was able to cite were numerous by 2018: Viktor Orbán in Hungary, Rodrigo Duterte in the Philippines, Trump in America. As Putin's admirers see it, the Russian leader inherited a country that had been humiliated by the breakup of the Soviet Union. Through strength and cunning, he had restored its status and global power and even regained some of the territory lost when the USSR broke up. And he had delighted nationalists, anti-Americans and populists the world over by successfully defying self-righteous American liberals like Hillary Clinton and Barack Obama.

But the idea that Putin's strongman leadership has been crowned with success is very questionable. The reckless lawbreaking of Putin's Russia – including invasions of neighbors and overseas assassinations – has led to the imposition of international sanctions, making Russia something close to an international pariah. The murder and imprisonment of Putin's domestic critics underlines how his continued rule ultimately rests not on success and popular consent but on force and repression. And Russia's long-term future looks bleak in many ways. The country's population is shrinking and aging. Russia's territory is vast, but its economy is roughly the size of Italy's. In a world that is decarbonizing, Russia's national wealth remains dangerously dependent on oil and gas.

Barack Obama caused outrage and anger in Moscow in 2014, when he dismissed Russia as no more than a "regional power."[31] But the remark also struck home because it had an element of truth to it. Vladimir Putin has been careful to avoid confronting Xi Jinping, the strongman leader to the east, even as China expands its influence across Eurasia and into the sphere of influence coveted by Moscow. Instead, Putin has sought to re-establish Russia's great-power credentials by flexing military muscle in the Middle East. But that has brought him into potential conflict with another regional strongman, who is also intent on rebuilding the glories of his country's imperial past: Turkey's Recep Tayyip Erdoğan.

2 Erdoğan – from liberal reformer to authoritarian strongman (2003)

The presidential palace constructed for Recep Tayyip Erdoğan looms over the west of Ankara, Turkey's capital city. Built on a hilltop on once-protected forest land, it is a vast edifice containing an art gallery, a convention center, a nuclear bunker and over a thousand rooms. The total area of the palace is larger than the Kremlin or Versailles. When President Erdoğan moved into his new residence in October 2014, it was confirmation of the Turkish ruler's growing megalomania. More than a decade in power had stripped away his claims to be a modest and unpretentious leader and revealed an ambition to be something closer to an Ottoman sultan.

The parallels between the careers of Putin and Erdoğan are striking. Both took power in the early years of the twenty-first century. Erdoğan first became prime minister in 2003.* Both leaders were initially regarded in the West as reformers who were prepared to govern within the constraints of a democracy. Both proceeded to take ever greater control of the state and society, while reasserting their country's power on the international stage. Both men have also become outspoken antagonists of the West and critics of liberalism. At home and abroad, Putin and Erdoğan have followed a similar playbook.

The rise of a strongman leader in Turkey is, in some ways, unsurprising. The founder of the modern Turkish republic was Kemal

---

* At that time, the job of prime minister was the most powerful in the country. Erdoğan's constitutional reforms later elevated the power of the presidency.

Atatürk, a charismatic leader whose personality cult continues to be celebrated, decades after his death in 1938. Before Erdoğan, modern Turkish history was punctuated by coups and periods of military rule. And yet Turkey plays an important part in the story of the Age of the Strongman. In the aftermath of the 9/11 attacks, the US and the EU became increasingly preoccupied by the political problems of the Middle East and the Islamic world. Western opinion-formers were on the hunt for "moderate" Muslim leaders, who could reconcile Islam with democracy and the West. Erdoğan looked like the man they were searching for.

Turkey was already a member of NATO, and while Erdoğan was much more religiously devout than Turkey's traditionally secular leaders, he had embraced capitalism and risen through democratic politics. Turkey is also a large enough country and economy – with a population of more than 80 million people – to look like a credible model for other Muslim nations. Robert Kaplan, an influential American journalist, captured the mood of the time when he argued in 2004 that "Erdoğan's moderate, reformist Islam now offers the single best hope for reconciling Muslims . . . with twenty-first-century social and political realities."[1]

I first saw Erdoğan in action in Brussels in 2004, at a press conference in support of his country's application to join the European Union. His willingness to sit in a back room of the European Parliament, patiently fielding questions from foreign journalists about Turkey's suitability to "join Europe," seemed to confirm that this was a leader who was comfortable with the cut and thrust of democratic politics. When I asked if he was worried about opposition to Turkish membership within the EU, he gave an answer well tailored to liberal sensibilities: "If the European Union has decided to be a Christian club, rather than one of shared values, then let it say so now."[2] Olli Rehn, the European commissioner in charge of handling Turkey's application for joining the EU, told me how he and Erdoğan had bonded over their shared love of football. What could be more European than that!

In the geopolitical context of the time, Turkey's application to join the EU was regarded as vitally important. If Turkey became an EU member state, it was widely believed that the dual threats of Islamism and military coups in the country would be safely banished to the past. Otto Schily, Germany's interior minister, argued that if Turkey joined the EU, it would "show the world that it is possible for Muslims and the West to live together on the basis of the values of the Enlightenment."[3] For a while those hopes were embodied in the figure of Recep Tayyip Erdoğan.

It was not just European politicians and Washington journalists who placed enormous faith in the Turkish leader. As US president, Barack Obama chose to give his first major speech on foreign policy in Ankara, and throughout his first term he spoke more frequently to Erdoğan than to any other foreign leader.[4] After the Iraq war, Obama's main foreign policy goal was to establish a new relationship between the US and the Muslim world and the Turkish leader seemed like a key figure.

Erdoğan's political history and his first years as prime minister did offer some evidence for the beguiling hope that he could provide a model for the reconciliation of Islam, democracy and modernity. Born in 1954 in a poor part of Istanbul, the son of a ferry captain, Erdoğan had joined the Islamist National Salvation Party (MSP) as a teenager. After spells as a semi-professional footballer and a factory worker, he became a full-time party worker and rose to head the party in Istanbul. His charisma and skills as a grassroots organizer saw him elected as mayor of the city in 1994. But in 1998, the Turkish courts ordered the closure of the Welfare Party (as the MSP had now become), because of its Islamist character. In the same year, Erdoğan himself was forced to step down as Istanbul's mayor and imprisoned for reciting a poem that judges said had incited religious hatred. It contained the lines "The mosques are our barracks, the domes our helmets, the minarets our bayonets and the faithful our soldiers."

Rather than ending his political career as Turkey's secular establishment had intended, Erdoğan's four and a half months behind bars in 1999 helped to catapult him to national power.[5] Many devout Muslims now regarded him as a hero, whom the state had failed to silence. On his release he formed and led a new breakaway Islamist party, Justice and Development (known by its Turkish initials, AKP), which won the Turkish general elections of 2002. When Erdoğan's ban from politics ended, he entered parliament through a by-election and became prime minister in 2003.

At this stage, even many Turkish democrats supported Erdoğan, who seemed to have triumphed over an effort to undermine democracy.

Liberals were encouraged by his opposition to military rule and his avowed commitment to democracy and pluralism. The new Turkish leader seemed to set himself against the very concept of strongman politics, proclaiming "the age of me-centred politics is over."[6] Some of his early actions in office also appeared to justify the hope that he would be a democrat and a reformer. As well as pressing ahead with Turkey's application to the EU, his government passed legislation strengthening minority rights and judicial independence and abolishing the death penalty.[7] It helped that, in his first years in office, Turkey was going through an investment- and construction-led boom, driven in large part by hopes that Turkey would soon join the EU. The surge in the economy boosted Erdoğan's credibility with both Turkish voters and foreign investors.

A few skeptics noted that Erdoğan's past contained plenty of evidence that he was no liberal. As a young activist in the 1970s he had starred as lead actor, joint director and part scriptwriter of a conspiratorial play called *Mason-Communist-Jew*.[8] As mayor of Istanbul in 1996, he had remarked, "Democracy is like a tram. You ride it until you arrive at your destination. And then you step off."[9] The destination, it could be assumed, was a Turkey in which the Islamic faith once again played a central role, reversing the secularism written into the Turkish constitution by Atatürk. It was notable that most of the liberalizing measures of the early Erdoğan years also helped Islamists strengthen their position in society. Western liberals welcomed Erdoğan's removal of a ban on women in headscarves studying at universities as a boost for freedom and women's rights;[10] Islamists welcomed it as an advance for religious piety.

As the years wore on, Erdoğan's strengthening grip on power and his ongoing struggle with the Turkish military brought his autocratic instincts to the fore. After the Turkish police claimed to have discovered evidence of a coup plot in 2007, scores of generals and military officers were arrested and put on trial. Once again some liberals approved, since they regarded the army as the historic foe of democracy in Turkey. But there were also concerns that much of the evidence had been fabricated.

The realization of just how strong Erdoğan's anti-democratic tendencies were dawned only slowly in the West. On a visit to Turkey in 2011, conversations with friends and contacts convinced me that

Erdoğan's dark side could no longer be ignored.* In an article with the (admittedly timid) headline "Don't Be Blind to Erdoğan's Flaws," I noted that the Turkish leader was undoubtedly popular and charismatic: he had won three successive elections by this stage and even his opponents generally regarded the votes as clean. But I also pointed out that "there are now considerably more journalists in jail in Turkey than in China." The prime minister's personal style was also becoming more dictatorial. On a visit to the UN in New York in 2011, some of his bodyguards had got into a fight with UN security personnel. Ominously, Erdoğan had announced that he intended to move from the prime ministerial office to the presidency after changing the constitution to boost presidential powers. He was clearly settling in for another decade in power which, as I noted in my article, would "make him Turkey's answer to Vladimir Putin."[11]

Domestic opposition – whether peaceful or violent – seemed only to strengthen Erdoğan's paranoia and his determination to crush all dissent. In 2013, many Turkish liberals and secularists took to the streets in the Gezi Park protests – prompted initially by news that the Turkish leader intended to build over one of the few parks in central Istanbul to re-create an old Ottoman-era barracks that had once been the base for a rising by Islamist officers. Erdoğan also planned to build a mosque in Taksim Square, the symbolic heart of Istanbul, right next to Gezi Park.

The power of social media helped turn an environmental protest into a massive anti-government movement, which at its height drew one million people onto the streets of Istanbul. The demonstrators who I saw gathered in Taksim Square, at one of a succession of rolling protests, were urban liberals who would have looked totally at home in New York or London. Few of the women in the crowd wore headscarves – unlike the wives of all senior AKP politicians. This was a Turkish "culture war" – and it provoked Erdoğan into a fury of paranoia and bitterness. He accused the demonstrators of being a tool of foreign powers and of the Jewish financier George Soros.

But even the paranoid have real enemies. The Gezi Park protests eventually fizzled out. But in August 2016, Erdoğan's enemies in the

---

* Some of my contacts were later imprisoned, put on trial or went into exile, so I would prefer not to list them.

military moved against him. Troops arrived to arrest the Turkish leader at his holiday hotel, or possibly assassinate him, but found that Erdoğan had been tipped off and had left just an hour beforehand. As fighter jets bombed the Turkish parliament, Erdoğan appeared on television – via FaceTime – and appealed to Turks to take to the streets to block the putsch. After twenty-four hours, the Turkish leader had regained control. But some 250 people had been killed. And Erdoğan himself was profoundly shaken.[12]

In the aftermath of the failed coup, Erdoğan declared a state of emergency which led to a massive crackdown on civil liberties. The president blamed the attempted putsch on the followers of a US-based preacher, Fethullah Gulen, with whom he had once been allied. There is indeed evidence that supporters of Gulen were heavily involved in the plot against Erdoğan.[13] In its aftermath, tens of thousands of civil servants, alleged to be "Gulenists," were arrested, the passports of 50,000 people were cancelled, 4,000 judges and prosecutors were sacked and more than a hundred media outlets were closed.[14] The purges extended well beyond Gulenists, sweeping up independent voices and liberal critics of the Erdoğan government.

One of the most important figures imprisoned in the crackdown was Selahattin Demirtas, a Kurdish politician and a key figure in the parliamentary opposition. Demirtas had led his political party to a historic success in the 2015 Turkish election, when the HDP had won enough seats to deny Erdoğan's AKP a parliamentary majority for the first time since it took power in 2002. The HDP had become the first Kurdish party to gain representation in the Turkish parliament. But it had also attracted support from a wider public, who saw Demirtas as an articulate and principled figure, capable of standing up to Erdoğan.

In the aftermath of the coup, Demirtas was arrested and accused of supporting terrorism, specifically the PKK, the armed Kurdish movement. He was detained in a remote prison and charged with various terrorism-related offenses that collectively carried a sentence of up to 142 years. Foreign jurists who looked at the case were unconvinced. In a scathing verdict issued in 2020, the European Court of Human Rights demanded that he should be released immediately and concluded that the Turkish state's actions had "merely been cover for an ulterior political purpose."[15] The ECHR was ignored. Erdoğan had resorted to one of the favorite tools of the strongman leader – the imprisonment of dangerous opponents. It was a tactic that Vladimir Putin has used with Alexei Navalny and Mikhail Khodorkovsky and that Xi Jinping has employed with the leaders of the Hong Kong democracy movement such as Joshua Wong, Agnes Chow and Jimmy Lai.

Visiting Turkey again, the year after the failed coup, I found an atmosphere of fear among my familiar circle of academics and journalists. Everybody knew somebody who had lost their job or been arrested or fled the country. Many of those who were still free feared for their livelihoods or their liberty. As one internationally respected scholar put it to me: "Things that I once thought unimaginable now happen on a daily basis."

It was a striking statement that resonated well beyond the borders of Turkey. I had heard similar laments from members of the liberal intelligentsia in cities as different as Delhi, Beijing and Budapest. Indeed, by 2017, I was hearing the same kind of incredulity and fear for the future of democracy even in Washington DC and New York. The advent of the Trump presidency had created an ironic inversion of the hopes that American pundits had once expressed about Erdoğan. Back in 2004, the idea was that the Turkish leader would direct his country towards liberal democracy and "twenty-first-century political realities" – in the self-assured phrase of Robert Kaplan. Now it seemed as if Trump was making the US look more like Turkey.

Viewed from Istanbul in May 2017, the comparisons seemed quite striking. Both Trump and Erdoğan were nationalists who had promised to make their nations respected and feared again. Both had turned governing into a family business and promoted their sons-in-law. The Turkish equivalent of Jared Kushner was Berat Albayrak, who Erdoğan had appointed first as energy minister and then as finance minister. Both presidents drew their political strength from small towns and rural areas. Both accused their country's bureaucracies of plotting against them. Indeed, the notion of a hostile, self-interested "deep state" which Trump popularized in America originated in Turkey.[16]

Both leaders also used their countries' bitter social divisions as a means of bolstering their political support. In Turkey, devout Muslims and the rank and file of the AKP seemed prepared to accept Erdoğan's slide into autocracy because he was seen as a defender of the faith and the nation, against their enemies in the secular establishment. In a similar way, Trump's most loyal base of support came from white evangelicals who saw the president as their champion against liberal America. A bitterly divided country makes it easier to persuade your followers to tolerate the erosion of civil liberties, in the interests of political victory over domestic enemies.

The similarities between the Trump and Erdoğan approaches to the media and the courts were also chilling. By 2017, Erdoğan was able to stage multiple arrests of journalists and sack judges. Trump was restricted to denouncing the "fake news media" and "so-called judges." Watching the interactions between the two presidents, some of Trump's aides came to the conclusion that their boss rather envied Erdoğan's impunity.[17]

One aspect of Erdoğan's period in power that Trump may well have envied was the Turkish leader's sheer longevity in office. In March 2018, he became the Turkish republic's longest ever serving leader – recording 5,500 days in office as prime minister and president combined, and so eclipsing the republic's founding father, Kemal Atatürk. But Erdoğan was not intent on simply notching up a longer term in power than Atatürk. In important respects, he was undermining his legacy and its emphasis on secularism. By reconnecting the Turkish state with Islam, Erdoğan was in essence pushing for a refounding of the Turkish republic. Rather than being a "Kemalist" state, it would be molded in Erdoğan's image.

A symbolic moment came in 2020, when the Erdoğan government reconverted the Hagia Sophia into a mosque. Built as a cathedral by the Emperor Justinian in 536, it became a mosque after the fall of Constantinople in 1453. Under Atatürk, the building was converted into a museum in 1935 and by 2020 had become the most visited site in Istanbul. For Turkey's Islamists, reconverting the Hagia Sophia back into a mosque was a long-standing goal. After seventeen years in office, Erdoğan finally achieved it. Leading the prayers in the Hagia Sophia on July 24, 2020, he proclaimed: "This was the greatest dream of our youth, and now it has been accomplished." For Erdoğan, this was a moment of global significance. The "resurrection of the Hagia Sophia" was, he claimed, "the will of Muslims all over the world."[18]

The claim to be a champion of the faith is fairly common among the new generation of strongman leaders. Vladimir Putin claims to see himself as the defender of 800 million Christians around the world, as he once told José Manuel Barroso, the president of the European

Commission.[19] In India, Narendra Modi is a proud Hindu national-ist. Indeed, just a week after Erdoğan presided over the reconversion of the Hagia Sophia into a mosque, Modi was laying the foundation stone of a new Hindu temple at Ayodhya, where a mosque had stood until it was destroyed by Hindu militants in 1992. For Modi, as for Erdoğan, this was the realization of a decades-long dream. If the strongman leaders of Turkey and India were rivals in a "clash of civilizations" – the one a champion of Islam, the other a Hindu nationalist – they were pursuing strikingly similar cultural and political projects: seeking to put religion back at the center of the nation and the state and to fight back against secular liberalism.

Rallying the faithful is a particularly useful stratagem at times of economic hardship. Erdoğan's triumphal moment at the Hagia Sophia was staged in the middle of a deep crisis brought about by years of economic mismanagement and compounded by the Covid-19 pan-demic. The Turkish leader's grasp of economics is extremely shaky. He has often insisted, for example, that raising interest rates causes infla-tion. Even before the Covid crisis struck, Turkey was on the brink of a debt crisis. As the Turkish economy sunk deeper into the mire, Erdoğan fell out with his own son-in-law, and Albayrak was forced to resign as the country's finance minister in November 2020.

The use of "culture war" distractions is one obvious tactic for a strongman leader facing domestic economic problems. Another is to employ nationalism and foreign military adventures to stir up patriot-ism at home. It worked for Vladimir Putin with the annexation of Crimea in 2014. In the aftermath of the post-coup crackdown, and with the Turkish economy in trouble, Erdoğan's foreign policy became increasingly aggressive too.

The fact that Turkish membership of the EU has become less and less likely during the Erdoğan period has also made it easier for the Turkish leader to adopt the methods of a strongman leader, both at home and abroad. Erdoğan never formally retracted Turkey's applica-tion to join the EU, and the EU never formally withdrew the invitation. But a process of mutual disillusionment has set in over his long years in power. As Turkey has become more and more autocratic, so it has moved further and further away from the democratic standards that the EU insists are adopted by would-be members. Erdoğan is also now regarded with deep suspicion in some EU countries, such as the

Netherlands and Germany, where the Turkish leader has been accused of intervening in domestic politics by appealing directly to ethnic Turks. In 2017, ministers in Erdoğan's government were prevented from campaigning on Dutch soil (some 400,000 Turks live in the Netherlands), in favor of a Yes vote in the Turkish referendum on constitutional change. In response, Erdoğan called the Dutch "fascists" and linked them to Nazism.[20] Erdoğan has also, on occasions, used wild rhetoric about the Greek, French, Cypriot and German governments. His willingness to lash out against EU members reflects his increasing bitterness towards the organization – and his eagerness to play to the nationalist gallery at home. In Brussels, Paris and Berlin, meanwhile, Erdoğan is no longer seen as a man who could lead his country towards a future in the EU. Instead, he is regarded as autocratic, unpredictable and potentially dangerous.

In his early years in power, when Turkey was still being talked of seriously as a future EU member – and Erdoğan himself was still regarded as a reformist liberal in Washington – the Turkish leader's approach to foreign affairs had been conciliatory. The slogan popularized by Ahmet Davutoğlu, Turkey's hyperactive foreign minister, was "zero problems with the neighbors." By 2020, however, Davutoğlu was long gone and Turks were joking that the new policy was "zero neighbors without problems." In defense of what he perceived to be Turkey's national interests, Erdoğan had become increasingly willing to run risks and to use force. Like Putin, he has sought – with some success – to reassert his nation's power beyond its borders. That, in turn, has bolstered his prestige at home.

The fragmentation of Syria, and America's alliance there with Kurdish militias, had fanned Turkish fears of Kurdish separatism. In response, Erdoğan deployed Turkish troops into Syria in 2016, who effectively occupied part of the country, creating a buffer zone. Turkey also intervened with troops and logistical support for the internationally recognized Libyan government, turning the tide against a rebel offensive backed by France, Russia and the Gulf States. In addition, the Turkish navy has flexed its muscles in the eastern Mediterranean in protest at gas exploration by Greece in waters claimed by Turkey. And in 2020, Turkey intervened decisively in a war between Azerbaijan and Armenia over the status of Nagorno-Karabakh. Military drones supplied by the Turks were crucial in swinging the long-festering conflict towards Azerbaijan. In December 2020, Erdoğan took the stand at a victory parade in Baku, the Azerbaijani capital, as the guest of honor. Surrounded by Turkish and Azeri flags, he proclaimed: "Today is a day of victory and pride for all of us. For the whole Turkic world."[21] In common with several other strongman leaders – such as Putin, Xi and Modi – Erdoğan sees his country as representing a civilization and a culture, as much as a state.

This kind of military adventurism inevitably means that Erdoğan has complicated and dangerous relations with many of the other strongman leaders in his neighborhood. He has long been at daggers-drawn with both Bashar al-Assad of Syria and Benjamin Netanyahu of Israel. The Turkish leader is an object of deep suspicion in Riyadh as well because the Saudis regard Erdoğan as a supporter of their sworn enemies in the Muslim Brotherhood. The antipathy is mutual, so Erdoğan was more than happy to leak the Turkish intelligence tapes of the murder of the journalist Jamal Khashoggi in the Saudi consulate in 2018.[22] The Turkish leader has also clashed repeatedly with Emmanuel Macron of France over Libya, Islam and the eastern Mediterranean. He has even suggested that the French president is mentally unstable.

Erdoğan's relationship with Vladimir Putin is particularly compli-cated. At times, the Turkish and Russian strongmen have seemed very close. Erdoğan appreciated the instant support that Putin offered him at the time of the 2016 coup attempt. Indeed, a common rumor in Ankara is that Putin actually telephoned Erdoğan on the night of the coup with the offer of military support. Putin also persuaded Erdoğan to buy a Russian air-defense system, which caused outrage among Tur-key's NATO allies. On the other hand, Turkish and Russian interests have clashed right across the region, in Syria, Libya and Nagorno-Karabakh. Turkish intervention in that conflict was particularly startling, since this former part of the Soviet Union is regarded in Mos-cow as Russia's backyard. Once again, there was an Islamic and cultural aspect to the conflict with the Muslim Azerbaijanis, backed by the Turks, squaring off against the Orthodox Armenians, who were closer to Russia.

When Turkey shot down a Russian plane in 2015 on the Syrian–Turkish border, Erdoğan eventually apologized for the incident. (He later alleged that the Turkish pilots involved had been traitors and Gulenists.) In 2020, thirty-four Turkish troops were killed by an air strike inside Syria that was carried out by the Syrian air force, perhaps with Russian participation. But, once again, the strongmen of Moscow and Ankara were careful to avoid the situation escalating into all-out conflict.

International conflicts always carry a risk for a strongman ruler. A quick victory, followed by a military parade and a stirring speech, is ideal. But military adventures can go wrong. The invasion of the Falklands in 1982 was meant to provide a propaganda boost for General Leopoldo Galtieri in Argentina, but instead ended in military defeat and his downfall. And conflicts that drag on too long can eventually drain away political support. By 2020, Turkish troops had been in Syria for four years, sustaining hundreds of casualties, but without a clear exit route.

Neither domestic repression nor foreign entanglements have been enough to completely secure Erdoğan's domestic political position. The Turkish leader can lock up and harass many of his political opponents, and has increasing sway over the courts, the media and business, but he has not extinguished electoral democracy.

That became dramatically evident in 2019, when Erdoğan's AK Party lost the mayoral elections in Istanbul, the president's original power base. Like Donald Trump a year later, Erdoğan was unable to accept defeat. He denounced the Istanbul election as fraudulent. Unlike Trump, the Turkish leader was able to force the election to be rerun. But the AKP lost again, with the opposition candidate, Ekrem Imamoglu, winning by an even larger margin second time around. The Turkish opposition was understandably jubilant. The *Cumhuriyet* newspaper, many of whose staff had been imprisoned on terrorism charges in 2018, proclaimed a "thrashing for one-man rule."[23] The Istanbul elections of 2019 were certainly a reminder of Erdoğan's potential vulnerability – and of the fact that Turkey remains a curious and unsettling hybrid, hovering between democracy and authoritarianism.

But as we will see, many other countries around the world, from the Philippines to Hungary, are in similar situations. Indeed, even the United States in the Trump era was teetering on the edge of losing its democratic safeguards. In June 2020, when the Washington-based Turkish analyst, Soner Cagaptay, listed "Erdoğan's 10 steps to power," the list seemed distinctly familiar to many in the US: "Attack 'nefarious elites'; Deliver prosperity; 'Make Turkey Great Again'; Create fake news; Say opposition's lying; Demonize press & courts; Frame opponents as terrorists; Curb their freedoms; Undermine and change the constitution."[24] Step 10 was an emoji of a crown.

Erdoğan has provided a model for how to move a fragile democracy towards strongman authoritarianism. The size and importance of Turkey, combined with Erdoğan's longevity in office and outspoken rhetoric, has turned the Turkish leader into an important global figure. He has helped to dash facile hopes about the reconciliation of Islam and liberalism. And he has made Turkey an increasingly significant player in the politics of both Europe and the Middle East.

But while Turkey is a significant member of the G20 group of leading economies, it is not and never will be a superpower. For strongman politics to change the world, the trend had to move beyond Moscow and Istanbul and establish itself in one of the world's major rising powers. And that is what happened in Beijing in 2012.

3 Xi Jinping – China and the return of the cult of personality (2012)

"The argument that strong countries are bound to seek hegemony does not apply to China," Xi Jinping declared. His tone was firm and did not invite debate. It was November 2013, almost exactly a year since Xi had been appointed as China's leader, and I was part of a small group of foreigners invited to meet him in the Great Hall of the People in Beijing.

The Chinese leader kept our group waiting for a few minutes, before striding into the room, shaking a few hands and posing for a group photo. Once seated in a comfortable armchair, Xi started our meeting by pronouncing himself "deeply moved by the sincerity you have shown." The ornate pleasantries offered by China's new leader were a striking contrast to the edginess and menace that I had seen Vladimir Putin radiate in Davos a few years earlier. Xi spoke deliberately and without notes. His air of calm authority was aided by the grandeur of his surroundings. A huge mural of the Great Wall of China decorated the wall behind him. Just outside was Tiananmen Square, the ceremonial heart of Beijing. Arrayed in front of him, listening intently, was a group that included former prime ministers, such as Britain's Gordon Brown and Australia's Kevin Rudd, corporate leaders like Google's Eric Schmidt, and a smattering of academics and journalists.

In a short speech, followed by questions, Xi explained his plans to eradicate poverty and establish China as a "moderately prosperous" country. He predicted confidently that the Chinese economy would continue to grow at 7 percent a year, powered by the continuing urbanization of the country. But this was balanced with a promise that China would never use its power to threaten the world. It all sounded reassuringly technocratic and rational. By the standards of the previous Chinese leader, Hu Jintao – who had often read robotically from notes – Xi's willingness to answer questions seemed refreshingly spontaneous.

Nicolas Berggruen, the German businessman who had organized the meeting, summarized the group's general impressions afterwards. He concluded that the new Chinese president stood in the tradition of Deng Xiaoping, the leader who had opened up the country and liberalized its economy from 1978 onwards. As Berggruen and Nathan Gardels put it: "Xi is a true disciple of Deng Xiaoping, albeit in these less harsh, more tempered times."[1]

Other Western commentators dared to be even more optimistic. Writing in the summer of 2013, John Simpson, the veteran BBC journalist, compared the rise of Xi to the appointment of Mikhail Gorbachev as the leader of the Soviet Union and floated the idea that "the next five to seven years will change everything" in China, leading to the emergence of a popularly elected parliament.[2]

It was an intoxicating thought. But, in retrospect, Western commentators should have been comparing Xi not with Gorbachev or Deng but with Mao Zedong. When I later read the historian Frank Dikötter's description of Mao, I was reminded of my first impressions of Xi: "He walked and spoke slowly, always with great gravitas. He smiled often and benevolently."[3] Unfortunately, the parallels between Xi and Mao went deeper than their personal comportment. As Xi settled into power, it became clear that his admiration for "the Great Helmsman" was deep and genuine. Like Mao, Xi set about consolidating power around himself, establishing a personality cult and reasserting the Communist Party's control of every facet of China's development. By 2017, he was speaking in unmistakably Maoist terms, proclaiming: "Government, military, society and schools, north, south, east and west – the party is the leader of all."[4] And the leader of the party was none other than Xi Jinping.

That statement was made by Xi in October 2017 at China's 19th Communist Party Congress. I was in Shanghai for a conference at the time, which gave me some insight into the intensity of the personality cult around Xi and the fear that it inspired. At the party congress, a new guiding ideology, "Xi Jinping Thought on Socialism with Chinese

Characteristics for a New Era," was written into the party's constitution. As a result, Xi became the first living leader since Mao to have his own ideas incorporated into the party's founding document.

The length of Xi's speech offered another clue to his incipient megalomania. The Chinese leader spoke for three hours and twenty-three minutes – and the whole country, right down to kindergarten classes, was encouraged to sit down and watch on television. An academic friend of mine told me that at one of China's leading universities, the heads of all the faculties were instructed to assemble in a room on campus and to watch the speech. Those who failed to turn up were called by party officials and asked to account for their movements and, in one case, even to send selfies of themselves watching the speech. Its contents reflected Xi's determination to identify himself with China's growing strength. He told his audience that "The Chinese nation . . . has stood up, grown rich, and become strong – and it now embraces the brilliant prospects of rejuvenation . . . It will be an era that sees China moving closer to centre stage."[5]

A few months later, Xi further cemented his personal power. In March 2018, it was announced that China was abolishing term limits for the country's presidency – opening the way for Xi to rule for life. The practical and symbolic impact of this decision was enormous. Term limits for the presidency had been introduced in 1982 by Deng, as part of a deliberate attempt to move away from the personalized rule of Mao and the concentration of power in one man. Now Xi was quite deliberately turning the clock back.

Each year seemed to mark an intensification of the Xi cult. On another visit to the country in early 2020, I watched in appalled fascination as a friend gave me a demonstration of the new "Xi Jinping Thought" app now installed on more than 100 million phones in China. All party members, students and employees of state companies were told to study Xi thought on a daily basis and their study-time and performance in quizzes was monitored. As one prominent Beijing academic complained to me, "We are increasingly living in a totalitarian state."* The signs of a personality cult proliferated: city streets were overlooked by banners with excerpts from Xi thought and street

---

* The number of unattributed quotes in this section is a reflection of the need to protect Chinese friends from retribution.

posters in Shanghai showed the great leader with rays of light emerging from his head.

Chinese liberals and intellectuals were both dismayed and disorientated by the speed of the change, and were trying to figure out where it had all gone wrong. One prominent economist told me that the moment he began to realize what was afoot was when Xi had given a speech in 2013 arguing that it was wrong to believe Deng's leadership had marked a sharp break with Mao. On the contrary, Xi had insisted, Deng had been building on Mao's legacy.

On both a factual and personal level, this was a peculiar argument to make. The country that Deng took over in late 1978 had been laid low by Mao. It was desperately poor and many millions had died as a result of Mao's political and economic experiments, the Great Leap Forward (1958–61) and the Cultural Revolution (1966–76). Deng had rejected the idea that all wisdom could be found in Mao's "Little Red Book" and instead pledged to "seek truth from facts." His pragmatism allowed China to embrace foreign investment and to unleash domestic entrepreneurship. The economic results were spectacular, indeed arguably unparalleled in human history. The country that Xi inherited in 2012 was more than fifty times richer than the one that Deng had taken over in 1978 – with a GDP estimated to have grown from a mere $150 billion to $8,277 billion.[6]

On a personal level, Xi had plenty of reasons to be deeply wary of Mao's legacy. He was born in 1953, four years after the establishment of the People's Republic of China. Xi's father, Xi Zhongxun, was a military commander and comrade of Mao's from the 1930s, who became chief of the Communist Party's propaganda department in 1962. The young Xi Jinping was a child of the elite, educated at the August 1st School, located in a former palace and known as "the cradle of leaders."[7] By 1962 his father had risen to the rank of vice premier.

But then, as was all too typical in that era, he fell from grace as a result of an obscure doctrinal dispute. Xi the elder was placed under house arrest and became a nonperson for more than fifteen years, spending long periods in detention or working as a factory-hand. Xi Jinping was forced to denounce his father. One of his sisters committed suicide. When his school was closed in 1968, Xi was sent into exile in the countryside to join a work brigade in Shaanxi province. Banishment was a common experience for members of the Chinese elite during the Cultural Revolution period and the young Xi, like many others, was forced to abandon his studies, and to become a farm laborer and construction worker.

But in 1975, the same year that his father was politically rehabilitated, Xi Jinping's period of exile was allowed to come to a close. The future Chinese leader returned to Beijing, where he was admitted to Tsinghua University – China's equivalent of Harvard or Oxford – as part of a cohort of places reserved for "workers, peasants and soldiers." Like many other future Communist Party leaders, Xi studied engineering.[8]

Official biographies of Xi have used his rural exile – including a period when he is said to have lived in a cave – to portray the Chinese leader as a man familiar with the hardship of life in the countryside. Xi himself has spoken of his rural exile as both formative and positive. In a long article written in 2002 and clearly aimed at burnishing his image as he rose up the Communist Party ladder, he wrote: "I arrived in the yellow earth (the countryside) when I was fifteen. I was lost, indecisive; when I left age twenty-two, I had clear life goals and self-confidence. The northern plateaux of Shaanxi province are my roots as a servant of the state."[9]

Some of the Chinese leader's liberal critics take a less charitable view of his period of rural exile, pointing out that Xi missed out on a crucial decade of education and suggesting that he is, as a result, crude and ill-informed in his approach to government. Xi himself has a tendency to make ostentatious references to his own learning. On a trip to France, he claimed to have read the works of nineteen leading French authors, including Diderot, Voltaire and Sartre.[10] On a trip to Russia, he claimed to have read not just Tolstoy and Dostoevsky, but also Pushkin, Gogol and a host of other Russian authors.

There can be little doubt that, for all the mythologizing of Xi's youth, his family's fall from grace must have been a searing experience. But Xi's reaction to the hardships that the Maoist system inflicted on him was revealing. Rather than rejecting the Communist Party, the young Xi strove desperately for rehabilitation, applying again and again to rejoin the party before finally succeeding on his seventh attempt in 1974.

By 1978 Xi had begun his long career as a Communist Party functionary, serving for four years as the secretary of Geng Biao, a member of the Central Military Commission. This gave the future leader a familiarity with military affairs, which would assume a new significance decades later when he presided over a rapid arms buildup and the construction of new military bases across disputed areas of the South China Sea. In 1982, however, Xi left Beijing and the military behind to take on the life of a party bureaucrat in the provinces – a traditional but arduous proving ground for Communist officials who eventually aspired to a big job in Beijing. From 1985 to 2002, Xi worked in the coastal province of Fujian, an area that was at the forefront of the rapid economic transformation of China, with close trading links to the booming capitalist economy of Taiwan. As Kerry Brown observes, Xi's years in Fujian from 1985 "form the backbone of his career before central leadership."[11] From Fujian, where he had finished up as provincial governor, Xi moved to run the Communist Party in Zhejiang, another fast-growing coastal province, before moving to Shanghai in 2007. That same year, Xi was promoted to the Politburo Standing Committee of the Communist Party, a seven-man body which stands at the very apex of political power in the country. He was now clearly marked out as a potential future leader of China, an impression that was strengthened when he was appointed to chair the committee preparing for the 2008 Olympic Games.

Rising political stars in China generally do not reveal too much of themselves – and those that do often come to a sticky end. But even before Xi took the top job and party propagandists set about creating a leadership myth, elements of his biography marked him out as something more than a colorless apparatchik, in particular the fact that the future Chinese leader was married to a famous singer. It was during his period in Fujian that Xi married his second wife, Peng Liyuan, who is both a former general in the People's Liberation Army and a TV star in China. Her performances singing patriotic songs, while clad in military uniform, can be found on YouTube and Chinese social media. The couple have a daughter, Xi Mingze, born in 1992, who was educated at a French-speaking school in China and did her undergraduate degree at Harvard in the US, where she studied under a pseudonym and graduated in 2014. One Chinese dissident told me that the only thing that had made him think positively of Xi was meeting his daughter. She was not the entitled brat he had expected, but came across as intelligent and open to the outside world. A European head of state who dined with the Xi family in Beijing also told me how impressed he had been by the president's daughter.

Xi's willingness to send his only child to be educated in the US suggests a certain open-mindedness. But other glimpses of the private man reveal a strong nationalist side, such as his remark when visiting Mexico in 2009, where Xi was recorded complaining to fellow countrymen about "foreigners with full bellies, pointing their fingers at China." This revealed that beneath the calm and statesmanlike exterior the Chinese leader likes to present to the outside world, there is also an edge of anger in his worldview.

As China prepared to anoint a new leader in 2012, one much-discussed candidate was Bo Xilai, the charismatic and ambitious leader of the giant city of Chongqing, whose nationalism and flirtation with the "red" themes and slogans of the Mao Zedong era alarmed Chinese liberals. When Bo was dramatically arrested that year and later imprisoned for conspiracy to murder, China seemed to have been saved from the threat of Caesarism. Instead, it was Xi who was appointed to the most important leadership role in China, General Secretary of the Communist Party, in November 2012. He was then elected president of China at the National People's Congress in March 2013. There were 2,952 votes in favor and one against, with three abstentions.

Xi's first distinctive initiative as China's leader revealed his populist and ruthless edge. It was an anti-corruption drive that took down some of the most powerful people in China, including an extraordinarily high number of senior party members. By some estimates 14 percent of the top cadres of the party were arrested and imprisoned as part of the anti-corruption campaign. Wang Qishan, Xi's trusted ally who was put in charge of the campaign, liked to shake up foreigners by boasting of the numbers he had sent to jail. One visitor to his office told me that Wang had opened the conversation by remarking: "People say that I've locked up hundreds of thousands of people. But it's more than that. It's over a million." There was no hyperbole in that statement. As Richard McGregor observed in 2019: "Since late 2012, the authorities have investigated more than 2.7m officials and punished more than 1.5m others. This includes seven at the top level (Politburo and cabinet) and about two dozen high-ranking generals."[12]

Arrests and imprisonment on this scale create a wider sense of insecurity and fear. Even outwardly loyal followers of Xi would occasionally reveal these sentiments to me. A stock market crash in 2015 led to a rash of arrests of officials involved in the regulation of finance, spreading panic among some of the bankers who were used to dealing with them.[13] One manager at a top-tier Western bank told me that she had noticed some of its employees had become reluctant to travel, fearing they might be arrested at the airport. A few years later, a prominent businessman told me in shocked tones that one of his close friends, a rising political star who was deputy head of the Communist Party in Chongqing, had thrown himself off the roof of a hotel in Beijing, after being accused of corruption at a party meeting. "I guess he just couldn't face spending the rest of his life in prison," mused my friend, who believed that the real cause of Ren Xuefeng's suicide might have been a political purge sparked by ideological differences with President Xi.[14] Even Chinese officials with significant international profiles were subject to sudden falls from grace. Meng Hongwei, who in 2016 became the first Chinese national to head Interpol, the international police body, was himself arrested on a return trip to China in 2018. A few months later, reports emerged in the Chinese press that Meng had admitted to corruption, although his family insisted that he had been targeted because of his reformist views.[15]

Party officials and apologists for the system, who might previously have dismissed stories of official corruption as overblown, quickly adopted the new line for the Xi era: that the Chinese system had faced a potentially terminal threat from corruption that Xi had responded to decisively. Any suggestion that the Xi family had itself acquired mysterious wealth was dealt with ruthlessly. When a story along these lines was reported by Bloomberg News, the news agency was placed firmly outside the great firewall that polices the Chinese internet.[16]

Inevitably, many have interpreted Xi's anti-corruption drive as a settling of political scores and a means to consolidate power. That may well be true. But Xi also seems to be genuinely frightened by the idea that corruption could lead to the Communist Party losing power in China. And he believes that the end of one-party rule would be fatal to his much-stated goal of the "great rejuvenation" of the Chinese people.

In particular, China's leader is haunted by the collapse of the Soviet Union. In 2013, his first full year in power, Communist Party members all over China were invited to showings of a documentary film about the collapse of the USSR. The film portrayed this event as a tragedy and the villain of the piece as Mikhail Gorbachev, the last Soviet leader whose reformist policies of openness and economic reconstruction are described not just as wrongheaded but as immoral and unpatriotic. In a speech given to the Communist Party Central Committee in 2013, Xi himself asked: "Why did the Soviet Union collapse? Why did the Soviet Communist Party lose its power?" His answer was that "The history of the USSR and of the party had been completely denied . . . Lenin was rejected, as was Stalin . . . Ideological confusion was everywhere . . . The army wasn't under the control of the party. Finally, the Communist Party of the Soviet Union . . . was dissolved like a flock of sparrows. The Soviet Union, which had been a great socialist country collapsed. This is the lesson we must learn from the errors of the past."[17]

Xi does not believe that the collapse of the USSR was simply a result of mistakes by Soviet leaders. He sees the West as deliberately driving the process, through the promotion of subversive liberal ideas, and he is determined to prevent any similar campaign in China. This line of thinking was laid out very clearly early in Xi's period in power, with the distribution to party cadres of a "Communiqué on the Current State of the Ideological Sphere." Referred to more succinctly as Document 9 (and later leaked), the communiqué outlines the hostile Western forces that China needs to guard against. These include ideas such as "universal values," "civil society" and "the West's idea of journalism."[18]

Xi and his acolytes see these ideas as dangerous imports, alien to China. But they know that they are also attractive to many Chinese intellectuals and to some in the rising middle class. Liberal intellectuals were an important part of the Chinese debate in the years before Xi came to power. The most internationally famous figures were the artist Ai Weiwei and the Nobel prizewinner Liu Xiaobo, but behind them stood a much larger group of academics, lawyers and journalists who all hoped to see China gradually evolve into a more democratic country, with independent courts and greater freedom of speech.

Chinese citizens brave enough to argue for these ideas were never safe from persecution. Liu Xiaobo was arrested and imprisoned in 2009 (and died in prison in 2017). Ai Weiwei was imprisoned in 2011 and eventually went into exile in 2015. But in the early twenty-first century, Chinese liberals dared to hope that things might gradually move their way. The idea of "constitutionalism" – which demands that all parts of society, including the Communist Party, should be subject to the rule of law – was openly debated in academic journals and in some daring newspapers, such as *Southern Weekly*. But these kinds of debates have been shut down during the Xi era. In 2015, a large number of human-rights lawyers were arrested. It was not just liberals whose dissenting voices were silenced. In a supreme irony, given that Xi had praised Marx as the "greatest thinker of modern times," student members of the Marxism societies at Beijing's leading universities were also arrested. Their offence was apparently taking Marx's strictures on class struggle a little too seriously and attempting to organize low-paid workers into unions.[19]

As a regular visitor to the country, the closing down of debate has been striking. In the years before Xi took power, I remember going to a dinner in a restaurant in Beijing, where conservative and liberal academics were willing to argue in public about whether China should become a democracy. Such an event would be inconceivable now. Indeed, China has stopped even pretending to encourage free inquiry. In late 2019, Fudan University, the most prestigious university in Shanghai, removed a commitment to "freedom of thought" from its statutes. A few weeks later, I interviewed Eric Li, a trustee of the China Institute at Fudan and noted pro-Xi intellectual. Li was unapologetic about the changes at Fudan. Indeed, he celebrated them as part of the necessary defeat of liberal ideas in China. "For a period of several decades, the Chinese nation has been debating what kind of society and government they want . . . There are people who are liberals, who want China to be a liberal country. I think that debate is over."[20]

Yet even as Li was speaking, the debate about freedom of speech in China and the Xi model of authoritarian strongman rule was about to burst open again. On my way to meet Li for lunch in Shanghai, I had been reading stories about a mysterious new viral disease that had broken out in the city of Wuhan, some five hundred miles away. At the time, it did not seem like a significant enough problem to be worth discussing. But within a couple of weeks that complacency had been shattered as the virus spread, killing hundreds and then thousands and prompting mass quarantines and lockdowns across China.

From the outset, the government in Beijing strove to portray Covid-19 as a natural disaster, with no fault attached to the central government or to President Xi. But this line of argument came under severe strain as the epidemic spread – particularly after the death from the virus of Li Wenliang, a young doctor in Wuhan. As the origins of the disease were probed, it emerged that in the early days of the crisis, Dr. Li had raised the alarm in an online chat group. This earned him a visit from the police, who forced him to promise to stop spreading rumors and to sign a confession. On his deathbed, Dr. Li made a statement that later went viral: "I think a healthy society should not only have one kind of voice." It was easy to read that as an indictment of the strongman style of Xi Jinping.

Some domestic critics of Xi were even more direct. In March 2020, Ren Zhiqiang, a party member and real-estate tycoon, published an open letter accusing the Communist Party of incompetence and condemning the "stupidity of the great leader."[21] Like other domestic critics of Xi, Ren was silenced. In September 2020, he was sentenced to eighteen years in prison on corruption charges.

The outpouring of emotion on social media that followed Dr. Li's death was probably the moment of maximum danger for Xi during the coronavirus crisis. But in the weeks that followed, the Chinese government regained control of the narrative. The official line was that far from blundering in the early stages of the crisis, Xi had acted decisively to rally the nation and contain the disease. Not just China, but the whole of humanity owed President Xi a debt of gratitude for buying the world time to prepare for the virus. If the West had failed to use that time properly – well, that was just further proof of the superiority of the Chinese system. China's propaganda efforts were aided by effusive praise from the World Health Organization, whose director general, Tedros Ghebreyesus, met Xi in Beijing on January 28 and emerged to commend China for "setting a new standard for outbreak control," praising Beijing for its "openness to sharing information."[22]

This Xi-friendly narrative gained traction throughout 2020, as China brought the pandemic under control and the Western world reeled from its impact. The first death caused by the coronavirus was recorded in the US at the end of February 2020 – by which time cases had already peaked and were declining in China. A year later, the United States had suffered over 500,000 deaths. Official figures in China, by contrast, recorded less than 5,000 deaths in the People's Republic.[23]

For President Xi, a potential disaster had turned into a public-relations triumph. At a ceremony handing out medals to ordinary citizens for their work on Covid-19, he declared that "the pandemic once again proves the supremacy of the socialist system with Chinese characteristics."[24] A year after Wuhan had been locked down in panic, the city hosted an exhibition on the successful Chinese battle against Covid-19 featuring, as the BBC reported, "models of medical workers in hazmat suits . . . and everywhere you look, giant portraits of Xi Jinping." At the same time, the Chinese government began to promote the idea that Covid-19 may not have originated in China, after all. As the signboards at the Wuhan exhibition put it, Covid-19 had emerged simultaneously "in multiple places all over the world."[25]

But while the Chinese government was able to control the narrative about Covid-19 within China itself, Xi's image had suffered in the outside world. A Pew opinion poll taken in the summer of 2020 showed that negative views of China's leader had soared across Europe and North America. In Germany, for example, 78 percent of respondents expressed no confidence in Xi to "do the right thing regarding world affairs," a negative shift of 17 points over the course of a year. Distrust of Xi was at similar levels in the US and Britain, and even higher in Japan and South Korea.[26] The Covid-19 pandemic was not the only factor darkening Xi's image in the outside world, however. China's crackdowns in Hong Kong and Xinjiang had revealed the harshness and intolerance of his rule.

In the summer of 2019, protests broke out in Hong Kong, sparked by fears that a new law was about to be passed that would allow Hong Kong citizens to be extradited to mainland China. The protest movement's agenda soon broadened to embrace wider concerns about protecting the territory's autonomy from Beijing – including cherished freedoms, such as independent courts and free media. At their height, the protests brought more than 2 million demonstrators onto the street, out of a total population of 7.4 million. The protests raged for months, often leading to pitched battles between the police and demonstrators. The return of Hong Kong to Chinese rule in 1997 is seen in Beijing as a key moment in the "great rejuvenation" of the nation – finally drawing a line under the colonial era, associated with the "century of humiliation" that had begun when Hong Kong was ceded to Britain in 1842. But the initial inability of Xi to bring an end to this near anarchy on Chinese soil – or even to risk a visit to Hong Kong – threatened to make China's strongman look weak.

As with the coronavirus, Chinese propagandists strove to create some distance between Xi and the problems in Hong Kong. It was said that the proposed extradition law that had sparked the original demonstrations had been a local initiative, not the idea of the leadership in Beijing. But on my own trips to Hong Kong, it was clear to me that Xi's strongman style was an important background factor that had led to the Hong Kong rebellion. Given that mainland China retained ultimate sovereignty over Hong Kong, the illiberal turn in Chinese politics and the decreasing space for dissent had frightened many Hong Kongers. Even pro-Beijing figures in the city were frustrated by their inability to persuade Xi to take a more flexible approach – and wondered if their advice ever made it to his desk. Many feared that Xi believed Beijing's own propaganda: that the problems in Hong Kong were the product of agitation by hostile foreign forces.

In the summer of 2020 – with the outside world distracted by the pandemic and the US presidential election – Xi moved decisively to crush the pro-democracy movement in Hong Kong. A new national security law, drafted on the mainland, was imposed on the territory, with party officials sent from Beijing to police and enforce the new system. Within months, the most prominent leaders of Hong Kong's democracy movement were under arrest and facing long jail sentences. The protests in Hong Kong would have posed a problem for any Chinese leader, since they touched upon the most sensitive issues facing the Communist Party – democracy and national unity. Nonetheless, Xi's heavy-handed response typified his reaction to any form of dissent within China.

China's crackdown on Uighur Muslims in the remote northwestern province of Xinjiang was a topic that often came up in my discussions with Hong Kong protesters. They saw Beijing's decision to intern over one million Uighurs in re-education camps as chilling confirmation of Xi's ruthless determination to impose his vision of national unity on all Chinese citizens, whatever the cost.

In retrospect, the week I had encountered Xi in Beijing in November 2013 may also have marked a crucial moment in the story of the Uighur province of Xinjiang. Five days beforehand, Uighur separatists had driven a car into a group of pedestrians near Tiananmen Square, killing five people.[27] A terror attack in the heart of the People's Republic of China was the kind of challenge Xi was never going to let pass, particularly given other violent incidents elsewhere in the country. The following year, China launched the "strike hard" campaign against terrorism. Fairly soon, however, it became apparent that this was no mere law enforcement campaign. Instead, it was an effort to force the entire Uighur population to assimilate with Han Chinese culture and to accept the will of the Communist Party.

Under Xi's watch, a network of camps was constructed across Xinjiang and a mass internment campaign was begun. By 2018 a UN committee estimated that over one million people had been detained – or roughly 10 percent of the Uighur population.[28] The Chinese government had initially denied the existence of the camps and then described them as "vocational education and training camps" designed to combat extremism and to help Uighurs to find jobs. But testimony from exiles and refugees painted a different, horrifying, picture. Allegations included the forcible separation of hundreds of thousands of children from their parents, torture and sexual abuse, as well as the compulsory study of Xi Jinping thought as part of a program of mass indoctrination. Stories of forced sterilization and abortions also emerged. Chinese government statistics, which showed a 60 percent reduction in the birth rate in Xinjiang, led to allegations that these measures went beyond brutal repression and were producing a cultural genocide.[29]

The Trump administration's decision to categorize China's actions in Xinjiang as genocide were dismissed in Beijing as the actions of a flailing, dishonest government. But in 2021 the Biden administration also endorsed the verdict, as did the Canadian parliament. A legal opinion commissioned from human-rights barristers in the UK called the charge of genocide "plausible" under international law and noted that "Mr Xi controls the overall direction of state policy and has made a range of speeches exhorting the punitive treatment of the Uighurs." The clear implication was that Xi was personally responsible for a genocide.[30]

Chinese nationalists dismiss the West's increasing focus on Xinjiang as a hypocritical effort to find fault with China so as to block the country's rise. But Xi's formula of authoritarianism at home and assertiveness overseas has made greater international scrutiny of China inevitable. The fact that China is the emerging superpower of the twenty-first century makes it harder for the country's leadership to argue that its "internal affairs" should be of no concern to outsiders.

Under Xi, the Chinese leadership has also begun to shed its inhibitions about promoting its model of governance overseas. Previous

Chinese administrations had sought to fend off Western pressure on human rights by suggesting that all countries should be allowed to pursue their own path to development. The West, they argued, should not preach to China and, in return, China would not preach to the rest of the world. In the Xi era, however, Chinese spokesmen have promoted a "China model" of development that is portrayed as an alternative to Western-style democracy, more suitable for developing nations.

In 2018, Xi himself gave a speech in which he suggested that China's "new type of party political system" could act as a model for other countries around the world – an idea that was then energetically promoted by the state media.[31] With the EU having just suffered the blow of Brexit, and the US bitterly polarized during the Trump years, the Xi model of political stability, economic strength and national assertiveness has attracted a variety of international admirers in Africa, Latin America and even Europe.

China has also expanded its international influence through Xi's "Belt and Road" initiative, which has involved billions of dollars in Chinese loans and investment to support infrastructure projects across Asia, Europe and Africa. Chinese investment and influence has even expanded into Latin America, an area once regarded as the US's backyard. When I interviewed Colombia's president, Iván Duque, in 2021, he was firm in his protestations of friendship towards America. But he also insisted that Chinese companies would continue to build the Bogotá metro – since they had offered the best deal.[32] Far from being alone, Colombia was a relative laggard in Latin America in its embrace of Chinese investment.

China's ability to win friends overseas through loans and investment is crucial to the expansion of its international power. But those efforts are complicated by the Xi government's increasing willingness to use force and bullying when confronted by international setbacks. Beijing's response to even mild criticism over Covid-19 has been ferocious. After the Australian government proposed an international inquiry into the origins of the disease, China imposed retaliatory tariffs on some Australian exports.

Meanwhile, China has ramped up the pressure in its various territorial disputes. Threats against Taiwan have been stepped up markedly, with fears rising in Washington that China may feel strong enough to attempt an invasion of a flourishing democracy of 23 million people, which Beijing regards as a renegade province. The Taiwan dispute goes back to the very origins of the People's Republic of China. The Kuomintang forces defeated by Mao in 1949 fled across the sea to the island, and set up their own regime there. Ever since, Beijing has been committed to "reuniting" Taiwan with the mainland, by force if necessary. In typically pragmatic fashion, Deng Xiaoping had suggested that the Taiwan issue could be left for future generations to settle. But Xi has changed Beijing's line, pointedly telling Taiwanese leaders that the issue can no longer be passed from generation to generation. Military exercises in the Taiwan Strait have been intensified.

China's increasingly aggressive line over Taiwan partly reflects a shift in the balance of global power. Over the past generation, Beijing has poured money into its armed forces. The Chinese navy now has more ships than the US navy. Given Xi's evident preoccupation with his place in the pantheon of Chinese leaders, Taiwan is a tempting target. If Mao was the hero who founded the People's Republic and Deng was the leader who set the country on the road to prosperity, Xi may see the next task as demonstrating that China is now a leading global power – by facing down the US over Taiwan. If Xi can be the leader who finally completes the "reunification" of the nation, by conquering Taiwan, his place in the pantheon would be secure.

Actually mounting an invasion of Taiwan would be an immensely risky undertaking. It would probably encounter fierce resistance and might require as many as a million troops. A Chinese attack on Taiwan might also well lead to war with America. Nonetheless, open fantasies about the conquest of Taiwan are now common in nationalist circles in China. Hu Xijin, the editor of the nationalist *Global Times* wrote a typical piece in October 2020 that proclaimed: "The only way forward is for the mainland to fully prepare itself for war and to give Taiwan secessionist forces a decisive punishment at any time. As the secessionist forces' arrogance continues to swell, the historical turning point is getting closer."[33] This kind of overheated rhetoric may not reflect the thinking of China's leaders. But in the tightly controlled media environment created by Xi, bloodcurdling threats towards Taiwan are, at the very least, tolerated. As a self-styled strongman, there is a danger that Xi may feel under pressure to play to nationalist sentiment at home.

In recent years, most Western discussion about potential Chinese aggression has focused on Taiwan and the South China Sea. But the most startling development in 2020 took place high in the Himalayan mountains. A clash between Indian and Chinese troops over disputed territory there saw some twenty Indian troops killed, along with an unknown number of Chinese casualties.

This fatal dispute raised the prospect that the two emerging super-powers of the twenty-first century, China and India, were heading towards conflict. In India and the West, the conflict was also portrayed as a clash between a giant authoritarian state and the world's largest democracy. So it was. And yet the picture was more complicated than that. For, from a very different starting point, democratic India has also moved towards the strongman model.

4 Modi – strongman politics in the world's largest democracy (2014)

Lutyens' Delhi is the seat of power in India. It is named after the British architect Sir Edwin Lutyens, who designed a spacious district, with carefully tended lawns, grand buildings and fountains, setting the area apart from the hubbub of the rest of the city. The district is the site for the most important government buildings in India – including the prime minister's office, as well as the ministries of defense, finance and foreign affairs. Visits to those key ministries are sometimes enlivened by watching the colonies of monkeys that scramble over the yellow sandstone window ledges.

India's top politicians and officials govern a country of 1.4 billion people from these buildings. But since the election of Narendra Modi as India's prime minister in 2014, some of India's most powerful people have sounded more like populist insurgents than a governing elite. One minister, ensconced in the heart of Lutyens' Delhi, nonetheless treated me in 2018 to a scornful denunciation of the "Lutyens elite." The group had traditionally run postindependence India but, he said, it was now being deservedly swept aside by Modi. The old elite had lost touch with the "real India." It felt like the Indian version of a lecture that I had also heard in Washington from officials in the Trump administration, and in London from triumphant Brexiters.

In India, the populist gospel was even delivered by politicians with impeccable "globalist" credentials, such as aviation minister Jayant Sinha, a former McKinsey consultant with an MBA from Harvard. As Sinha said to me, semi-mockingly, "I can do Davos with you all day long, if you like."[1] Like Steve Bannon, Sinha was using "Davos" as a synonym for the rootless globalism that he claimed to be rejecting. He argued that Modi, unlike the opposition Congress Party, was in touch with the India of faith and spirituality. His project was to correct the errors of modern India's founding fathers, in particular Jawaharlal Nehru, who had mistakenly embraced Western ideas, believing them to be universal. Instead Modi was basing India's governance on its own unique culture. "In our view," Sinha proclaimed, "heritage precedes the state. People feel their heritage is under siege. We have a faith-based view of the world, versus the rational-scientific view."

In India, as elsewhere, the rise of populism is intimately connected with the strongman style of leadership. Like Xi and Putin – as well as Trump in America and Erdoğan in Turkey – Modi presents himself as a man with a direct relationship with the people. He promises to take on the corrupt elite at the top of society and bring justice and prosperity to the common man. To bring the powerful to heel, the leader has to be tough – both morally and physically. In the 2014 election campaign, the sixty-four-year-old Modi was portrayed as a literal strongman – with much made of his "56-inch chest."

Modi's victory was a crucial moment in the Age of the Strongman. Two years earlier, Xi Jinping had taken power in China. Now, Modi brought the strongman style to India. With populations of about 1.4 billion people each, China and India together account for roughly 40 percent of the world's population and these two countries are the emerging superpowers of the "Asian century."* Within the space of two years, they had both succumbed to the strongman style of leadership.

Some might question whether it is legitimate or enlightening to bracket a democratically elected leader like Modi with Xi, who is the head of a one-party state, or even with Putin. Doesn't the idea of a "strongman style" become meaningless if it encompasses leaders operating in such different political circumstances and cultures? Xi and Putin, for example, have changed their countries' constitutions to allow them to rule for life, while Modi has to face the electorate every five years. It is also true that Indian intellectuals and some of the media

---

* In real terms China's economy is now five times larger than that of India – and is the second largest in the world. Measured as purchasing power, China has the largest economy in the world and India has the third largest.

still air scathing criticisms of their national leader in a way that is unthinkable in China and increasingly difficult in Russia.

Nonetheless, there are some characteristics of strongman leadership that span both democracies and dictatorships and which are very evident in Modi's India. The first and most obvious is the encouragement of a cult of personality. A charismatic speaker, Modi is in his element addressing large crowds – and very rarely submits to unscripted questions. As well as stressing his strength in the face of India's enemies, Modi's image-makers have carefully cultivated the idea that the Indian leader is a religious and ascetic figure, whose only concern is the good of the people.

Unusually for a serving leader in a democratic country, Modi has allowed monuments to be named after him, while still in office. In 2021, India's largest cricket stadium was renamed the Narendra Modi Stadium. The prime minister's social media team tweeted triumphantly: "World's largest stadium dedicated to the world's largest personality."[2] A few days later, an Indian satellite was launched with Modi's face engraved upon it. Praise for the prime minister from his party colleagues is often wildly sycophantic. Shivraj Singh Chouhan, the chief minister of the state of Madhya Pradesh, called Modi "God's gift for India." Popular films about Modi's life have been produced, portraying the prime minister in a saintly light. Suresh Prabhu, a cabinet minister, called *Come Let Us Live*, a film about Modi's childhood, "motivational, inspirational."[3]

The Indian leader plays up many of the populist and nationalist themes central to the appeal of strongman leaders elsewhere in the world. In different ways, they all promise to restore a lost era of national greatness; yet the distinctively Indian twist is Modi's championship of the ideology of "Hindutva" or Hindu nationalism. His promise is not just to make India great again but, more specifically, to make Hindus great again. Some 80 percent of Indians are Hindus. But Modi and many of his followers embrace a version of Indian history in which Hindus are portrayed as a historically downtrodden group. In a speech to the Indian parliament in June 2014, shortly after winning the election, Modi referred to Indians suffering from "1200 years of slave mentality."[4] The underlying idea was that Indians were not just "enslaved" during the roughly two hundred years of British rule, which began in the mid-eighteenth century. Instead the oppression stretched much further back in history, encompassing the previous thousand years during which the most important rulers of the country were first Buddhists and then Muslims, with both groups cast as foreign interlopers.

As many of Modi's followers see it, even Indian independence in 1947 did not end Hindu subservience. For most of the post-independence era, India was led by the Congress Party, which Modi and his Bharatiya Janata Party (BJP) accuse of relying on a Muslim "vote bank," in return for which India's roughly 200 million Muslims, they argue, have been granted special privileges.* Subramanian Swamy, a BJP member of the Rajya Sabha (the upper house of India's parliament), was playing on this sense of Hindu grievance when he complained that "We are 80 percent of the population, but we are treated like 10 percent."[5] In a vast country where the competition for jobs, educational opportunities and resources is fierce, any suggestion that minorities are being given unfair privileges is politically potent. The BJP's identity as a Hindu party is underlined by the stark fact that in the 2014 election, there was not a single Muslim among the 282 BJP members returned to the Lok Sabha, the more powerful lower house of parliament.

Modi's own life and career is deeply intertwined with the Hindu nationalist movement. Born in 1950 in the small town of Vadnagar in the state of Gujarat, Modi joined a Hindu nationalist organization called the Rashtriya Swayamsevak Sangh (RSS) when he was eight years old and he has remained a member ever since. Founded in 1925, the RSS was dedicated to the idea that India is in essence a Hindu nation. Its founder, K. B. Hedgewar, was an admirer of European fascists such as Italy's Benito Mussolini, and emulated their fascination with uniforms and paramilitary training.

It was a former RSS activist and Hindu nationalist, Nathuram Godse, who assassinated Mahatma Gandhi in 1948, shortly after the achievement of Indian independence. Gandhi's nonviolent campaign for freedom from British rule means that he is widely described as the "father of the nation." But many in the RSS despised Gandhi because of his insistence that Hindus "could have no quarrel with Islam." The partition of India that accompanied Indian independence created two states, India and Pakistan, the latter a majority-Muslim state. The

---

* The complaint is reminiscent of the way in which Donald Trump mobilized white American resentment against "affirmative action" for racial minorities.

forced population transfers and communal violence that accompanied partition led to the death of as many as two million people. In that context, Gandhi's insistence on the ideal of peaceful coexistence with Islam was denounced by the RSS as "appeasement,"[6] creating the tumultuous background against which he was murdered. The RSS's militarist ethos contrasted strongly with Gandhi's pacifism.

Today Modi and the RSS publicly endorse the conventional view that Gandhi was a national hero and "father of the nation." But some BJP members of parliament are prepared to give public voice to a radically different view: the idea that Gandhi's assassin was a national hero – and that Modi, as a Hindu nationalist, should be regarded as the true founder of the Indian nation.[7] Modi's continuing personal and political connection with the RSS remains a subject of much conjecture, but there is no doubt that his membership in the organization provided him with a springboard to move from humble, provincial origins to national leadership.

He was born into a low-ranking caste and, as a teenager, helped his father run the family tea shop near the train station in Vadnagar. His origins as a humble tea seller are now crucial to Modi's image and certainly make a powerful contrast with the highborn Gandhis, who continue to dominate the Congress Party – and whose political dynasty had provided three prime ministers, Nehru, Indira Gandhi and Rajiv Gandhi.* At the age of thirteen, the young Narendra got married but the arranged marriage swiftly broke down. Instead, Modi made the RSS his family, rising quickly through its ranks. To this day, Modi remains unmarried and (it is claimed) celibate.[8] Modi's lack of personal family ties is a key political asset in a country in which politicians are routinely, and often accurately, accused of corruptly favoring members of their own family. Talk to his most ardent followers, and you will often be told that Modi is a selfless and ascetic man, who has dedicated his life to the welfare of ordinary people.

By 1987, Modi had joined the BJP, the political party closely affiliated with the RSS. It was opportune timing. At the time, the BJP had only two members of parliament; by 1996 it had become the largest

---

* Indira Gandhi, prime minister from 1966 to 1977 and from 1980 until her assassination in 1984, was not related to Mahatma Gandhi. She was, however, the daughter of Nehru and the mother of Rajiv Gandhi.

party in the Indian parliament. Its meteoric rise had been fueled by the party's championship of the destruction of a mosque in the city of Ayodhya, which it claimed had been built on a site holy to Hindus. The Ayodhya controversy fueled Hindu–Muslim clashes across India in 1992, which in turn mobilized support behind the BJP. At the time, Modi was an obscure party official. But his drive and charisma led to rapid promotion through the party's ranks and he became general secretary of the BJP in 2001. That same year, Modi was appointed as chief minister of his native Gujarat, after the incumbent stepped down through ill health.

Gujarat is a state of over 60 million people on the west coast of India. During Modi's period as chief minister, the state's economy grew much faster than the Indian national average, cementing his reputation as a pragmatic and business-friendly politician. The economic success of Gujarat under his leadership was crucial to Modi's rise to national power. It allowed the BJP leader to be portrayed as, above all, an economic reformer rather than a Hindu nationalist.

Indeed, one characteristic that Modi shares with many other strongman leaders is that he was initially hailed in the Western media as just the kind of energetic reformer his country needed. I wrote one of those pro-Modi articles myself. On a visit to India in 2013, I had been taken aback by the widespread pessimism and cynicism I encountered. The country's prime minister at the time was Manmohan Singh – whom I had met in the 1990s and admired as a courageous and principled reformer.[9] But, by 2013, the scholarly and introverted Singh seemed to have lost energy, and the Congress Party was once again clearly under the thumb of the Gandhi dynasty. The economy was slowing, Indian businessmen were grumbling, and there had been mass demonstrations against corruption in the streets of Delhi and other Indian cities. Many of those clamoring for a change were promoting the leadership prospects of Narendra Modi, who was promising to bring the "Gujarat economic miracle" to India as a whole.

But there was also a much more frightening side to Modi's reputation. He had been chief minister in 2002 when anti-Muslim riots had broken out in Gujarat, leading to the deaths of around a thousand people. Ever since, Modi has been accused of tacitly encouraging the anti-Muslim pogrom. India's court system found that there was insufficient evidence to prosecute him in 2012. But his reputation was sufficiently besmirched for him to be banned from entering the US, right up until his election in 2014.

Nonetheless, in an article published just before the 2014 election, I argued that "India needs a jolt and Modi is a risk worth taking."[10] Modi's humble origins in small-town India made a refreshing contrast to the born-to-rule credentials of Rahul Gandhi, the standard-bearer of the Congress Party, whose father, grandmother and great-grandfather had all been prime ministers of India. Modi's rise, I said, "would send an invigorating message across a country where too many people's chances are still blighted by poverty, class or caste." As for the Gujarat massacres, they "took place more than a decade ago." Since then "Mr. Modi's tenure as chief minister has been distinguished more by his focus on economic reform than communal grievances."[11]

I now read those words with some embarrassment. But more distinguished figures than me were coming to similar judgments about Modi at that time. In 2015, President Obama, writing in *Time* magazine, praised the new Indian prime minister as reflecting the "dynamism and potential of India's rise."[12] Many prominent Indian liberals and intellectuals were also prepared to give the new prime minister the benefit of the doubt. After some thought, Raghuram Rajan, a distinguished economist who had been persuaded to leave the University of Chicago to run the Indian Central Bank in 2013, decided to stay on and serve in the Modi government.

In fairness to Modi, his early years in office did not confirm the worst fears of his critics. There was little intercommunal violence, the worst examples of which still belong to the pre-Modi era, such as the anti-Sikh riots and killings of 1984.

Yet returning to India in May 2018, I found plenty of evidence of a coarsening of the national discourse and a culture of violence and hatred within the rank and file of the ruling BJP. In one case – much discussed in Delhi at the time – an eight-year-old Muslim girl had been gang-raped and murdered in northern India. Some local BJP leaders had taken part in rallies and marches in support of the accused killers, who were Hindus. The prime minister himself had been conspicuously slow to speak out about the case. In response, forty-nine retired senior civil servants had written an open letter to Modi, accusing him of fomenting a "frightening climate of hate, fear and viciousness in India," adding that "in post-independence India, this is our darkest hour."[13]

Yet the despair of Delhi liberals seemed to be a source of contempt and even amusement among the BJP's supporters and pro-Modi intellectuals. Rather like Trump supporters in Washington, they tended to argue that they represented the sentiments of hardworking ordinary folk, rather than the hand-wringing liberal elites in the capital city. S. Jaishankar, the Indian foreign minister, himself born into the Indian elite – his father had designed the country's nuclear weapons program – told me that Modi's foreign and domestic critics needed to understand the depth of the prime minister's relationship with the India that lay beyond Delhi.[14]

Others were much blunter and more flamboyant in their rejection of Western liberal values. Subramanian Swamy, who has a doctorate in economics from Harvard, even called for all Indian Muslims to lose the vote, unless they acknowledged "their ancestors were Hindus." (It is common in the BJP to argue that most Indian Muslims were originally Hindus, who were forcibly converted during the Mughal period.) As Swamy saw it, the current state of international politics demonstrated that "where the Muslim population is large, there is always trouble."[15] While Modi himself rarely put things this directly, he was happy to let senior figures and foot soldiers in his party indulge in this kind of rhetoric. As one Delhi journalist put it to me: "Modi doesn't say the worst stuff himself. He just poses for selfies with those who do."

But would Modi actually *do* the worst stuff? I left Delhi in 2018, undecided. Modi was clearly popular. He had delivered decent economic growth and championed important social reforms, such as the provision of toilets to the homes of the hundreds of millions of Indians who live without that basic necessity. But some of his economic reforms had demonstrated a taste for arbitrary and dramatic gestures. In 2016 he had suddenly abolished 80 percent of the country's currency. The government's claim that this would be an effective anti-corruption drive drew upon the popular image of the corrupt rich with piles of ill-gotten cash lying around their houses. In reality, it was India's poor who were much more reliant on cash – while the super-rich were more likely to favor overseas bank accounts. Demonetization was a classic populist move that hit the economy, but did no lasting damage to Modi's popularity.

Unfortunately, strongman leaders have a tendency to become steadily more autocratic and arbitrary the longer they stay in office.[16] Putin and Erdoğan both became more radical during their second and third terms in office. And a similar pattern set in during Modi's second term.

The Indian leader headed into the 2019 election facing what looked like a serious challenge from Congress and from India's plethora of regional parties. But the campaign was transformed to Modi's advantage by a military confrontation with Pakistan, with whom India has fought three post-independence wars. On February 14, 2019, forty Indian policemen were killed in Kashmir by a suicide bomber in an attack claimed by a Pakistan-based Islamist group. In 2008, the government led by Manmohan Singh had refrained from retaliating against nuclear-armed Pakistan, after terrorists trained there killed 166 people in attacks in India's largest city, Mumbai. But the Modi government took a more aggressive and bolder line, authorizing air strikes on alleged terrorist bases in Pakistan on February 26. The Indian government claimed to have killed hundreds of terrorists in an attack on a Jaish-e-Mohammed training camp, a claim derided by the Pakistani government.

Whatever actually happened in the raid, the response in much of the Indian media was ecstatic. The attack came just a couple of months before voting started in the Indian election and so was perfectly timed to burnish Modi's strongman credentials. In one of his closing campaign rallies, the prime minister boasted that "When you vote for Lotus [the BJP's poll symbol] you are not pressing a button on a machine, but pressing a trigger to shoot terrorists in the chest . . . Do you think this approach is good? Are you happy? Aren't your heads held high? Don't your chests puff up with pride?"[17] It was an extremely effective message. In the vote, which began on April 11, the BJP substantially increased its parliamentary majority, winning 55 percent of seats in parliament on the basis of a 37 percent vote share, up from 31 percent in 2014. The Balakot raid had been a turning point.

Any wave of anti-Pakistan feeling in India is liable to spill over into increased antagonism towards India's Muslim minority, who are often portrayed by ardent Hindu nationalists as a "fifth column." And indeed, within months of winning re-election, the BJP's Hindutva agenda became both more explicit and more radical. In August 2019, the Modi government abolished the special constitutional status of the country's only majority-Muslim state, Jammu and Kashmir, and followed up with a broad crackdown on civil liberties, including the detention without trial of leading Kashmiri politicians. Foreign correspondents based in Delhi and opposition politicians were banned from visiting the region. The Indian government did invite me on a special "fact-finding" tour of the state but I declined the invitation because the *FT* 's Delhi correspondent was still being denied access to Kashmir. One group who did accept the Modi administration's invitation to go on a government-sponsored trip to Kashmir was a group of nearly thirty members of the European Parliament – drawn largely from far-right parties, with France, Poland and Britain heavily represented.[18]

The Modi administration defended the abolition of Kashmir's special status as representing the correction of a constitutional anomaly. Its argument was that, henceforth, all Indians should be treated equally. But in fact, it seemed that Muslims were now being singled out for special, and worse, treatment. In the state of Assam, bordering the Muslim-majority nation of Bangladesh, a citizenship registration exercise saw some two million mainly Muslim residents deemed to be illegal immigrants – with no right to live in India.

The Modi government then moved to extend citizenship registration across the whole of India. Millions of people faced the potential loss of their citizenship unless they could produce papers proving their right to live in India. In a country with poor levels of literacy, weak record-keeping and a creaking legal system, the threat was terrifying. The construction of detention camps across India raised fears that Modi's India might even emulate Xi's China by incarcerating millions of Muslims. The sense that Muslims were now regarded as second-class citizens was heightened by a Citizenship Amendment Act, which was passed in December 2019, giving any Hindu fleeing persecution abroad the right to Indian citizenship – a right that was to be denied to Muslims in the same situation. (The BJP argument was that there was only one state in the world where Hindus could take refuge, whereas Muslims could seek asylum in a number of Muslim-majority states.)

In democracies, an independent judiciary, a free press and vibrant non-governmental organizations are the traditional guardians of civil liberties. But, in Modi's India, these institutions are under increasing threat. Government pressure on media owners and editors – re-enforced by advertising boycotts, selected sackings and social media harassment – were shrinking the space for criticism of the government. Amartya Sen, a Nobel prizewinning economist now resident in the US, remarked that his friends in India were reluctant to criticize the government on the phone, adding, "People are afraid, I've never seen this before."[19]

Talking to Indian intellectuals in Delhi or Mumbai reminded me increasingly of speaking to their counterparts in Istanbul or Moscow. There were still brave and principled people prepared to criticize the government in strong terms. But there was a growing sense that such criticism put careers – or even personal freedom and safety – at risk. There were cases of prominent editors and news anchors who had lost their jobs after speaking up against the BJP. Pratap Bhanu Mehta, an eminent Indian academic and outspoken critic of the government, wrote in 2019 that "The noose is tightening around all independent institutions in India."[20] As if to prove the point, Mehta resigned suddenly from his job as vice chancellor of Ashoka University, a private institution, that same year and then quit the university altogether in 2021, prompting more than 150 academics to sign a letter protesting against the "political pressure" that had led to his resignation.

Amnesty International was forced to close its doors in India in 2021 after its bank accounts were frozen on the grounds that it had illegally received money from overseas. Amnesty argued, plausibly, that the real reason it had been singled out was because of its work on the treatment of Muslims and on Kashmir.[21] Attacking non-governmental organizations because they are allegedly tools for foreign interference is also common in Russia and China.

In 2014, Brijgopal Loya, a judge hearing a case against Amit Shah, one of Modi's key political allies, died in mysterious circumstances. Loya's family claimed that when his body was returned to them, it had been covered in blood. They asked for an official investigation but it was denied. The new judge swiftly dismissed the case against Shah, who is now minister for home affairs.[22] Shah himself is not shy about encouraging violence. When protests broke out in Indian universities in 2020 against Modi's discriminatory new citizenship laws, Shah suggested that the students involved should be "taught a lesson and punished." Not long afterwards, Delhi police stood by as a violent mob, armed with weapons, beat up students at Jawaharlal Nehru University.

In this atmosphere, some prominent Indians chose to write in code. Shivshankar Menon, one of India's most eminent retired diplomats, who was once the country's top national security adviser, seemed to make his point in a review of Frank Dikötter's book, *How to Be a Dictator*. Menon noted how the twentieth-century dictators that Dikötter studied "All conflate the person of the leader with the nation, use ultra-nationalism or xenophobia . . . race and ethnicity to identify an enemy such as Jews or Muslims and present the leader as simple, spartan and hardworking." Naming no names, Menon finished his review by noting the book's "contemporary resonances, in our politics of hate, ultra-nationalism and personality cult . . . There is a warning for all of us here."[23]

For the Modi government – as for the Trump administration in the US – criticism from retired officials or university professors was simply treated as evidence of the rottenness of the country's intellectual elite. India's universities were regarded as suspect institutions and the home of untrustworthy virtue-signaling liberals.[24] As Shruti Kapila, a historian based at the University of Cambridge saw it, Modi was now "at the epicentre of a global arc of antagonism and anger against traditional elites, the media and intellectuals, as democracy is remade under authoritarian populism."[25]

The extent to which things have changed in India was acknowledged in the 2021 *Freedom in the World* report, issued by Freedom House, a US-based NGO. For the first time since 1997, India was downgraded from a free to a "partly free" country. Freedom House justified its downgrade by pointing to a "multi year pattern" of erosion in freedoms, and lamented that "Modi and his party are tragically driving India toward authoritarianism." Given that India accounts for roughly 20 percent of the world's population, changes in that country alone go a long way in shifting the global balance from democracy and towards authoritarianism.

The ideological and personal affinity between Trump and Modi and the movements that support them was underlined by joint appearances of the two leaders in India and the US. In September 2019, Modi addressed a large and ecstatic rally, largely made up of expatriate Indians in Houston, Texas, in an event that was quickly dubbed "Howdy Modi." A few months later, Trump visited India and spoke to a rally of 125,000 people in Modi's home state of Gujarat. Both politicians had put the battle against "Islamic terrorism" at the center of their electoral appeals. One of Trump's first acts as president in 2016 was his attempt to enact a "Muslim ban," preventing citizens of several Muslim countries from entering the US. Modi's second-term efforts, potentially restricting Muslims' claims to Indian citizenship, reflected similar thinking. Observing Trump's 2020 visit to India, Jason Stanley, a political philosopher at Yale University, argued that in their common emphasis on ethno-nationalism, both Modi and Trump were flirting with fascist themes. As Stanley saw it, "The core of fascist ideology is realised in changing citizenship laws to privilege a single ethnic group . . . Trump's triumphant visit to India demonstrates just how global ethno-nationalism has become."[26]

Yet accusations of fascism hurled at Trump or Modi by liberal academics were not necessarily unwelcome to the two leaders. Both thrived off the political polarization created by their domestic policies. The Trump–Modi meetings in Delhi in February 2020 took place against the background of deadly clashes between Hindus and Muslims elsewhere in the city, sparked by protests against India's new citizenship law. In Delhi, as in America later that year, the police were accused of participating in violence against minority groups.

In contrast to Trump, however, Modi's domestic political standing in 2020 looked increasingly secure. His country's parliamentary system allowed India's strongman to strengthen his position on the basis of little more than one-third of the electorate's support. Unlike Trump, Modi left the most divisive messaging to his political surrogates, allowing him to polish his image as a selfless man-of-the-people, who stood above the political fray. The Indian media and courts were also much more pliant than the forces facing Trump. While the Indian Supreme Court remains formally independent of the government, some judges seemed uncomfortably close to Modi. One of the justices described the prime minister as an "internationally acclaimed visionary"; another called him "our most popular, loved, vibrant and visionary leader."[27]

Mishandling Covid-19 – which did so much to undermine Trump's leadership – was less damaging for Modi. Imposing a lockdown or social distancing was always going to be extremely difficult in a poor, densely populated country like India. Nonetheless, Modi botched India's response – not once, but twice. His impetuous decision to impose a harsh lockdown, with just four hours' notice, in March 2020 had the counterproductive effect of causing manual laborers, who had lost their jobs, to stream out of India's major cities back to rural areas. That led to the disease being spread even more rapidly around the country. When the lockdown proved to be economically and socially unsustainable, India was left facing one of the worst epidemics in the world.

Modi's personal popularity was seemingly unaffected by this debacle. In mid-June 2020, with the pandemic raging, the Indian leader's approval ratings stood at a sky-high 74 percent. As Gilles Verniers, a political scientist at Ashoka University, saw it: "People believe the prime minister means well. They trust him to take strong and courageous decisions, and they don't hold him responsible for the actual consequences."[28]

By February 2021, the BJP was exulting that Modi's India had successfully ridden out the Covid crisis. The ruling party passed a motion that triumphantly proclaimed: "It can be said with pride, India . . . defeated Covid-19 under the able, sensible, committed and visionary leadership of Prime Minister Modi. . .The party unequivocally hails its leadership for introducing India to the world as a proud and victorious nation in the fight against Covid."[29] To ram home the message that this was Modi's victory, vaccinated Indians were given a certificate with the prime minister's portrait on it.

But declarations of triumph over Covid proved to be tragically premature. In the spring of 2021, India was hit by a massive second wave of the pandemic, which was worsened by the Modi government's willingness to allow mass election rallies to take place in West Bengal, addressed by the prime minister himself. The Kumbh Mela, a Hindu religious festival, had also gone ahead, allowing millions of pilgrims to descend on a single town. When the second wave hit, hospitals all over India ran out of beds and oxygen – and mass cremations took place in public parks and even in car parks. Tragic television images were broadcast all over the world, making India a symbol of Covid mismanagement. Even so, Modi's approval ratings barely dipped. In the summer of 2021, as the second wave of the pandemic raged, his approval ratings were at 64 percent. Cynics noted that the prime minister had changed his style, growing a long beard of the type favored by Hindu ascetics, speculating that this might be an attempt to position himself as a spiritual leader, above the fray of day-to-day political and pandemic management.[30]

The appeal to national pride, as much as any claim to spiritual authority, was vital to Modi's continuing political strength – as became evident when his government faced huge demonstrations by farmers. The trigger was three laws, passed in September 2020 and intended to liberalize farming. The Modi government proposed abolishing the old system through which farmers sold their produce to the state at a fixed price. Instead, producers would be free to sell directly to the private sector. This is the kind of liberalizing reform that appeals to economists and technocrats in places like the World Bank. But it sparked a backlash that had not been anticipated by a BJP leadership that prides itself on its feel for the "real India."

Some 50 percent of Indians still make their living from the land and many were alarmed by the idea that guaranteed prices might be scrapped. More than 500,000 demonstrators descended on Delhi and camped outside the city. Successive rounds of negotiations and promises that implementation of the laws would be deferred failed to end the protest movement. The Modi government was clearly rattled and suggested that the demonstrations were being stirred up by "anti-national" or foreign forces. Disha Ravi, a twenty-two-year-old climate activist, was even arrested for sharing a document that listed ways for activists to support the protesting farmers. Ravi was accused of being in league with Greta Thunberg, the Swedish climate activist. Other foreigners, accused of meddling in Indian affairs, included the pop star Rihanna, who had tweeted her concern for the farmers. These kinds of outbursts by BJP supporters often provoke bafflement or scorn outside India. But inside the country, nationalism is a highly effective tool for rallying support for Modi and intimidating his critics.

Western critics of India are frequently accused of lingering colonialism. But the West is no longer a plausible threat to Indian security. By contrast, the deadly clash between Indian and Chinese troops in the summer of 2020 shocked the Delhi establishment and Indian public opinion. The hyper-partisanship of Indian politics was dropped briefly with Modi holding emergency consultations with opposition leaders. The Indian government sought to lessen its growing economic entanglement with China by banning some popular Chinese apps. Indian strategists also moved to strengthen military and diplomatic ties with the US, Japan and Australia.

As US antagonism with China rose – and talk of a second Cold War intensified – so Washington increasingly looked to India as a crucial member of an emerging alliance of democracies that could resist Chinese expansionism. As a strategic move it made sense. But anyone familiar with the ideological drift of Modi and his party also knew that

Western politicians were in danger of embracing a seriously oversimplified world view – in which democratic India acted as an ideological bulwark against authoritarian China. In reality, it could equally well be argued that India's own slide into illiberalism was actually strengthening the global trend towards authoritarianism.

These inconvenient nuances, however, were not welcome in Western capitals. In Washington, the increasingly single-minded focus on rivalry with Beijing made Modi look like an indispensable ally. In London, India was once again regarded as the "jewel in the crown" – this time, not of the British empire, but of a new post-Brexit strategy for "Global Britain." And even inside the European Union, there was an influential movement that shared Modi's deep suspicion of Islam. Indeed, the fear of Muslims and migrants has also spurred the rise of strongman politics inside the EU.

5 Orbán, Kaczynski and the rise of illiberal Europe (2015)

"Hello, dictator" is an unusual greeting to extend to the head of an EU member state. But those were the words used by Jean-Claude Juncker, the president of the European Commission, as he welcomed Viktor Orbán, Hungary's prime minister, to an EU summit in May 2015.

It was an edgy joke to smooth over a deeply uncomfortable situation. The EU is meant to be a community of liberal democracies. It proudly boasts that it has helped to guarantee political freedom in the countries of Eastern and Central Europe, which endured so many years as part of the Soviet bloc. To join the EU, Hungary and other newcomers, such as Poland and Romania, had to sign up to the "Copenhagen criteria," a statement of political values with democracy at its core.

But, by the summer of 2015, it was clear that Viktor Orbán's Hungary was heading in the opposite direction. With a two-thirds parliamentary majority behind him, Orbán was steadily eroding the country's independent institutions as he brought the courts, media, civil service, universities and cultural institutions under the control of his party, Fidesz. Non-governmental organizations that objected to Orbán's increasingly authoritarian style were subject to tax raids or closed down. The prime minister's cronies meanwhile were rewarded with top jobs and lucrative public contracts.

It was classic stuff from the strongman playbook. But Orbán was also a theorist. He was keen to spell out an alternative ideology to the liberal lessons handed out from Brussels and Washington. In a series of speeches and political interventions, he set out the case for "illiberalism." The Hungarian leader caricatured liberalism as an elitist ideology, favored by "globalists," intent on erasing national borders and cultures. The year before Juncker's unorthodox greeting, Orbán had set the alarm bells ringing in Brussels with a speech in which he pledged "to construct a new state built on illiberal and national foundations within the European Union."[1]

Juncker's barbed greeting may have been intended to serve as a coded warning to the Hungarian leader. If so, it failed. In fact, the Orbán project was about to take off. The rocket fuel was the refugee crisis that hit Europe in the summer of 2015, alongside Islamist terrorist attacks that shook Europe throughout that year.

The murderous terror attack on *Charlie Hebdo*, a French satirical weekly in January 2015, gave Orbán a first opportunity to establish himself as one of the loudest voices in Europe, sounding the alarm about immigration from the Muslim world. Along with many other world leaders, Orbán marched in Paris to demonstrate solidarity with the French. But he also went further, declaring "Zero tolerance against immigrants . . . We do not want to see in our midst any minorities whose cultural background differs from our own. We want to keep Hungary for the Hungarians."[2]

In some respects, this vocal opposition to immigration from the Hungarian leader was peculiar. Less than 5 percent of his country's population was born abroad and most of those were ethnic Hungarians who had moved to the country from Romania.[3] (This compares to 12 percent of the population of France and the US who were foreign born, and 14 percent of the population of the UK.) But despite being culturally homogeneous, Hungary has a small population of just 10 million and a history that has allowed Orbán to portray his country's culture as threatened with extinction. Throughout his political career, he has obsessively returned to the iniquities of the Treaty of Trianon of 1920, which saw Hungary lose some two-thirds of its territory, after being on the losing side in the First World War.

For Orbán, the central flaw of Brussels-style liberalism is its failure to accept the importance of the nation. He argued that the EU's alleged insistence on open borders threatened to inflict another Trianon on Hungary by different means: "Not with a stroke of a pen, as happened a hundred years ago at Trianon; now they want us to voluntarily hand our country over to others, over a period of a few decades . . . to foreigners coming from other continents, who do not speak our language."[4]

Having stated his vocal opposition to immigration from non-Hungarian cultures at the beginning of 2015, Orbán was perfectly placed to capitalize politically as the refugee crisis developed across Europe. Four years of devastating civil war in Syria, and more than a decade of conflict in Afghanistan and Iraq, had created millions of refugees on Europe's borders. Most of the displaced Syrians had been bottled up inside Turkey. But when the Turks relaxed frontier controls in 2015, many Syrians, as well as other unfortunates from Afghanistan, Iraq and elsewhere, began to make the journey west across the Balkans to Western Europe.

Hungary lay squarely along their path. And although very few refugees showed much intention of settling there, the Orbán government harassed them. Amid chaotic and distressing scenes near Budapest station, Syrians and others were shown scant sympathy and frequently denied food or shelter. The Hungarian government also moved swiftly to construct a 175-kilometer-long barbed-wire fence along Hungary's border with Serbia and later Croatia.

The decision by the German chancellor Angela Merkel to open her country's borders to more than a million refugees was motivated, in large part, by horror at what was happening inside Orbán's Hungary. The images of harried refugee families – fleeing war and packed onto crowded trains – were too painful and resonant for many Germans to accept after the Holocaust.

But while Orbán became an ogre for liberals, he was regarded as a hero by a new breed of populist right-wingers, as well as by traditional conservatives who were alarmed at the idea that the EU had lost control of its borders. In September 2015, he was pointedly invited to speak at the party conference of Germany's CSU, the Bavarian sister party of Merkel's CDU. The "C" in both parties' names stands for Christian and the Hungarian prime minister told the assembled German conservatives that "The crisis offers the chance for the national Christian ideology to regain supremacy not only in Hungary but in the whole of Europe . . . We are experiencing the end of all the liberal babble. An era is coming to an end."[5]

The sense that the future of Europe might indeed belong to nationalist populism was given further momentum that year by political change in Poland. In May, Andrzej Duda, the candidate for the Law and Justice Party (PiS), won the Polish presidential election. In October

2015, against the backdrop of the refugee crisis, the PiS, which was led by Jaroslaw Kaczynski, consolidated its grip on Poland by winning parliamentary elections, after a campaign that capitalized on fears of Muslim immigration. Law and Justice was the party of small towns and the countryside. Its politics were nationalistic and reactionary in tone, wrapped up in complaints about corrupt elites that were selling the country out to foreigners. It also adopted the most conservative form of Catholicism.

The promotion of strongly conservative social values was central to the rejection of Western liberalism that tied together the Orbán and Kaczynski projects. As Ivan Krastev and Stephen Holmes put it, these two leaders were representative of an "anti-Western counter elite, with predominantly provincial origins," which drew its support from "outside the globally networked metropolitan centres."[6] Both Orbán and Kaczynski have described their politics as "counter-revolutionary" and argued that they are supporting traditional values, against a new form of totalitarianism that will brook no opposition – liberalism.

These events in Europe were eagerly picked up by the nationalist right in the US, on websites such as Breitbart and Drudge. And they took place just as a maverick candidate was gearing up his unlikely bid for the US presidency, on the back of a promise for a "total and complete shutdown" of all Muslims entering the United States.[7] Steve Bannon, Trump's campaign manager in 2016, described Orbán as a "hero" and the "the most significant guy on the scene right now."[8]

The Trumpists had only contempt for the cautious, pro-migrant Merkel. The Europe they identified with was the continent of Orbán and Kaczynski. Kaczynski shared much of Orbán's illiberalism, as well as his nationalism and reactionary social values. As the de facto leader of Poland, one of the EU's big six nations, he had a bigger stage available to him than Orbán.

Kaczynski is the dominant figure within the ruling party – much more than President Duda. But he is also a recluse who does not speak English and is more comfortable at home with his cats and his books than strutting the world stage. When he served briefly as Poland's prime minister from July 2006 to November 2007, Kaczynski chose to live with his mother, not at the official state residence, and donated 20 percent of his salary to a cat charity.[9]

On returning to power, he was content to cast himself as a student of Orbán, telling the Hungarian leader in 2016 that "Viktor Orbán has demonstrated that in Europe things are possible. You have given an example, and we are learning from your example."[10] These modest words masked a rather sinister reality. Like Orbán, Kaczynski had drawn lessons from his own first period in office. Both leaders had decided that if they were to effect real, lasting political and cultural change, they needed to control the institutions of the state, in particular the courts, the media and the schools. For his part, the cynical, tactical Orbán found his mystical Polish ally rather peculiar. After the two men held a daylong meeting on the Polish–Slovak border in January 2016, Orbán reportedly told a confidant: "I have just spent the day with a madman."*

With Kaczynski uninterested in building a profile outside Poland, it was left to Orbán to become the face of illiberal strongman politics within the EU. The global reputation that he gathered during the 2015 refugee crisis did not fade with the passage of time. Four years later, he was featured on the cover of *Foreign Affairs* – coffee-table reading for the American establishment – under the headline "Autocracy Now." For Orbán to be on the cover alongside Putin and Xi, as well as the leaders of Turkey and the Philippines, represented a striking level of recognition for the leader of a nation of just 10 million people.

The experience of gaining a global audience and lecturing affluent Western Europeans about the future of politics was intoxicating for the Hungarian leader. For decades, ever since the fall of the Berlin Wall, the post-Soviet countries had been cast in the role of students and supplicants, as they were told how to restructure their economies and political systems by the EU. Now it was their turn to hand out the lessons. In his state-of-the-nation speech, at the beginning of 2020, Orbán proclaimed: "We used to think that Europe was our future. Today we know that we are the future of Europe."[11] But the Hungarian prime minister's ability to command global attention as Europe's leading populist autocrat was also an ironic culmination of a political journey that had begun in 1989, when Communist rule came to an end in Hungary.

Orbán was born in 1963, in a village around fifty kilometers from

---

* This story was told to me by a friend of Orbán's. I have no independent evidence for it. But I include it because it made me laugh.

the Hungarian capital, Budapest. He grew up in poverty, in a house without running water; he later described the "unforgettable experience" of his first encounter with a modern bathroom at the age of fifteen.[12] But although he came from a family of agricultural workers, Orbán's father had a university degree and Viktor himself was a bright student, who won a place at a selective school and later university. As a political leader, Orbán has retained a connection to his roots – and to his youthful passion for football, overseeing the construction of a large new football stadium in Felcsút, where he grew up. At law school in Budapest, Orbán stood out for his domineering and charismatic personality. He became part of a close-knit group of liberal students and benefited from internships, grants and scholarships bestowed by the Hungarian Jewish philanthropist, George Soros.

The turning point of Orbán's life and career came in the summer of 1989, when the Soviet Union's grip over Central Europe began to weaken. On June 16, Hungarian opposition groups organized a demonstration in Budapest's Heroes' Square, which drew over 200,000 people. The speeches were televised live and a bearded young activist, aged just twenty-six, seized his opportunity. Taking the stage last, Orbán gave a seven-minute speech that made his reputation. "If we trust our own strength, then we will be able to put an end to the Communist dictatorship," he declared. "If we are courageous enough then we can compel the ruling party to face free elections."

It was an appeal for democracy that has echoed down the years and become a historical landmark. It also helped to establish Orbán as a leading political figure in post-Communist Hungary. In 1991, an opinion poll showed that Orbán was already the third most popular politician in the country.[13] Two years later, he became the leader of Fidesz, a liberal party whose youthful leadership and unstuffy and informal style contrasted powerfully with the former apparatchiks of the Communist Party.

But the Hungarian elections of 1994 were a disappointment for Fidesz, which performed badly. It was a turning point for Orbán. He began to break with the older, urban liberals of Budapest – many of them Jewish – and embraced a more conservative and nationalistic politics that proved popular in the small towns and in the countryside. This new strategy turned the party's fortunes round: in 1998 Fidesz won the elections and Orbán became prime minister, serving in office for four years. His rightward drift had yet to be fully noticed outside the country. When I first visited Hungary in the early 2000s, to follow the country's application process to join the EU, I arrived with the belief that Orbán was still the liberal hero of 1989. I soon came to realize that the reality was rather different.

Orbán's real breakthrough came in 2010. Out of power for eight years, Fidesz's fortunes were again transformed, this time by a corruption scandal that scuppered the governing Socialists as well as by the aftermath of the financial crisis of 2008. In the 2010 election, the party swept to power. Crucially, it won a two-thirds majority in parliament, allowing Orbán to push through constitutional change.

In what was to become an all-too-familiar pattern for other strongmen, the Hungarian prime minister used his democratic mandate to erode democracy; and he took advantage of his legal powers to roll back the rule of law. In 2011, a new constitution was pushed through parliament that gave a parliamentary majority the power to appoint judges to the constitutional court. The court was gradually packed with judges sympathetic to Orbán and stripped of some of its review powers. Trusted Fidesz officials were put in charge of the state media and Orbán's friends and business cronies began to buy up the rest of the press.

Friends of mine working in the media in Hungary soon told me horror stories about the crude promotion of falsehoods and pro-government propaganda. Some of them went into exile. Attila Mong, one of the country's most respected reporters, protested against the new media law in 2010 with a minute's silence on his public radio show. He was fired and eventually left the country.

But other former liberals made their peace with the regime and learned to profit from it. On a visit to Budapest shortly after Orbán returned to power in 2010, I had dinner with György Schöpflin, whom I had first got to know during the Cold War, when he lived in exile in London. An academic at the LSE, Schöpflin had been a regular in the studios of the BBC World Service and a staunch opponent of Communist rule in Hungary. But now he was a member of the European Parliament for Fidesz, smoothly justifying Orbán's policies as a necessary defense of the Hungarian nation in an expensive restaurant in Budapest.

The tactics that Orbán was prepared to use to defend his conception of Hungary and his own political position became more radical the longer he was in power and the more confident he became. In the aftermath of the refugee crisis, Orbán decided to demonize George Soros, his onetime benefactor. The denunciation of an alleged "Soros plan" to flood Hungary with Muslims became central to his re-election campaign in 2017 – with a grinning Soros featured on election posters that were plastered all over Hungary. There was no such plan. What is true is that in 2015, as the European refugee crisis was coming to the boil, Soros had written an opinion piece arguing that the EU needed to redefine its asylum policy and should admit at least a million refugees a year, sharing them out across the bloc.[14] He was also a generous backer of refugee charities. During the 2017 election Soros, who was not running for office, was made the face of a shadowy international plot that was allegedly planning to flood the Hungarian nation with Muslims.

The dark nature of the anti-Soros campaign became even clearer a year later, when Orbán gave a speech commemorating the anniversary of the 1848 revolutions in Europe. Orbán alluded to Soros and employed classic anti-Semitic imagery, declaring that Hungary faced "an opponent who is different from us": "Their faces are not visible, but are hidden from view . . . They are not national, but international. They do not believe in work, but speculate with money. They have no homeland, but feel that the whole world is theirs."[15]

After winning another election victory, Orbán continued his vendetta. One of Soros's most generous gestures to the land of his birth had been to found the Central European University in 1991 and to base it in Budapest. Over the next decades, CEU built a global reputation, attracting talented students and lecturers from all over the world, such as Michael Ignatieff, the biographer of Isaiah Berlin, and Tim Crane, who left his position as head of the philosophy department at Cambridge to join CEU. But the university's openness to ideas from around the world and its connection with Soros made it a target for Orbán, who passed legislation forcing it to move from Budapest to Vienna in 2019.

The longer Orbán was in power, the more he strengthened his grip on the institutions of the state and of civil society. By 2019, the Hungarian journalist Paul Lendvai could observe that "every single media outlet is now controlled by the regime."

As so often, the crushing of an independent media and judiciary opened the door to corruption. Many of Orbán's old friends have become rich in business. By 2018, Transparency International estimated that some 40 percent of public contracts in Hungary were awarded after a process involving only one bidder.[16] In 2017 an investigation by OLAF, the EU's corruption watchdog, recommended that István Tiborcz, Orbán's son-in-law, should be prosecuted because his companies had rigged bids for tens of millions of euros in EU contracts for municipal lighting. Unsurprisingly, Hungary ignored this recommendation and there was nothing that OLAF could do about it.[17] Tiborcz is now one of the hundred richest people in Hungary. The second richest man in the country was thought to be Lörinc Mészáros, a boyhood friend of Orbán.

The whiff of corruption around the Hungarian leader did not inhibit him from playing the role of philosopher-king. As a student, he had written a dissertation on Antonio Gramsci, the Italian Marxist philosopher who argued that political power often flowed from the control of powerful cultural institutions. As prime minister, he embarked on a Gramscian program of societal transformation. His goal, he declared, was to create "a new cultural era." Even the Hungarian kindergarten curriculum was reshaped to promote "national identity, Christian cultural values, patriotism."[18]

Orbán continued to promote his ideas of "illiberal" democracy outside Hungary too and showered praise on strongman leaders such as Vladimir Putin. He was the first EU leader to endorse Donald Trump for the presidency in 2016. He regularly praised Xi's China and forged a close relationship with Benjamin Netanyahu of Israel. The Israeli leader was prepared to overlook Orbán's use of anti-Semitism in domestic political campaigns in return for a valuable ally around the EU table. Within the EU, Orbán argued against sanctions on Russia, saying that the EU needed to recognize that "Putin has made his country great again."[19] Like Putin, Xi and Erdoğan, Orbán had no plans to pull back from power any time soon. "I will remain in politics for the coming 15 or 20 years," he announced in 2016.[20] In September 2021, after Angela Merkel stepped down as leader of Germany, Orbán became the longest-serving prime minister in the twenty-seven EU member states.

The emergence of a strongman leader in its midst was a huge challenge for the EU. One embarrassing open secret was that the German government had tolerated Orbán because he was useful to them. For much of the Orbán–Merkel years, the votes of Fidesz in the European Parliament helped to secure the working majority of the European People's Party (EPP), which was dominated by Merkel's Christian Democrats. As a result, the CDU did its utmost to shut its eyes to the erosion of democracy within Hungary lest a showdown with Orbán cost the EPP its precious parliamentary majority. When at an event in Brussels, just after the refugee crisis, I asked Manfred Weber, the parliament's president and a member of the CDU's sister party the CSU, about why his party continued to work with Fidesz, Weber, looking slightly uncomfortable, informed me that Orbán had not yet crossed any red lines.

A turning point was eventually reached in 2019, when Orbán attacked Jean-Claude Juncker, accusing the commission president of being in league with the hated George Soros in a plot to force refugees on Hungary. Juncker is a much revered figure in the European Parliament and now a red line had clearly been crossed. By 2021, with Fidesz on the verge of being thrown out of the EPP, Orbán chose to quit the group instead.[21]

But membership of Europe's main center-right grouping was not the only protective cloak around Viktor Orbán and Fidesz. There were also procedural reasons that made it hard for the EU's democracies to crack down on Hungary's strongman. The obvious sanction under EU law was to suspend Hungary's voting rights – or to stop the flow of EU money into Hungary, which provided so many of the juicy contracts on which Orbán's associates had feasted. The difficulty is that, under the EU's complex legal rules, far-reaching decisions of this nature often have to be taken unanimously. And by 2016, after recent elections, Orbán had a crucial ally in the shape of Poland's Law and Justice Party. An informal axis had emerged within the EU: Poland would protect Hungary and Hungary would protect Poland – and Europe's liberals were left fuming on the sidelines.

In Poland, the Law and Justice Party had acted swiftly to bring independent institutions under its control. In a move that emulated developments in Orbán's Hungary – and anticipated events in Trump's America – the new government targeted the constitutional court. After winning the 2015 elections, Law and Justice refused to approve new judges appointed by the outgoing Civic Platform Party and instead appointed five new government-friendly justices. It also changed the law to make it harder for the court to overrule the government. Kaczynski was frank about his motivations. Without these changes, he pointed out, "All our actions could be questioned." In a parliamentary speech that drew a standing ovation from Law and Justice MPs, Kornel Morawiecki, a pro-government legislator proclaimed: "The good of the nation is above the law."[22] As Law and Justice saw it, the "good of the nation" involved pushing Poland irreversibly in a more nationalistic and culturally conservative direction – rejecting the cosmopolitan liberalism of Brussels, with its emphasis on gay rights and internationalism.

In the last days of 2015, new statutes were pushed through parliament, allowing the government to sack senior civil servants and employees of the state media. Once again, pro-government legislators were frank about their motives. Elżbieta Kruk, a Law and Justice MP, argued that "Instead of creating a media shield for the Polish national interest, journalists often sympathize with negative opinions about Poland."[23] The deterioration in the standards of the state media was swift and startling. When I visited Poland in late 2017, one prominent academic told me he believed the state media was now even more slavishly pro-government than in the 1970s, when the Communist Party was still firmly in charge. One crucial qualification to that bleak judgment was that independent newspapers and other media continued to operate and to criticize the government. But the government's core constituency, outside the big cities, was much more likely to get its news straight from the main television stations.

For those who had cherished the idea that Poland was the model of a one-party state that had transitioned successfully to a liberal democracy, these developments were depressing. But, in retrospect, the warning signs had been there for some time. I first realized that something disturbing was happening beneath the surface of Polish politics on a visit to Kraków in 2013, two years before Law and Justice won back control of the presidency and parliament.

Over dinner, I was told about the popularity of the Smolensk conspiracy theory. The Smolensk air disaster had taken place in 2010, when a plane carrying the Polish president, Lech Kaczynski, the identical twin brother of Jaroslaw, had crashed over Russia, killing the president and many other senior government officials, including the president of the central bank, military leaders and eighteen members of parliament. Successive investigations, including by the Polish government itself, had concluded that the crash had been a tragic accident, involving heavy fog and pilot error.

But Jaroslaw Kaczynski – perhaps blinded by grief or perhaps sensing political advantage – never accepted that the air disaster that killed his brother had been an accident. Instead he and his acolytes promoted the theory that Russia had plotted to murder much of Poland's elite and that the Polish government had deliberately covered up the evidence. At times, Kaczynski even suggested that his Polish political opponents were directly responsible for his brother's death, shouting in parliament at the opposition benches, "You destroyed him. You killed him."[24]

Given the long history of Russian aggression against Poland – and the memory of the Katyn massacre of the Polish elite by the Soviet Union in 1940 – it is not surprising that many Poles were suspicious about an accident on Russian soil that wiped out much of the country's government. But successive investigations failed to find any evidence for foul play – let alone the notion that Poles themselves had been in league with the Russians. Nonetheless, by 2013, as I was told in Kraków, this evidence-free conspiracy theory was helping to frame Polish politics, with around one-third of Poles believing that Smolensk was a mass assassination that had been covered up.

At the time, it was tempting to dismiss the significance of poll results of this nature. Perhaps they were a symptom of an immature democracy: after all, Poland was just a generation away from decades of one-party rule. In fact, as events were to prove, it was not just Poland that was susceptible to conspiracy theories promoted by far-right parties and irresponsible leaders. At the same time that the Law and Justice Party won the Polish elections, after promoting the Smolensk conspiracy theory, Donald Trump was launching his presidential campaign, after promoting the "birther" conspiracy theory that Barack Obama had not been born in the US. And several years later, in the US, Donald Trump and the Republicans were able to convince around 70 percent of their voters – roughly a third of the total electorate – that the 2020 US presidential election had been stolen. In that same year, opinion polls in Poland were suggesting that 45 percent of the population believed that "foreign powers are deliberately contributing to the spread of the coronavirus."[25] With Kaczynski, as with Trump, conspiracy theories were not an incidental detail: they were absolutely central to their politics. As one of the Polish leader's confidants put it: "In his political thinking, there is no such thing as an accident . . . If something happened, it was the machination of an outsider. Conspiracy is his favourite word."[26]

Unlike Trump and Orbán, Jaroslaw Kaczynski continued to hover in the background. Law and Justice's front man was Andrzej Duda, who was elected as president in 2015 and re-elected in 2020. Duda seemed affable and a little bland. I shared a conference platform with him twice in 2020, in Davos and in Tallinn in Estonia, and he was friendly enough. In Davos, he spent such a long time straightening his tie and smiling at himself in the mirror before our event that there was no time to exchange more than a few words. In Estonia, he confined himself to pitching confidently (and in English) for foreign investment in Poland and he shook my hand warmly at the subsequent drinks reception. (I was a little disturbed to discover, a couple of days later, that Duda had come down with the coronavirus; fortunately, I was spared.)

But while Duda struck a conventional pose overseas, at home he and his party colleagues were waging an all-out culture war and push-ing through deeply reactionary policies. Law and Justice was often accused of flirting with anti-Semitism, but in the 2020 election, the chosen enemy were gays. At a campaign rally, Duda called the push for LGBT+ rights an ideology that was "worse than communism." As ever, the party line enjoyed strong support from the public television, which ran news stories with captions proclaiming that "LGBT ideol-ogy is destroying the family."[27] With re-election secured, Law and Justice pushed forward with a new law that all but abolished the right to abortion. The move provoked hundreds of thousands of people to take to the streets of Warsaw in protest.[28]

The global significance of what happened in Hungary and Poland was not apparent in 2015, when Orbán and Kaczynski made their breakthroughs. But in retrospect, these events were a warning to other Western democracies. The strongman style of politics would no longer be confined to Asia or to countries on the fringes of Europe, such as Russia and Turkey. It was now entrenched within the European Union. The following year populist strongman politics was to make a shock-ing breakthrough in two countries that were widely regarded as having the most secure liberal democracies in the world: the United Kingdom and the United States.

6 Boris Johnson and Brexit Britain (2016)

I first met Boris Johnson at an English country wedding in 2002. He was already a political and media star, who carried around with him a whiff of danger and scandal. Boris, as he was universally known, had been elected to Parliament the previous year and was editor of the *Spectator*, a small-circulation magazine that was big in Tory Britain. He was also a man with a large and adoring following on the Euroskeptic right, dating from his time as the *Daily Telegraph*'s correspondent in Brussels from 1989 to 1994. With a mixture of humor, flair and fantasy, Johnson's reports had whipped up conservative outrage about the EU's supposed plans to create a European superstate that threatened Britain's ancient liberties and independence.

In 2002, I too was working as a foreign correspondent in Brussels, for *The Economist*, so my first conversation with Johnson was about mutual friends in the EU capital. A few months earlier, I had written an article in *Prospect* magazine arguing that it would be a mistake for Britain to join the newly launched European single currency, the euro. Standing in the wedding marquee, with a glass of champagne in his hand, Johnson told me that he had read my article and that he agreed with my side of the argument.[1] I thanked him and said: "But you know a lot of your friends in Brussels think that you are secretly in favor of the EU." Johnson looked back at me, with a faintly hurt expression. "Of course, I'm in favor of the EU," he exclaimed. "How could you not be?"

It was a remark that was, in retrospect, deeply ironic. In 2016, some fourteen years after our conversation, Johnson was to lead the successful campaign for Britain to leave the EU. Brexit was the worst blow to the European project since its foundation in the 1950s.

Johnson's central role in delivering Brexit means that his name will forever be linked in history with that of Donald Trump and with the populist revolt that swept the Anglo-American world in 2016. By coincidence, Trump was actually in Britain on June 23, the day of the Brexit referendum, playing golf at his Turnberry resort. He immediately latched on to the result, predicting that America would have its own "Brexit moment" in the US presidential election in November.[2] Steve Bannon, Trump's campaign manager, remarked later that the moment he "knew" Trump would win was when Britain voted for Brexit. As Bannon saw it, Trump's victory and the successful Brexit campaign, led by Johnson, were both part of a populist revolt against "globalism."

Trump himself got on best with Nigel Farage, the leader of the UK Independence Party who had helped put Brexit on the agenda, years before Johnson joined the cause. Farage even managed to be the first foreign politician to visit Trump after his improbable victory. But once Johnson emerged as prime minister and the standard-bearer of Brexit, Trump claimed him as one of his own, even labeling him as "Britain Trump." The American left saw things the same way, routinely bracketing Johnson with their enemy. As Joe Biden pointed out, there was even a certain physical resemblance between the two leaders. Their personal lives were also similar. Trump's third wife, Melania, is twenty-four years younger than him. Johnson's third wife, Carrie, is twenty-three years younger than him.

Indeed, wherever I traveled in recent years – from Delhi to Beijing to Moscow – political analysts bracketed "Trump and Brexit." But for many ardent Boris-backers, putting their hero in the same category as Donald Trump – let alone Vladimir Putin or Xi Jinping – is unfair. As they see it, labeling Johnson a "strongman" is an unjustified insult from Remainers unwilling to accept their defeat. To his fans, Johnson is a democrat through and through, whose campaign for Brexit ensured that the will of the people prevailed over that of the elite.

Many of Johnson's bitterest opponents would also reject the idea that he is a "strongman" leader – but for different reasons. They regard Johnson as indecisive and unable to come to terms with the demands of office, a charge that gained in force as Britain stumbled through the first stages of the coronavirus crisis. Far from being strong and decisive during the pandemic, Johnson was portrayed by his critics as too weak to take control of the situation.

All of these qualifications to the idea of Boris Johnson as a "strong-man leader" have some force. But there are clear similarities – in themes and methods – between Johnson and Trump. Both men ran as tribunes of the people against the elite. Both argued that elitist politicians had put foreigners ahead of their own countrymen. Trump's slogan was "America First." Campaigning for Brexit, Johnson toured Britain in a bus demanding that Britain stop paying £350 million a week (a much disputed figure) to the EU, demanding: "Let's fund our NHS instead." In foreign policy, both took aim at their country's traditional alliances. Johnson's most important policy was to take Britain out of the European Union. Trump made it clear that he regarded NATO as biased against American interests and toyed with withdrawing from the Western alliance. The "liberal international order," constructed by previous generations of American and British statesmen, was severely disrupted by the twin impacts of "Brexit and Trump."

Both Trump and Johnson also capitalized on hostility towards mass immigration. For Johnson, this was something of a departure. As mayor of London from 2008 to 2016, he made a point of his enthusiasm for leading a multicultural city, a third of whose inhabitants were born overseas. When I followed Johnson on the mayoral campaign trail in 2008, I watched him attend a "citizenship ceremony" for new Britons, after which he told me how moved he had been. Doubtless, he felt this was the right sort of thing to say to a representative of a pro-immigration newspaper. But, despite his record of making occasional off-color jokes about race, I didn't really doubt his pro-immigration sentiments. Those kinds of views were standard in the liberal London circles in which we both moved.

Johnson's campaign for Brexit, however, deliberately exploited hostility to mass immigration. The Brexit campaign's slogan "Take Back Control" was widely understood to refer, above all, to the demand to take back control of Britain's borders. One of the most controversial aspects of Britain's EU membership was the free movement of people between EU member states. After Poland and other relatively poor countries from Central Europe had joined the EU in 2004, well over 2 million Europeans had moved to Britain. This had caused a backlash and concerns that Britain was being "swamped" by immigrants.

The Brexit campaign – masterminded by Dominic Cummings, who

played a Bannon-like role as campaign strategist and philosopher –
deliberately stoked these fears of migration, by claiming that Turkey, a
Muslim country, was poised to join the EU. Campaign posters stated
baldly: "Turkey (population 76m) is joining the EU." "Since the birth-
rate in Turkey is so high," explained one Vote Leave statement, "we
can expect to see an additional million people added to the UK population from Turkey alone within eight years."[3] Turkey was, in fact,
nowhere near joining the EU. Its application process had fallen into
abeyance, since the formal opening of negotiations in 2004. But in
the closing weeks of the campaign, Vote Leave hammered away at
the themes of Turkey and immigration. These scare tactics were
particularly effective after one million Syrian refugees had entered
Germany the previous year.

Johnson's willingness to use such tactics testified to the lengths he
was prepared to go to get to the top. On other occasions, he had
stressed his pride in his own Turkish ancestry. His great-grandfather,
Ali Kemal, had been a liberal Turkish journalist, who had served
briefly as a government minister. Insider accounts of the Brexit campaign suggest that, behind closed doors, Johnson expressed qualms
about the Turkey-bashing campaign and even "erupted with rage."[4]
But he never expressed misgivings in public. He was willing to do
what was necessary to win, even if that involved lying and dabbling in
race-baiting.

Vote Leave's decision to stoke fears about immigration was shrewd.
The Remain campaign was focused almost entirely on the economic
benefits of British membership of the EU. But polls later revealed that
Leave voters were not influenced primarily by economics. As Roger
Eatwell and Matthew Goodwin argued, in a post-referendum analysis,
"Remainers were talking endlessly about economic risk while Leavers
were chiefly concerned about perceived threats to their identity and
national group." Six in ten Leave voters said that significant damage to
the British economy would be a "price worth paying for Brexit."[5]

In the aftermath of the Brexit vote, a lot of attention was focused on
economically "left-behind" areas that had voted Leave, in particular
parts of northern England that had been hit hard by deindustrialization. But the Leave vote in Britain – like the Trump vote in the American
Rust Belt – was more complicated than a simple cry of economic
anguish. The Leave campaign successfully targeted people who were

upset by immigration and social change – and who often linked immigration with economic decline and insecurity. Some 64 percent of Leave voters thought that immigration had been bad for the economy and an even higher proportion, 72 percent, believed that it had undermined British culture. Many Leave voters had stopped voting in general elections but seized upon the Brexit referendum as a chance to change "the system." Voter turnout in the referendum was 72 percent – higher than in any election for twenty-five years.[6] It was this mobilization of new voters, as much as anything, that threw out the calculations of the Remain campaign.

As mayor of London, Johnson had praised its dynamism and diversity. But London voted heavily to remain. He led Leave to victory by mobilizing the discontent of non-metropolitan Britain.

Johnson's transformation into a champion of "left-behind" Britain was not the only way that Brexit represented a disavowal of his own past. Perhaps uniquely among the top echelon of British politicians, his own life had been bound up with Brussels and the European project. Johnson's father, Stanley, had worked for the EU and, for two years, the young Boris attended the European School in Brussels, an educational establishment for the children of EU officials. It was at the European School, in the suburb of Uccle, that he first met Marina, who was to become his second wife and to whom he remained married for twenty-five years. Most of Johnson's family are devoted Europhiles. His brother Jo attended the College of Europe in Brugge, a training school for the EU elite, and later resigned from Johnson's government in protest at his brother's policies on Brexit. His sister, Rachel, vociferously opposed Brexit and joined the Liberal Democrats, Britain's most pro-EU party.

But while Brussels was part of Boris Johnson's life and background, his truly formative years were spent in the most traditional, British elite institutions. His secondary education was at Eton College, which had produced nineteen other British prime ministers before Johnson. Contemporaries remember Boris as a social and intellectual star, far more memorable than his Eton schoolmate, David Cameron. But some of Johnson's teachers also glimpsed his flaws. In a letter to his parents, Martin Hammond, an Eton master, noted: "Boris seems affronted when confronted with what amounts to a gross failure of responsibility . . . I think he honestly believes that it is churlish of us not to regard him as an exception, one who should be free of the network of obligation that binds everyone else."[7]

It was a perceptive insight. Johnson seems to feel that great men and big personalities should not have to play by the same rules as everybody else. In a 2003 article for the *Spectator*, he expressed sympathy for the Italian prime minister Silvio Berlusconi, a billionaire whose rise to power as a populist outsider anticipated the later ascent of Donald Trump. Berlusconi stood accused of corruption and abuse of power – he was later convicted of tax fraud and sentenced to prison – but Johnson found him charming and compared him favorably to the "bossy" bureaucrats of Brussels, declaring that Berlusconi was "better than the whole damn lot of them."[8]

After Eton, Johnson went on to study classics at Balliol College, Oxford – and became president of the Oxford Union, a rite of passage for some previous prime ministers, such as Heath, Asquith and Gladstone. A famous photo taken of Johnson at Oxford shows him posing in white tie and tails with fellow members of the Bullingdon Club, alongside fellow Old Etonian and future prime minister David Cameron. The Bullingdon is famous for its brand of upper-class, drunken hooliganism. One member later recounted to me his initiation into the society by Johnson: "They all burst into my room and smashed it up. Then Boris turned round and shook my hand and said, 'Congratulations, man, you're in.'"

As his journalistic and political career took off, Johnson used his charm and his sense of humor to refashion his image – from upper-class lout into jolly man-of-the-people. Like Trump, Johnson built his public profile on popular television programs, in his case the television quiz show *Have I Got News for You*. While *The Apprentice* portrayed Trump as ruthless and decisive, Johnson cultivated a bumbling and comic persona. By making people laugh, he came across as somebody very different from the normal, slickly packaged politician. His shock of tousled blond hair made him an instantly recognizable figure who quickly achieved the holy grail for politicians of being universally known by his first name. (Actually Boris is his second name; his real first name is Alexander and some members of his family still call him Al.)

Johnson's image as an anti-politician has allowed him to survive incidents and embarrassments that would have finished off the careers of other politicians. Like another right-wing charmer, US president

Ronald Reagan, Johnson seems to have something of a "Teflon" coating. In 2004, he was forced to resign from the Tory front bench, after lying about an affair to the party leader, Michael Howard. In 2012, in a publicity stunt during the London Olympics, Johnson found himself stuck in midair on a zip wire, haplessly waving some Union Jacks, until he could be rescued. As David Cameron, by then prime minister, pointed out with a mixture of fondness and exasperation, for almost any other politician this would have been a public-relations disaster. But Johnson somehow turned it into a triumph. In fact, it became one of the most famous images of Johnson – helping to mold his image as a lovable, patriotic joker.

In 2016, Johnson's popularity and his skill as a campaigner made his position on Brexit crucial to the national referendum that had been called by David Cameron. But just a few months before the vote, it was still unclear which side he would back. At the time I asked Christopher Lockwood – the mutual friend at whose wedding I had first met Johnson – what did Boris really think about Europe? Lockwood, who had served as Johnson's deputy at the *Telegraph* office in Brussels, shrugged. "I think he is genuinely schizophrenic about the subject." That split personality played out as decision time approached. Unable to make up his mind about which side to back, Johnson wrote two columns for the *Telegraph*: one in favor of Brexit, one against. The popular legend goes that he liked the pro-Brexit column better – and the rest became history.

In reality, rather more calculation had gone into Johnson's decision. There had perhaps been clues about which way Boris might jump in his biography of his political hero, Winston Churchill. There, Johnson had written: "To some extent all politicians are gamblers with events. They try to anticipate what will happen, to put themselves on the right side of events." Johnson even interpreted Churchill's opposition to Nazism in this rather cynical light, writing that in the early 1930s, when Churchill's fortunes had been at a low ebb, he had "put his shirt on a horse called anti-Nazism . . . and his bet came off in spectacular fashion." I thought of that passage in February 2016, when Boris announced that he would campaign for Brexit, and wrote in an article: "Mr Johnson has put his bet on a horse called Euroscepticism. He is clearly hoping that his bet will also come off in spectacular fashion and carry him, like Churchill, all the way into 10 Downing Street."[9]

Johnson's campaigning did indeed help to deliver an unexpected victory for "Vote Leave," by 51.89 percent to 48.11 percent. But appearing outside his London house the morning after the vote, Johnson looked shocked and disconcerted rather than exultant. The fact that he was greeted by a baying crowd of angry young Remainers clearly rattled a man who was used to being popular – and who had always expected, and perhaps hoped, that Vote Leave would lose narrowly. David Cameron later revealed that when Johnson had informed him that he intended to campaign for Leave, he had swiftly followed up their conversation with a text predicting that "Brexit will be crushed like a toad under the harrow." Cameron concluded that Johnson had genuinely believed that Brexit would lose, "but he didn't want to give up the chance of being on the romantic, patriotic, nationalistic side."[10]

The unexpected Leave victory had consequences for both men. That same morning Cameron resigned as prime minister. Johnson was immediately installed by the bookmakers as his likely successor. The route to 10 Downing Street, which he had eyed ever since as a child he had proclaimed an ambition to be "world king," lay wide open.

And yet, at the very last, the prize was snatched away. Michael Gove, who had fronted the Leave campaign with Johnson, announced that close proximity to Johnson had convinced him that Boris was unfit for the highest office in the land. Casting around for a better candidate, Gove glanced in the mirror and saw just the man. Johnson's reaction to being challenged by his close colleague was not the kind of thing one would have expected from "a man of destiny" or a strongman leader in the making. He folded. Rather than fight his corner, Johnson did a quick calculation of the electoral arithmetic inside the Conservative Party, which was now moving against him, and withdrew from the contest to be the next party leader. But Gove's act of spectacular backstabbing did him no good. Instead, the relatively colorless figure of Theresa May – who had voted Remain – was elected Tory Party leader and became the next prime minister.

May well understood that if she was to retain the backing of her party, she had to deliver Brexit and convince Tory Leavers that she was now one of them. So she swiftly appointed Johnson as her new foreign secretary. What seemed to be a clever compromise never really worked for either of them. Johnson was widely seen as an ineffectual foreign secretary, and May as a hapless prime minister. Unsurprisingly, she was unable to conclude a Brexit deal with the EU that delivered on the Leave campaign's impossible promise of frictionless trade without any of the encumbrances of EU membership. Within the Conservative Party this failure was not blamed on the unrealistic promises made by the Leave campaign. Instead unhappy Leavers argued that May had never really believed in their cause and so had been led down the path to disastrous compromises by a "Remain establishment" embedded in the British Civil Service.

The growing discontent with May presented Boris Johnson with a second shot at the top job. In the summer of 2018, he resigned as foreign secretary, positioning himself once again as the champion of true Tory Euroskeptics. Johnson's argument was that May had been too weak in her dealings with Europe and with the "Remain establishment" in Britain. Only he had the strength to deliver Brexit. Shortly before quitting as foreign secretary, Johnson told a group of fellow Tory MPs: "I am increasingly admiring of Donald Trump . . . Imagine Trump doing Brexit. He'd go in bloody hard . . . There'd be all sorts of breakdowns, all sorts of chaos. Everyone would think he'd gone mad. But actually you might get somewhere. It's a very, very good thought."[11]

Freed from ministerial responsibility, Johnson dabbled in Trump-style conspiracy theories, suggesting that if Brexit was not achieved, "I think that people will feel betrayed and I think they will feel there's been a great conspiracy by the deep state of the UK, the people who really run the country, to overturn the vote in the referendum." He also hinted at violence on the streets, saying that those who were trying to thwart Brexit were "playing with fire" and would "reap the whirlwind."[12]

By May 2019, discontent with Theresa May inside the Tory Party had grown to such a pitch that she was forced out as prime minister. This time, with much more time to prepare a proper leadership campaign and with a team of ambitious people around him, Johnson finally achieved his goal. At the age of fifty-five, he was leader of the Conservative Party and prime minister of the United Kingdom of Great Britain and Northern Ireland.

Installed in 10 Downing Street and reunited with Dominic Cummings, Johnson began to deliver on his promise to be a strong and ruthless leader. May had been unable to get her Brexit deal through Parliament because too many "hard Brexiters" in the Tory Party, aligned with Johnson, had consistently voted against it – believing that May's deal left Britain still too closely tied to the EU. Johnson faced the opposite problem. If he went for too hard a Brexit or threatened to leave the EU without any sort of deal, he would lose his parliamentary majority, because too many former Remainers in the Tory Party would refuse to back him. Egged on by Dominic Cummings, Johnson made a move from the strongman playbook: he prorogued Parliament at the end of August 2019. This meant that the sitting of the House of Commons was suspended in an effort to prevent it getting in the way of Brexit. When several leading members of his own party objected to these tactics, Johnson took the ruthless decision to expel twenty-one MPs from the Conservative Party. The victims included Sir Nicholas Soames, Churchill's grandson, and Kenneth Clarke, a veteran of the Thatcher era and the longest-serving MP in the house.[13]

Outraged Remainers challenged the legality of Johnson's decision to prorogue Parliament and managed to get it overturned in Britain's Supreme Court. The fact that the court's decision was handed down on the very day that the House of Representatives in Washington DC announced impeachment proceedings against Donald Trump served to re-enforce the Johnson–Trump parallels, suggesting that there was a rule-of-law crisis building on both sides of the Atlantic.

Cummings was openly contemptuous of the legal constraints normal governments operated under. In a blog entry in March 2019 – typically scattered with block capitals, and random literary and scientific references – Cummings had advised Brexiters to ignore promises that the May government was making to the EU, writing: "A serious government – one not cowed by officials and their bullshit legal advice . . . will dispense with these commitments and any domestic law enforcing them."[14]

Johnson's willingness to break the law to force Brexit through had been repudiated by the Supreme Court and outraged liberal Britain. But it chimed with the mood of the public. A poll taken earlier in 2019 showed that 54 percent of people agreed with the statement that "Britain needs a strong ruler, willing to break the rules"; only 23 percent disagreed.[15] The public tolerance, even desire, for some kind of strongman leader was wildly at odds with the image of a tolerant, law-abiding nation, cherished by the British elite. But it was in line with global trends.

At the Conservative Party conference that year, which was held just after the Supreme Court had ruled against Johnson, the prime minister was greeted as a conquering hero. In the corridors of the Manchester convention center, I encountered one Tory MP and Brexiter looking stunned as he left the meeting of his regional party association. "It's like a fucking Nuremberg rally in there," he said, reporting that Johnson had only got two sentences into his speech, before being interrupted by thunderous chants of "Boris, Boris." The cult of personality, a key part of the strongman style, had been established.

On the surface, defeat in the Supreme Court was a major setback for Johnson. But the bigger picture was that it played into the Cummings strategy, which was to force a general election in Britain that would allow him to reprise Vote Leave's successful "people versus the elite" strategy of 2016. The idea was to portray the difficulties in getting Brexit past Parliament and the courts as the product of an elitist plot to thwart the will of the people. Unexpectedly, and disastrously for them, the opposition Labour Party and Liberal Democrats decided to give Johnson his wish and agreed to a rare winter election in December 2019. Cummings, a master of the three-word slogan, came up with "Get Brexit Done" as the campaign theme. Johnson was also hugely aided by the fact that the Labour Party was led by Jeremy Corbyn, an elderly far-left activist, dogged by accusations of anti-Semitism.

The election, held on December 12, delivered Johnson a moment of pure political triumph, as he led the Conservative Party back into power with a majority of eighty seats in the Commons. All the political and moral compromises he had made on the path to power – and all the setbacks and humiliations – seemed to have been brushed aside. As a victorious prime minister with a new mandate, he negotiated a new "hard" Brexit deal that took Britain out of both the European single market and the EU's customs union.

In reality, the Johnson deal also involved some major concessions on Northern Ireland. To avoid a hard border being re-established between Northern Ireland and the Republic of Ireland that would endanger the Good Friday peace deal, Britain had agreed that some goods coming into Northern Ireland from the rest of the UK would be subject to customs checks – effectively establishing an internal border inside the UK, running across the Irish Sea. It was an extraordinary erosion of the UK's control of its own territory, which should have been anathema to any sovereignty-minded nationalist. Indeed, Theresa May had declared that no British prime minister could ever agree to such a deal. But Johnson simply refused to acknowledge the reality of what he had signed up to, denying that there would be any checks on goods traveling between Northern Ireland and the rest of the UK. As so often in his life, he got away with it – at least for a while. The inconvenient details of the deal were largely ignored, amid the excitement of the suspension of Parliament and the election.

At the end of January 2020, Britain finally left the EU. Johnson had delivered on his campaign promise to "Get Brexit Done." With a large parliamentary majority and Dominic Cummings by his side, Johnson seemed perfectly placed to govern for five years, remaking Britain and the country's place in the world.

But January 31, 2020, the day that Brexit finally happened, was also the day that Britain announced its first case of coronavirus. Boris Johnson's libertarian rhetoric – which had been so well suited to a campaign against the European Union – was dangerously out of place when dealing with Covid-19. As other countries in Europe and Asia were locking down, Johnson was slow to react, fretting not just about the economic damage, but about the difficulty of asking Britons not to go to the pub.

Even after it became clear that the coronavirus had become a global problem, Johnson, preoccupied by his impending divorce and the pregnancy of his soon-to-be third wife, missed five consecutive meetings of Cobra, the government committee charged with dealing with national emergencies. In early March, when the pandemic had already taken hold in Italy, Johnson boasted of "shaking hands with everybody" during a hospital visit. Packed sessions of the House of Commons continued, with politicians jammed together in the traditional fashion. By the time events forced Johnson to impose a lockdown on the country, Italy, Spain, France and Germany had already acted.

The slowness of the Johnson government's response was an important contributory factor to the heavy death toll in Britain, which was the highest in Western Europe. Unlike Donald Trump or Brazil's Jair Bolsonaro, once Johnson imposed a lockdown, he made a show of following scientific advice – while occasionally railing against it in private.*

---

* His adviser, Dominic Cummings, later revealed how Johnson had fought lockdowns in private and blamed him for thousands of unnecessary deaths.

But the country and Johnson himself paid a heavy price for his early casualness. In early April 2019, Johnson became the first world leader admitted to hospital with Covid-19. Shortly afterwards, he was moved into intensive care and for a few days his life seemed to hang in the balance. The reaction of some of his most ardent supporters went well beyond the usual shock and sympathy, and showed the extent to which parts of Britain had succumbed to a leader cult. Allison Pearson, a prominent columnist, wrote in the *Daily Telegraph*: "Boris is loved – really loved – in a way that the metropolitan media class has never begun to understand . . . Make no mistake, the health of Boris Johnson is the health of the body politic and, by extension, the health of the nation itself."[16]

When Johnson emerged from hospital, his supporters (and much of the country) hoped that his recovery would inject some of his trademark optimism and energy into Britain's fight against the coronavirus. Instead the prime minister initially appeared a diminished figure – ill, uncertain and lacking in energy and direction. Sir Humphrey Wakefield, Dominic Cummings's father-in-law, unhelpfully compared Johnson to a permanently disabled horse, remarking, "If you put a horse back to work too early, it will never recover."

In the event, it was Cummings whose political career came to an untimely end. In May 2020, it emerged that he had broken the government's own lockdown rules. Infected by the coronavirus, Cummings had chosen to drive his wife and child more than two hundred miles north, to convalesce on his parents' farm in County Durham. Cummings survived the resulting scandal, but was finally forced out of 10 Downing Street towards the end of 2020, after numerous rows with colleagues. He swiftly became an outspoken critic of Johnson, labeling him completely unfit for the job of prime minister.

With Brexit done and Cummings gone, there was a clear opportunity for Johnson to abandon the strongman style and become a more conventional prime minister. After the early mishandling of the coronavirus, Johnson's personal ratings recovered on the back of Britain's relatively successful vaccination campaign against Covid-19. The contrast between the speed with which Britain had vaccinated its population and the floundering EU campaign was portrayed by Johnson as a retrospective justification for Brexit.

But Johnson was not quite ready to abandon the strongman style. The main problem was that the contradictions and strains inherent in the Brexit deal that he had negotiated were coming back to haunt him. Despite his protestations, Brexit involved a substantial increase in bureaucracy and nontariff barriers for British exports. In January 2021, the first month in which the new trading arrangements were fully in place, British exports to the EU dropped by 41 percent. Some of this was attributable to the effects of the pandemic. But much of the fall was a result of Brexit itself. The situation was even worse in Northern Ireland, where the new customs controls were hitting supplies to supermarkets.

The response of the Johnson government was to search for an enemy – and to threaten to break international law. Lord David Frost, Johnson's chief EU negotiator, argued that the root of the problem was that the EU had failed to accept Britain's democratic decision to leave. The UK also moved to unilaterally suspend aspects of the Northern Ireland protocol – which meant violating an international treaty that the prime minister had recently negotiated.

Johnson's personal style remained affable and outwardly friendly. He avoided the cold menace of a Putin or the ranting paranoia of an Erdoğan. But, in a very English way, he had introduced important elements of the strongman style of politics into Britain. He had shown a willingness to break both domestic and international law. He had demonized opponents as elitist enemies of the people. His political allies had extended the same description to the courts and had repeatedly questioned the impartiality of other important national institutions, such as the Civil Service and the BBC. Johnson had bent the truth out of shape in the Brexit referendum campaign in a way that went far beyond the normal cut and thrust of politics. And he had established a leader cult within his own Conservative Party, which forced MPs to abandon their principles to save their careers.

In some ways, Britain is particularly vulnerable to the strongman style of politics. The country has an unwritten constitution and has relied on what the historian Peter Hennessy calls the "good chap" model of governance – a belief that all establishment politicians will behave with a "sense of restraint" and respect for time-honored conventions. Outwardly, Boris Johnson looks like the very epitome of a "good chap." But in reality, as his Eton housemaster once astutely observed, he feels himself unconstrained by "the network of obligations that binds everybody else."

Given Britain's position as one of the world's oldest democracies, the election of a populist rule-breaker as UK prime minister marked a significant shift in European and world politics. Rush Doshi, director for China policy in the Biden White House, argues that Xi Jinping and his circle took the Brexit vote very seriously, seeing it as part of a "trifecta" of blows to the Western-led world order, made up of "Brexit, the election of Donald Trump and the West's poor initial response to the coronavirus pandemic."[17]

In office, Johnson and his supporters continue to argue that Britain's decision to leave the EU was rooted in liberal, democratic instincts, such as support for free trade and nation-based democracy. For that reason, they argue, Brexit should be seen as an assertion of core liberal principles. But when I put that view to analysts outside Britain – whether in Moscow, Washington or Beijing – it is almost invariably met with incomprehension or derision. Outside the UK, Brexit was understood for what it was: a serious blow to the power and coherence of the West and the liberal democratic values that the Western alliance has traditionally upheld.

Britain, however, is just a middle-ranking power. Brexit alone could not turn international affairs upside down. The emergence of the strongman style in the United States, the world's most powerful nation, was the genuinely transformative moment for global politics.

7 Donald Trump – American strongman (2016)

In November 2015, a year before Donald Trump was elected, I visited Washington DC. My goal was to get a feel for the upcoming presidential election. But I left the city feeling puzzled. The opinion polls were showing that Trump was the clear front-runner for the Republican nomination for the 2016 presidential election. A Democrat had been in the White House for eight years, so it seemed reasonable to think that it was the Republicans' turn to win the presidency. But even in right-wing think tanks I couldn't find anyone who believed that Trump would win the nomination, let alone the presidency itself. None of my Republican contacts had signed up to work for the Trump campaign, which, in a city full of ambitious people, was telling confirmation that he was written off as a no-hoper. The general tendency to dismiss Trump's chances was summed up by a television clip that later went viral: it showed the television host George Stephanopoulos and his guests dissolving into laughter at the very suggestion that Trump might win.[1]

Even at the time, it struck me as rash to be quite so dismissive. In a column on the rise of radical politics across the West that November, I suggested that it was complacent to write off Mr. Trump's chances, arguing that "Many Democrats chortle that if the Republicans are mad enough to nominate Mr Trump, he would certainly be trounced by Hillary Clinton in the presidential election. But even that cannot be assumed. The most recent national poll on a Trump v Clinton contest had Mr Trump winning by five points."[2] It wasn't hard to identify the factors that were fueling the rise of a candidate like Trump. They were "a loss of faith in traditional political elites," combined with "an increase in economic insecurity, a backlash against immigration, a fear of terrorism and the decline of traditional media."[3]

All that was evident enough a year before Trump was elected. So, in retrospect, it is interesting to ask why the US establishment was so unwilling to acknowledge a political phenomenon that was staring them in the face. The answer, I think, lies in American exceptionalism – the sense that US politics and society were immune from the political pathologies that plagued other, less fortunate countries. The idea was summed up by the (ironic) title of a 1935 novel about the rise of a dictator in the US – *It Can't Happen Here* – which found many new readers after Trump's victory.

Such exceptionalism was not unique to America: I recognized a similar complacency in the British establishment. The British, like the Americans, take pride in their long history of democratic stability – political extremism and vulnerability to dictatorship are widely felt to be continental European vices, alien to Britain. But countries with too powerful a faith in their own exceptional political virtue may as a result become more vulnerable to political vices. The French could see a candidate like Marine Le Pen and get a strong whiff of Vichy France. The Germans are forever on their guard against anything that smacks of Nazism. But many American pundits took a look at Donald Trump and simply burst out laughing. The man was a joke, an entertainer. It couldn't happen here.

But many of the political and social forces that fueled the rise of strongman politics elsewhere in the world were also present in the US. As Fiona Hill, who served in the Trump White House as the senior adviser on Russia,* later put it: "We were arrogant enough to think that what happened to Ukraine and Moldova could never happen to us."[4] Hill was referring to Russian interference in elections. But, as she also argued, the Russian experience provided broader lessons for the West too. The pain of this economic dislocation helped to drive the appetite for a strongman leader – somebody who could make Russia great again.

Ignored by much of the American elite, a rise in "deaths of despair" that was reminiscent of Russia in the 1990s was taking place in the US, in the years before the election of Donald Trump. In November 2015,

* And later played a starring role in the Trump impeachment hearings.

the same month I was touring the Washington think tanks, the economists Angus Deaton and Anne Case reported on a startling rise in death rates among white working-class Americans. They found that the mortality rates of non-college-educated whites had increased by 22 percent between 1999 and 2014. Over the same period, the inflation-adjusted income for households headed by a high-school graduate had fallen by 19 percent.[5] Significantly, there was no similar fall in life expectancy among college-educated whites. Deaton and Case reported that the increasing mortality among the white working class was being driven "by an epidemic of suicides and afflictions stemming from substance abuse: alcoholism, liver disease and overdoses of heroin and prescription opioids."[6]

The social group afflicted by what Deaton and Case identified as "deaths of despair" turned out in huge numbers to vote for Donald Trump in 2016. Reflecting on those figures, I came to wonder whether pundits (myself included) who complained about the many lies that poured from Trump's mouth were partly missing the point. To his most loyal supporters, Trump was telling a larger truth: that things in the US were bad and getting worse and that the American elite was corrupt and self-serving.

Talking to Trump voters on the campaign trail in 2016, I heard many variations on that theme. At a rally in Portsmouth, New Hampshire, in January, I had my first experience of watching the rambling, incoherent style of Trump unplugged on the campaign trail. Afterwards, I fell into conversation with one of his supporters, who had driven up from Michigan to see his hero speak. When I tried to suggest that Trump told lots of lies, the response was: "He's the only one who tells it like it is." Later that year, I would have a similar conversation with a Leave voter in Britain, a few weeks before the Brexit vote. I had suggested that leaving the EU would damage the British economy. "It can't get any worse for me," came the reply. "Something has to change. And maybe this can be it." The despair of those economically "left behind" was one common factor that linked the rise of Trump to populist and strongman politics elsewhere in the world. But another even more powerful factor was ethnic and racial tension.

In countries such as India, Israel and Hungary, the rise of strongman politics has been closely linked to the fears of a majority group that is traditionally dominant in society but now feels under threat from demographic change and immigration. The most ardent supporters of Narendra Modi argue that India's Hindu culture is being undermined by the country's Muslim minority. In Israel, Benjamin Netanyahu backed the successful effort to declare Israel a Jewish state, a move linked to fears of the rising share of the population accounted for by Arabs. In Hungary, Viktor Orbán has often suggested that the very survival of the Hungarian nation is under threat from Muslim immigration. Both Netanyahu and Orbán have built physical walls to protect their countries' borders from interlopers – a demand that was to be echoed by Trump's famous demand to "Build the Wall" at the US border with Mexico in 2016.

In Hungary, Israel and India, the majority status of ethnic Hungarians, Jews and Hindus isn't actually under threat. Ethnic Hungarians make up 85 percent of the population of Hungary; Jews are just under 75 percent of the Israeli population; and Hindus constitute 80 percent of the Indian population. By contrast, in the US it is now projected that whites will make up less than 50 percent of the population by the mid-2040s, although they will still be the largest single group.[7] Among the youngest age group – the under eighteens – whites are already less than half the population. The biggest single emerging minority is the Hispanic population of the US, who are projected to make up 24.6 percent of the US population by 2045, compared to 49.7 percent for whites, 13.1 percent for Blacks and 7.9 percent for Asians.

Fears of demographic change and of immigration were central to Trump's appeal in 2016. Those fears were expressed in an article called the "Flight 93 election"* by Michael Anton, who was later appointed to the staff of the National Security Council in the Trump White House. Anton fulminated against the "ceaseless importation of Third World foreigners" into the United States. He hailed Trump as the only candidate willing to stop immigration and to thereby say, "I want my country to live. I want my people to live. I want to end the insanity."[8] For those who shared Anton's world view, Trump's demand for a wall along the US–Mexican border and for a "total and complete shutdown" of

---

* The reference was to the flight on 9/11 in which passengers had seized control of the plane from hijackers who had been intent on crashing it into the White House or Congress in Washington. The flight crashed into a field killing everybody aboard.

Muslim immigration into the US was compelling evidence that he was just the kind of strongman that America needed to "end the insanity."

Trump won a majority of white votes in both the 2016 and 2020 presidential elections. As the Pew Research Center noted, shortly after the 2016 election, Trump had recorded the largest winning margin among whites without a college degree of any candidate since 1980. Four years later, Trump still won the white vote comfortably, although his slightly reduced margins may have been the difference between victory in 2016 and defeat in 2020.[9]

The fact that Trump won the white vote is not, in itself, conclusive evidence that racial fears and antagonisms fueled his vote. But social science research certainly points in that direction. *Identity Crisis*, an in-depth study of the 2016 election, concluded that attitudes to race and ethnicity were the single best predictor of a vote for Trump.[10] Trump became the champion of white voters who felt economically or socially insecure and who, crucially, blamed their situation on ethnic minorities. The authors, John Sides, Michael Tesler and Lynn Vavreck, point out that opinion surveys of Republican voters show that "Worries about losing a job were less strongly associated with Trump support than were concerns about whites losing jobs to minorities."[11]

By the time Trump was running for the presidency, such fears were dominant among Republican voters, two-thirds of whom agreed that "discrimination against whites has become as big a problem as discrimination against blacks."[12] Trump became the champion of those who believed that the nature of America was under threat and that whites were being unfairly treated. Economic stress was just one part of the picture. Many Trump voters were also driven by a sense of lost status, as well as direct economic loss. As Cameron Anderson, a social psychologist at Berkeley pointed out: "It is very very difficult for individuals and groups to come to terms with losing status and power . . . They respond to those threats with stress, anxiety, anger and sometimes even violence."[13]

Fears that whites were losing control of the US were reflected in a marked swing against the very idea of democracy and a demand for a strongman leader. A study of Republican voters carried out by Larry Bartels, a political scientist at Vanderbilt University, found that 50.7 percent agreed that "The traditional American way of life is disappearing so fast that we may have to use force to save it." A further 47.3 percent agreed that "Strong leaders sometimes have to bend the rules in order to get things done." The results of the survey anticipated the willingness of a majority of Republicans to accept Trump's assaults on democracy, which culminated in his effort to overturn the 2020 presidential election result and the storming of the Capitol in January 2021. Their willingness to accept Trump's unfounded allegations of election fraud reflected their belief that he was acting in the interests of a higher good: the preservation of the traditional American way of life, which they associated with a white-majority country.[14] By 2016, therefore, large parts of the American electorate were ready and waiting for a "strongman leader." They found their man in Donald Trump.

Trump's political philosophy had been clear for decades. It was perhaps set out most thoroughly in an interview that he gave to *Playboy* magazine in 1990, at a time when he was still no more than a flashy businessman, famous for building casinos, cheating on his wife and sounding off on television. That interview later became required reading for diplomats and correspondents heading for Trump's America, much as previous generations trying to understand China or the Soviet Union might have attempted to read Mao's "Little Red Book" or Lenin's *What Is To Be Done?*.

Trump's instinctive authoritarianism was already on full display in 1990. At the time, Mikhail Gorbachev, the leader of the Soviet Union, was a hero to many Americans because of his role in ending the Cold War and liberalizing the Soviet system. But Trump displayed contempt for Gorbachev. "He's shown extraordinary weakness," he complained, "he's destroying the Soviet Union."[15] Trump's prediction of the collapse of the USSR became reality at the end of 1991. Trump contrasted the Chinese Communist Party's clampdown on the country's fledgling democracy movement favorably with Gorbachev's weakness. The Tiananmen Square massacre had taken place just nine months before Trump spoke to *Playboy*, and commenting on the events, he expressed an unusual view for a prominent American: "They were vicious, they were horrible, but they put it down with strength. That shows you the power of strength. Our country right now is perceived as weak."[16]

Other themes that were to become all too familiar during Trump's presidency were already on prominent display in 1990. There was the self-pitying paranoia: "We're laughed at by the rest of the world." And the protectionism: "I'd throw a tax on every Mercedes-Benz coming into this country and on all Japanese products." But Trump also showed a shrewd appreciation of his own potential political strengths: "I know what sells and I know what people want."

In 2016, he demonstrated that intuitive grasp of "what sells" and "what people want." Time and again, Trump would make statements that outraged the political establishment and led many to predict that he was finished: Barack Obama was not born in the United States; John McCain was not a war hero; grabbing women "by the pussy" was just "locker-room talk." But these statements failed to destroy Trump. In fact they may have strengthened his support. For the large segment of the public convinced that America was on the wrong track and longing for a strongman leader willing "to bend the rules in order to get things done," Trump's taboo-breaking talk was the signal that here was the man they wanted.

By 2016, then, some of the social and economic conditions that had led to the rise of strongman politics elsewhere in the world had also established themselves in the United States. With the emergence of Donald Trump, the US produced a politician with the ideology and political instincts to capitalize on this latent desire for a strongman. Fortunately for the United States, however, the country also had institutions and political conventions that had developed over centuries of democratic politics. The story of the Trump presidency is, in many ways, the story of the struggle between the strongman style of the president and the democratic constraints established by American law, institutions and precedent.

From the very beginning of his run for the presidency, and throughout his four years in office, Trump's instinct was to govern like an authoritarian strongman rather than a democratically elected president. His politics were built around a personality cult. In his acceptance speech to the Republican convention in 2016, Trump denounced the corruption of the American system and proclaimed: "I alone can fix it." By 2020, the Republican Party was so completely in his thrall that it dispensed with the publication of a detailed policy platform and announced instead: "The Republican Party has and will continue to enthusiastically support the President's America-first agenda."

As president, Trump quickly made it clear that his appointees should be loyal to him personally, rather than to the law. When James Comey, the director of the FBI, was invited to a one-to-one dinner with the new president, Trump repeatedly asked him to proclaim his "loyalty." Comey demurred and was fired a few months later.[17] The letter sacking him was hand-delivered by a man who understood what the president meant by loyalty – Keith Schiller, Trump's former bodyguard. At his first full cabinet meeting, Trump extracted embarrassing pledges of loyalty from his cabinet members in front of the television cameras. Mike Pence, the vice president, set the slavish tone by proclaiming: "The greatest privilege of my life is to serve as vice president to the president who's keeping his word to the American people." Reince Priebus, Trump's chief of staff, thanked the president and called it a "blessing to serve your agenda." "It's an honor to be able to serve you," declared Jeff Sessions, the attorney general.[18]

But all these men found that loyalty was not reciprocal and that abasing yourself before Trump was no guarantee of job security. A month later, Priebus was fired. Sessions, who had been the first Republican senator to endorse Trump for the presidency, angered his boss by recusing himself from the "Russia investigation" into possible collusion between the Trump campaign and the Kremlin. In November 2018, he too was fired. Pence lasted until the very bitter end but was eventually denounced by the president – who accused him of betrayal, for failing to support Trump's effort to overturn the 2020 presidential election. Pence had to take shelter in a secure location while a Trump-supporting mob rampaged through Congress shouting "Hang Mike Pence."

In his dramatic, if belated, break with the president, Pence refused to go along with Trump's lies about electoral fraud. But as Pence knew, lies had been fundamental to Trump's political career from the start. Once again, this is a characteristic of the new era of strongman politics. Vladimir Putin and his propagandists established the technique of a "firehose of falsehoods" as a fundamental political tool. The idea is to throw out so many different conspiracy theories and "alternative facts" (to use the phrase of Trump's aide, Kellyanne Conway) that the truth simply becomes one version of events among many.[19]

For strongman leaders, a "firehose of falsehoods" can serve important purposes. Importantly, it makes it easier to evade responsibility. All the evidence might suggest that Covid-19 originated in China or that Russian missiles shot down flight MH17, but Chinese and Russian spokesmen will spin out a variety of alternative theories to obscure the reality of what actually happened. Indeed, establishing false narratives has been fundamental to most of the strongman leaders of our era – whether it is Viktor Orbán insisting that George Soros is planning to flood Hungary with refugees, Jaroslaw Kaczynski insisting that the Smolensk air disaster was a Russian plot, Recep Tayyip Erdoğan claiming that an "interest-rate lobby" is plotting against Turkey, or Boris Johnson suggesting that a "deep state" was thwarting the vote for Brexit. There will always be takers for these theories among loyalists who badly want to believe the best of their leader or their country. This is a phenomenon that psychologists call "motivated reasoning": a form of biased thinking that leads people to the conclusions they find most emotionally satisfying, rather than those that are justified by the evidence.

Trump instinctively understood the power of such wishful thinking – perhaps because he himself lived in a fantasy world, in which everything he touched turned to gold and he was always a "winner," despite numerous bankruptcies. So those Americans who could not bear the idea that they had a Black president were fed the emotionally satisfying lie that Barack Obama was not born in the United States and was therefore not a legitimate president. Trump loyalists who could not accept the idea that he had lost the 2020 election were told instead that their hero had been the victim of electoral fraud. Senator Ted Cruz, who had once accurately called Trump a "pathological liar," ended up defending Trump's biggest and most consequential lie, about a stolen election, from the floor of the Senate.

If Trump's presidency ended with a big lie, it also began with one: the self-evidently false claim that record crowds had assembled in Washington to applaud his inaugural address. Throughout his term in office, the president continued to flirt with and sometimes endorse outright lies, retweeting conspiracy theories, such as the idea that Osama bin Laden was still alive. He also praised as "patriots" the conspiracy theorists of QAnon, who believed that the president was leading a battle against an elite band of pedophiles and sex traffickers, and who were prominent in the crowd that stormed the Capitol in 2021. Indeed, there seemed no conspiracy theory that was too deranged or distasteful for Trump to encourage. In December 2015, he even appeared on the talk show of Alex Jones, who had repeatedly claimed that the 2012 Sandy Hook massacre of twenty children – aged six and seven years old – had been a hoax. "Your reputation is amazing," Trump said to Jones, "I will not let you down."[20] All told, the *Washington Post* tabulated some 22,000 false and misleading statements over nearly four years of the Trump presidency.[21]

A true dictator can force an entire society to accept his lies. He does this, in large part, by establishing his absolute authority over all the institutions of the country. Trump made moves in this direction, repeatedly firing cabinet officers and officials who were deemed to be insufficiently pliant and attempting to put loyalists in their place. But, in the end, America's key institutions held. The "firehose of falsehoods" that the Trump team spewed out in an effort to prove that the 2020 election was "rigged" were rejected by court after court. Evidence and truth still mattered in the legal system. Shamefully and dangerously, a majority of Republican members of the House of Representatives went along with Trump's big lie about the 2020 election, as did eleven members of the Senate.

It was clear throughout his term in office that Trump envied the world's other "strongmen" leaders – genuine autocrats who really were able to imprison their opponents and bend the state's institutions to their will. Trump was often savage in his criticism of democratic leaders, calling Canada's Justin Trudeau "very dishonest and weak" and making his distaste for Germany's Angela Merkel evident. By contrast, even as his administration embarked on a trade war with China, Trump praised Xi Jinping as a "great leader" and a "very good man."

The memoirs of John Bolton, Trump's national security adviser in 2018–19, and of Fiona Hill, the director for Russia on the NSC from 2017 to 2019, both provide remarkable insights into Trump's collegial and admiring relationship with Xi and other autocrats, such as Putin and Erdoğan. Close observation of her boss convinced Hill that Trump was suffering from "autocrat envy."[22] She describes how Trump nicknamed Erdoğan "the Sultan" and "often bantered with him about how, he, Trump was jealous of Erdoğan's seemingly boundless ability to get his way at home."[23] To the discomfort of Bolton, Trump got on very well with Viktor Orbán, when the Hungarian leader visited him in the White House in May 2019. David Cornstein, Trump's ambassador to Hungary and an old friend of the president, later said that "Trump would love to have the situation that Viktor Orbán has, but he doesn't."[24]

In line with his own authoritarian tendencies, Trump not only dropped America's traditional pressure on China over human rights but actively encouraged Xi in some of the worst abuses. Bolton records that at a G20 summit, "Xi explained to Trump why he was basically building concentration camps in Xinjiang. According to our interpreter, Trump said that Xi should go ahead with building the camps, which he thought was exactly the right thing."[25] When the White House drafted a statement to mark the thirtieth anniversary of the Tiananmen Square massacre, it was personally blocked by Trump.[26]

It was a similar story with Vladimir Putin. Trump blocked a statement criticizing Russia on the tenth anniversary of its invasion of Georgia and also initially opposed sanctioning Russia, after Moscow's use of chemical weapons in the UK, during the attempted murder of Sergei Skripal, a former Russian agent. None of Trump's relationships with foreign heads of state was more closely scrutinized than his dealings with Putin. The clear evidence of Russian intervention in the 2016 presidential election prompted a long investigation of possible collusion between Moscow and the Trump campaign, a probe that Trump consistently labeled "the Russia hoax." Even Trump's officials would admit that, at times, they had no idea of the real nature of the relationship between the Russian and American presidents. Bolton notes enigmatically that Trump's "personal take on the Russian leader remained a mystery."[27] One British official who sat in on meetings with Trump later told me, "There's definitely something going on there. He's incredibly evasive on Putin and on Russia."[28]

It is possible that there was some hidden aspect to the Trump–Putin relationship that has yet to come to light. But, in truth, no special explanation is needed for Trump's indulgent behavior. Both in word and deed, Trump made it very clear that he admired strongman authoritarian rulers and preferred both their politics and their company to that of wishy-washy liberals. As he told Bob Woodward, "The tougher and meaner they are, the better I get along with them."[29]

In fact, Trump not only got along well with strongman authoritarian leaders – in many ways he envied them for breaking free of the legal and institutional constraints that still bound a US president. Bolton records Trump reassuring Erdoğan that he could stop a New York–based prosecution of Halkbank, a Turkish bank accused of violating Iran sanctions: "It was as though Trump was trying to show he had as much arbitrary authority as Erdoğan."[30] Trump's conception of diplomacy centered around the idea of strongmen doing favors for each other, and in so doing, demonstrating their power and magnanimity. Chris Ruddy, the head of Newsmax and a friend of the president, told me that Trump had been particularly delighted by one exchange with Xi, in which the US president had asked for the release of three American basketball players who had got themselves into trouble in China: "Xi said, it will be done – and Trump liked that."[31] Fiona Hill concluded that Trump aspired to belong to an exclusive club of super-rich autocrats, "an elite of their own, very rich, very powerful and very famous" and that he "wanted to govern like them. He wanted raw power without much in the way of other checks and balances."[32]

It was not just the arbitrary powers of Xi, Putin and Erdoğan that Trump admired. He also envied their ability to stay in power for decades. At a meeting with Xi in 2018, Trump claimed falsely that there were moves afoot in the United States to repeal the two-term constitutional limit on the presidency, so that he too could stay in office for decades. Xi proved adept at playing to Trump's vanity, telling the president in a later phone conversation that China hoped that the constitution would be amended.[33] These private conversations shed a revealing light on Trump's public comments, in which he talked about emulating China's abolition of presidential term limits. His remark about the extension of Xi's term, "I think it's great . . . maybe we'll have to give it a shot someday," was dismissed as a joke by Trump apologists.[34] But his conversations with Xi – as well as his efforts to overturn the 2020 presidential election – suggest that Trump genuinely desired to become a ruler for life. Fiona Hill did not believe that the president was simply joking when he referred to Xi's ability to rule for life: "The frequency of the references told a different story. He was deadly serious."[35]

Throughout his period in office, and particularly during the disastrous climax to his presidency, Trump reveled in the rhetoric of strength. In the speech he made on January 6, 2021, urging his supporters to march on the Capitol, Trump declared: "You'll never take back our country with weakness. You have to show strength and you have to be strong."[36] The speech demonstrated many of the defining traits of Trump's brand of strongman politics. There was the big lie: "We won this election and we won it by a landslide." There were the conspiracy theories about the "fake news media." And there was the characteristic effort to play on the racially driven insecurities and grievances of his almost entirely white audience: "You're the real people. You are the people who built this nation. You're not the people who tore down our nation."[37] Trump accused his opponents of tearing down the nation, even as he tore at the fabric of American democracy. And his followers chanted "stop the steal," to further Trump's own efforts to steal the election.

Fortunately, the steal was thwarted and Joe Biden was inaugurated on January 20, 2021. But while Trump's efforts to subvert US democracy and institutions failed he had succeeded in subverting many American minds, leading a large part of the US electorate down a dark pathway of conspiracy theories and authoritarianism. Polls taken immediately after the storming of the Capitol suggested that a majority of Republican voters sympathized with the invasion of the seat of American democracy.

As a result, the end of the Trump presidency in 2020 did not end America's entanglement with the Age of the Strongman. The authoritarian themes that Trump had injected into US political discourse will survive his term in office. They include the belief that the American system is so rotten that a strongman "willing to break the rules" is needed to put things right. Indeed, the fear and resentment of many white voters that drove Trumpism is likely to be further strengthened by Trump's defeat – particularly since it coincided with the resurgent demands for a better deal for Black Americans, associated with the Black Lives Matter movement. The question seems to be not whether Trumpism will survive beyond 2021 but whether Trump himself will remain the figurehead of the movement, or whether a member of his family or another ambitious Republican will take the cause forward.

The crisis that Trump has created in the world's leading democracy is a huge boon to China and Russia and strongman leaders. After all, how can America lead a pushback against strongman authoritarianism, when its own democracy is so gravely wounded? Given the military, political and cultural power of the US, what happens in America sets the tone of politics all over the world. The United States was by no means the first country in the world to fall prey to the lure of strongman politics – as we have seen, Russia, Turkey, China, India and parts of Europe got there before. But the election of an American strongman in 2016 gave a fillip to populist authoritarianism all over the world. From Brasilia to Riyadh to Manila, would-be Trumps took heart and learned lessons.

8 Rodrigo Duterte and the erosion of democracy in Southeast Asia (2016)

"I just wanted to congratulate you because I am hearing of the unbelievable job on the drug problem . . . Many countries have the problem, we have a problem, but what a great job you are doing and I just wanted to call and tell you that."[1]

Donald Trump's congratulatory words to Rodrigo Duterte in April 2017 were part of a pattern of schmoozing with the world's strongman leaders. Kim Jong-un was "very open, terrific" and Xi Jinping was "a strong guy."[2][3] But with Duterte, Trump had decided to praise the most infamous and brutal policy that the president of the Philippines was associated with: the summary execution of people accused of dealing or using drugs.

Rodrigo Duterte was elected as president of the Philippines in May 2016, just six months before Trump won the presidency in the US. The Filipino leader was sworn into office on June 30, 2016 at the age of seventy-one. Almost immediately, the death squads were unleashed. In his inauguration speech, Duterte assured his audience that he fully intended to stay within the bounds of the law. But just a few days later, he was urging a Manila audience to take the law into their own hands: "If you know of any addicts, go ahead and kill them yourself."[4] According to Amnesty International, more than 7,000 people were killed in the first six months of Duterte's presidential term as part of his "war on drugs."[5]

The routine described in numerous journalistic accounts and human-rights reports went as follows. Duterte would publicly name hundreds of suspects.[6][7][8] Then the deaths would start. Sometimes the suspects were shot by the police "resisting arrest." On other occasions, masked vigilantes on motorcycles kidnapped and murdered them. The victims were slain in the streets, at home with their families, or even, on one occasion, on the operating table in front of horrified hospital staff, after the first hit had failed. Dozens of children were killed in the cross fire, which Duterte dismissed as "collateral damage."[9] The overall death toll for the "war on drugs" remains disputed: official figures put it at about 6,000 as of July 2020, but the Philippines' Commission on Human Rights suggests it could be as high as 27,000.[10][11] In fear for their lives, hundreds of thousands of suspects have surrendered to the government, meaning the Philippines now has one of the world's most overcrowded prison systems.[12] After the initial onslaught, following Duterte's inauguration, the pace of killing slackened. But the policy of state-sanctioned murder has never been abolished.

Of all the leaders to emerge in the Age of the Strongman, Duterte stands out as the most overtly thuggish. While Trump once joked that he could shoot someone on Fifth Avenue without losing voters, Duterte actually put the theory to the test. He openly boasts of having killed people: of stabbing someone to death in a drunken beach brawl, of gunning down suspected murderers, of hurling another murderer from a helicopter.[13][14][15] Not only did these boasts not cost him voters: they were an important part of his appeal. He relished the nickname, "Duterte Harry," after the vigilante cop played by Clint Eastwood in the Dirty Harry movies.

Duterte had not disguised his intention to unleash death squads during his presidential campaign. On the contrary, it was his signature pledge: "All of you who are into drugs, you sons of bitches, I will really kill you. I have no patience."[16] Brutal leaders are not a great novelty. But there are three additional reasons that make Duterte a significant global figure in the Age of the Strongman. The first is that he perfected and sometimes pioneered populist techniques that were then used effectively by Trump and others – attacks on elites, innovative use of social media, persistent lying and "simplist" politics. The second is that, having won an election, Duterte then demonstrated how a populist strongman could consolidate his power and erode democracy by building up a cult of personality, systematically intimidating and jailing opponents and undermining the independence of the media and the judiciary. These were techniques that were also used in Russia, Hungary and India – and attempted by Trump in the US. A third reason why Duterte is important to the Age of the Strongman is that both the Philippines and Southeast Asia as a whole have played a key role in the global struggle between authoritarianism and democracy over the last forty years. Given that Southeast Asia is China's "backyard," the region's significance as a bellwether for international democracy will probably increase in the coming years.

For most Europeans and Americans, it is 1989, the year of the fall of the Berlin Wall, that stands out as an *annus mirabilis* in the triumph of democracy over authoritarianism. The huge demonstrations that helped to bring down one-party states in East Germany, Czechoslovakia and Romania came to be known as "people power" revolutions. But the phrase "people power" had actually been popularized by the massive demonstrations in the Philippines in 1986 which brought down the military dictator Ferdinand Marcos and his shoe-loving wife, Imelda.

Marcos's twenty-year grip on power was weakened by the popular backlash against a stolen presidential election and the assassination of Benigno Aquino, a leading opposition politician. After the US withdrew its long-standing support for Marcos, he fled the country; Aquino's widow, Corazon, became president in his place. The "people power" revolution in the Philippines was the first of a series of transitions towards democracy across East Asia – with South Korea (1987), Taiwan (1987–96) and Indonesia (1998) to follow. In those three countries, as in the Philippines, the heyday of autocracy was associated with an authoritarian leader: Park Chung-hee of South Korea, Chiang Kaishek of Taiwan and Suharto of Indonesia.

The Philippines, however, provides the most dramatic example of an East Asian country that has now moved backwards politically. One of Duterte's first acts as president was highly symbolic – the reinterment of the body of Ferdinand Marcos in the National Heroes' Cemetery. He also dissolved the task force which was still trying to recover the billions of dollars Marcos had plundered from state coffers. Duterte is visibly turning the clock back towards the era of autocracy – and he is doing so with the vocal support of a significant part of the Filipino population. As Sheila Coronel noted in 2019, at the midpoint of his presidential term, Duterte enjoyed a satisfaction rating that was nearly 80 percent.[17] In part, Duterte's popularity stems from high-profile spending programs, such as salary rises for public-sector workers and the provision of free tuition in state colleges. But the "war on drugs" and the strongman contempt for the rule of law also poll well.

There is reason to fear that this return to autocracy is becoming a regional trend. When I was based in Thailand in the early 1990s as *The Economist*'s Southeast Asia correspondent, that country was re-establishing its democracy after a military coup in 1991. Democracy was gradually re-established over the course of a decade. But since a coup in 2014, Thailand has been back under military rule. Neighboring Burma (Myanmar) moved towards democracy later, with the release from imprisonment of Aung San Suu Kyi in 2010, but the military took back control in February 2021 and Suu Kyi was rearrested.*

Indonesia, the largest country in the region and the fourth most populous nation in the world, is run by a low-key civilian president, Joko Widodo. When I met Jokowi (as he is always known) in London in 2016, he made for a refreshing contrast with the regal Suharto, who governed Indonesia for a generation from the mid-1960s as the head of a brutal military regime. Indeed, Jokowi struck me as probably the most unassuming world leader I'd ever met, leaving most of the talking to his trade minister, Tom Lembong, and quietly deflecting difficult questions about historic human-rights abuses committed by the military. Jokowi's outward modesty and humble background have burnished his reputation as a man of the people, primarily concerned with the quality of life of ordinary Indonesians. But, as time has worn on, even Jokowi has become more autocratic. He has shored up his political position by embracing hard-line Islamists and military figures from the Suharto era. Jokowi is no Duterte but the earlier breathless descriptions of him as "Indonesia's Obama" now look predictably naive.[18]

Unlike the self-effacing Jokowi, Duterte has become a globally recognizable figure. Partly this is because of his deliberately outrageous

---

* After her release in 2010, Suu Kyi's complicity in the brutalisation of Burma's Rohingya minority was a source of disillusionment to many in the international community. But Burma remained a democracy. It was the military anger at the outcome of elections in 2020 – accompanied by Trump-like accusations of fraud – that prompted the coup of 2021.

style. But there are reasons beyond his grotesque showmanship for the international community to pay attention to the Filipino president. Duterte was one of the first strongman leaders to demonstrate that somebody regarded as completely unsuitable for national leadership by elite opinion was capable of winning the most powerful position in the country, with a new brand of populist politics.

Duterte's successful presidential election campaign in 2016 demonstrated the power of a big lie that struck a chord with voters – because it felt true. In Duterte's case, it was the claim that the Philippines was at risk of becoming a "narco state." Experts scoffed at this statement. There is certainly a drug problem in the Philippines, particularly with use of methamphetamine or "shabu" in the country's poorest areas. But according to the UN, overall drug abuse in the Philippines is below the world average, with about 1 percent of the population taking meth in 2016.[19]

But, as with Trump's various false claims about immigration, such as that immigrants are disproportionately responsible for crime, Duterte's purported drug epidemic became a focus for more general anxieties and insecurities. Like Trump, Duterte specialized in outrageous statements that kept the focus of attention on him, and made his rivals seem dull and cautious by comparison.

In another parallel with Trump, Duterte benefited from quirks in the electoral system. Both men won the presidency without winning a majority of votes. In Trump's case it was the electoral college that delivered a narrow victory in 2016. For Duterte, it was a one-round presidential election that gave victory to the candidate who won a plurality of votes. On May 9, 2016, Duterte beat four other candidates and recorded 39 percent of the vote, with his nearest rival, Mar Roxas, winning 23.45 percent.

It was a clear enough victory to be a decisive mandate. As so often, in an era of populist nationalism, liberal internationalists were left scratching their heads about what had just happened. To many outsiders, the Philippines had seemed to be on the up during the Aquino years. It had become, according to *The Economist*, "boring and successful," with economic growth averaging 6 percent a year.[20]

But Duterte found a political base in the precarious middle class, fearful of crime and angered by the political establishment's failure to tackle it. Like Modi and Trump, Duterte also exploited popular distrust of politicians and disgust with corruption. Three-quarters of the members of the National Congress in the Philippines come from traditional political dynasties, which are perceived, with some justification, as corrupt and uncaring.[21] Gloria Macapagal Arroyo, president from 2001 to 2010, was accused of plundering the state lottery, while her predecessor Joseph "Erap" Estrada, a former film star, was convicted of massive embezzlement of public funds. (He was also a heavy drinker, who I will always remember as the only politician to have actually fallen asleep while I was interviewing him.)

Duterte won power by running against the tainted elite of "Imperial Manila." He professes to be uncomfortable in their company, with his provincial background and regional accent. At law school in Manila, he claims to have shot and wounded a snooty student who mocked his speech.[22] (The incident did not prevent him graduating with a law degree.) He still insists on spending part of his week back in his home city of Davao, where he governed for decades, and prefers his old title of "mayor" to that of "president."

In Duterte, folksiness and crudity merge. His speeches are incoherent streams of consciousness, peppered by vulgarity and switching between Bisaya, Tagalog and broken English. As with Trump and Bolsonaro, this boorish style marks him out from the more decorous political establishment. Yet while Duterte is clearly aware that his style is a political asset, his manner is not put on. A psychological assessment he had to undertake as part of his divorce in July 1998 identified a "pervasive tendency to demean [and] humiliate others" and concluded he had narcissistic personality disorder.[23] His overall persona – his anger, misogyny and resentment – comes across as genuine because it is. In a country where the political class is seen as fundamentally duplicitous and the elite as remote from the struggles of ordinary people, many people share his rage.

Despite his antiestablishment appeal, once he assumed the presidency, Duterte proved predictably happy to do favors for members of the Manila elite. He is close to Senator Bongbong Marcos, the son of Ferdinand Marcos. When ex-president Arroyo was acquitted of the graft charges against her, in the first months of the Duterte administration, she publicly thanked the new president for having "provided the atmosphere" which led to her exoneration.[24] In November 2020, Duterte made her a presidential adviser.

This accommodation with the likes of Arroyo and Marcos is not particularly surprising because, like them, Duterte is, in fact, a hereditary member of the Filipino political elite. Despite his carefully cultivated image as a common man, his father Vicente was a provincial governor who later served in Marcos's cabinet. Duterte was a weak student and was expelled from multiple schools. But, helped by his mother's connections, he became vice mayor of Davao, the third largest city in the country, in 1986, shortly after the fall of the Marcos regime. Two years later, he was elected mayor and served in that position, with a couple of gaps, for over twenty years.[25]

As with Putin and Erdoğan, Duterte's start in big-city politics proved a useful power base and an opportunity to learn political skills on a smaller stage. In the 1980s, Davao was in the middle of a war zone. The New People's Army (NPA), a Communist guerrilla group strong on the southern island of Mindanao, assassinated police officers. Vigilantes hunted leftists. Muslim separatists from the Moro people waged a terror campaign. On top of it all, there was a crime wave, associated with drug gangs. To regain control, Duterte employed a divide-and-rule strategy. He welcomed ex-Communists into his administration – his campaign manager and chief of staff, Leoncio Evasco Jr., was an ex-NPA member. He also appointed a deputy mayor to represent Moro interests and granted amnesty to separatists if they put down their arms. But those groups who did not acquiesce to Duterte's new order were pursued ruthlessly, above all anyone involved in drugs.

In 2009, a team from the Philippine Commission on Human Rights entered a disused quarry outside of Davao. There, they found thousands of human bones, the remains of the victims of the Davao Death Squad (DDS), a vigilante group which had murdered over 1,400 drug users and dealers during Duterte's tenure as mayor.[26] The inquiry, led by the leading Duterte critic Leila de Lima, was quickly shut down by Vitaliano Aguirre II, a friend of Duterte's from law school, whom he would later appoint as justice secretary.

In September 2016, shortly after Duterte's election as president, de Lima, now a senator, led a new inquiry into the DDS, which produced explosive testimony. Former members of the death squad testified to the Senate Justice Committee that Duterte had personally overseen their operations and had himself executed drug suspects. They claimed that the group was funded by diverting the salaries of nonexistent city hall employees. Duterte's revenge against Senator de Lima was swift and brutal. After pressure from the president, she was removed from the Senate Justice Committee. In February 2017, she was arrested on trumped-up charges of drug trafficking, based on the testimony of police officers and prison inmates. The offenses were not eligible for bail. In 2021, she was still in prison awaiting trial – but announced her intention to run for re-election to the Senate in May 2022.

Although Duterte denied the allegations aired by the Senate Justice Committee – and did his utmost to discredit the investigation – he has a complicated public position on the DDS. He has frequently praised their actions and boasted personally of killing drug dealers. Once, during his Sunday-morning TV show as mayor, he seemed to confess: "They say I am the Death Squad? True, that is true." He later claimed this was a joke, but his overall intent seemed clear: to claim credit for the DDS killings without admitting his role outright. "I am your last card," he told a rally during his presidential campaign. "I promise you I will get down and dirty just to get things done."[27] That was the classic strongman pitch: the system had failed and only he could restore order, by taking measures no one else would. Davao, and implicitly the DDS, was Duterte's proof, or as he put it, "Exhibit A." The irony of Duterte's promise to run the Philippines like Davao is that Davao is still a dysfunctional place: it remains the murder capital of the Philippines.[28] And if Davao is safer and richer than in the 1980s, so is the vast majority of the Philippines.

Duterte's embellishment of his record in Davao, however, was only one part of a wave of disinformation he unleashed during the presidential campaign. Outspent by political rivals, Duterte's social media team knew it had to find ways to promote his message without relying solely on paid advertising. They quickly resorted to Facebook. Duterte's outrageous statements, however mendacious, were perfect for provoking the shares, likes and comments that would send them viral. Without spending anything, the campaign could already reach the over 70 million Filipinos (of a total population of 108 million) who use Facebook. But the campaign did throw additional funds at social media outreach, spending $200,000 on an army of bots and trolls to peddle fake news on Duterte's behalf. This stretched from stories that he had been praised by British royals or the pope to fake sex tapes of his political opponents and graphic images of supposed criminal violence. A picture, apparently of a Filipina mother grieving over her child cut down by a gang, turned out to have actually been taken in Brazil.[29]

The Philippines was at the forefront of the fake news epidemic – "patient zero," as one Facebook executive put it.[30] But despite this, the company did little to tackle the problem in the run-up to the May 2016 election. That August, in the aftermath of Duterte's victory, Maria Ressa, a prominent journalist and CEO of independent news site Rappler, tried to alert Facebook to the issue. She provided senior Facebook staff with evidence of phoney accounts spreading pro-Duterte propaganda and issued a warning: that the US presidential contest in November would be similarly targeted. Quickly, she was proved right.

After the US election, Facebook finally took action and eliminated the pro-Duterte accounts Ressa had identified. But much of the damage had already been done. Duterte's exploitation of social media had helped propel him to victory in the Philippines. It also served as an exemplar to strongmen around the world of how fake news could be used for political benefit. As Ressa argued, "they test the tactics of how to manipulate America in our country. If it works, they 'port' it over to the rest of the world."[31]

Unsurprisingly, Duterte has a sour relationship with those who challenge his version of events. He threatened to ban Facebook in September 2020 after it took down a fake news network which was traced back to the Philippine military and police. He accused Rappler, which identified the network, of being funded by the CIA, and remarked that impudent journalists were "not exempt from assassination." His press secretary chides journalists for not understanding the president's unique humor, advising them to take him "seriously but not literally" (a phrase borrowed from defenders of Donald Trump). But Duterte's threats are not just bluster, for he has ruthlessly pursued his media critics. Ressa herself has been served with ten arrest warrants for spurious offenses, largely libel and tax evasion, and potentially faces years in jail.[32]

Duterte has also targeted ABS-CBN, a major Philippine news broadcaster, which he castigated for its coverage of the drug war. After its license expired in May 2020, it was forced off air. The Philippine House of Representatives, controlled by Duterte's allies, voted not to renew the license and, with a massive loss of advertising revenue, ABS-CBN's local channels also folded. This is a common strongman tactic: Bolsonaro threatened in 2019 to pull the license of the top Brazilian broadcaster, while the Hungarian media, as we have seen, have been brought under much tighter control by Orbán.

Duterte's crushing of dissent has extended to the judiciary as well. After Conchita Carpio-Morales, the top anti-graft official in the country, opened an investigation into Duterte's personal finances, the president threatened to impeach her and ordered her to suspend her deputy, Arthur Carandang. Carpio-Morales refused, but after her term expired, Duterte replaced her with a loyalist who fired Carandang. At the Supreme Court, Chief Justice Maria Lourdes Sereno was removed through an obscure legal mechanism, after questioning the legality of Duterte's drug war and his declaration of martial law in Mindanao. She was accused of having failed to fully disclose her assets – something Duterte himself has never done. With a largely compliant judiciary at his disposal, Duterte has never been held to account for human-rights violations carried out in the war on drugs or in the "war on terror" in Mindanao, which was facilitated by Duterte's declaration of martial law on the island.

What sets Duterte apart from many other strongmen, such as Orbán, Putin and Xi, is his lack of ideology. He possesses an inchoate nationalism and a contempt for the educated "chattering classes." But he has not attempted an intellectual justification for his actions or articulated an anti-liberal project of the sort that guides other authoritarians. This puts Duterte closer to Trump and Bolsonaro. Like those two leaders, Duterte operates on instinct and patronage, appointing government officials on the basis of loyalty and personal friendship. A childhood school friend, Carlos Dominguez III, was made finance minister in his administration; another classmate, Bingbong Medialdea, became executive secretary, the most senior position in the president's office. Other former classmates of his have been appointed foreign and justice ministers. His daughter, Sara, is now mayor of Davao, and has stood in for her father at international events, while his son Paolo is vice mayor. Duterte has suggested that Sara would be his natural successor.

The president's instinctual, unsystematic style extends to foreign policy. Early in his term in office, Duterte caused consternation in Washington with a visit to Beijing, during which he announced his country's "separation" from its traditional alliance with the US. Before a highly appreciative audience in the Great Hall of the People, the Filipino president declared: "I've realigned myself in your ideological flow and maybe I will also go to Russia to talk to Putin and tell him that there are three of us against the world – China, Philippines and Russia. It's the only way." Duterte's comments partly reflected his personal anger towards President Obama, whose administration had expressed concern about his record on human rights. In response, Duterte had called Obama a "son of a whore" and told him to "go to hell."[33]

Unusually in the Philippines, Duterte has long nurtured a strong strain of anti-American sentiment, for a mixture of personal and political reasons.

He was denied a visa in 2002 to visit his girlfriend, Honeylet Avancena, in the US, due to concerns over his connections to death squads. Even before his row with Obama, he had called the US ambassador a "gay son of a whore" after he had criticized a remark Duterte made during the presidential campaign, implying that he wished he had participated in the gang rape of a missionary, murdered in a 1989 prison break in Davao. After the Obama incident, Duterte briefly canceled joint naval exercises with the US in the South China Sea, where China has made aggressive territorial claims.

But it is hard for any president of the Philippines to persist in an anti-American stance. International surveys indicate that the Philippines is one of the most consistently pro-American countries in the world. Rather than stoking lasting resentment, the country's history as an American colony from 1898 to 1946 has generally produced a cultural affinity. Over half of all Filipinos speak English, there is a large American expatriate community, and basketball is the country's most popular sport. The US Pacific Fleet uses bases in the Philippines and the two countries' navies frequently carry out joint exercises. The two foreign leaders Duterte quoted in his inaugural address were Franklin Roosevelt and Abraham Lincoln.

The Philippines also has a long-standing territorial dispute with China over the strategically important South China Sea, through which a third of the world's maritime traffic passes. This is a topic that appeared to preoccupy Duterte, who somewhat uncharacteristically recommended a serious book, Robert Kaplan's *Asia's Cauldron*, to reporters wanting insight into the issue. At times, Duterte has taken anti-Chinese or nationalist stances on this issue. During the presidential campaign, he struck a belligerent tone, saying he would ride a jet ski to one of the artificial islands constructed by China in disputed waters and plant a Philippine flag on it.

Duterte has also felt pressure from the Philippines military which, given its long-standing cooperation with the US, is staunchly pro-American. Equally, the Philippine public is generally hawkish on defending their country's maritime claims. As a result, Duterte has toughened his stance towards Beijing. Perhaps lulled into a false sense of security by Duterte's early acquiescence, China also overplayed its hand. In April 2019, after a buildup of Chinese forces near the disputed island of Thitu, Duterte lashed out, declaring he would send troops on "suicide missions" against the Chinese if they did not pull back. Addressing the UN General Assembly in September 2020, Duterte touted an international tribunal's ruling in favor of the Philippines' claims in the South China Sea. The next month, he ordered the resumption of oil and gas exploration in the disputed waters.

Nonetheless, it is striking that during his first four years as president, Duterte held six meetings with Xi Jinping – and met Donald Trump face-to-face only once. Although the US president made it clear that he personally had no intention of making an issue of human-rights abuses, he was not in full control of US foreign policy. Suggestions that members of his entourage would be barred from the US ensured that Duterte never accepted Trump's invitation to the White House.

But when the two men were able to meet, they got along famously. At a summit of the Association of Southeast Asian Nations in Manila in November 2017, Duterte serenaded Trump with a popular Philippine song. "You are the light in my world, a half of this heart of mine," he sang.

The episode was typical of relations between two strongman leaders, in which kitsch and mutual flattery in public merged with violence and lawbreaking offstage. That same combination of public glitz and private brutality was also characteristic of the strongman leader who, more than any other, could claim to have built a special relationship with the Trump White House – Mohammed bin Salman of Saudi Arabia.

9 The rise of MBS and the Netanyahu phenomenon (2017)

When Donald Trump was sworn into office in January 2017, there was a sense of foreboding in much of Europe. But the leaders of America's two closest allies in the Middle East – Israel and Saudi Arabia – were elated. Benjamin Netanyahu, the prime minister of Israel and Crown Prince Mohammed bin Salman of Saudi Arabia, both regarded the Obama administration's policies in the region as dangerously naive. With Trump in the White House, they once again had a US president who would prioritize regional stability over democracy and harden policy towards Iran.

Bibi and MBS – to use the nicknames by which they are always known – are key figures in the Age of the Strongman. Both came to personify the politics of their nations more completely than any of their recent predecessors. In July 2019, after thirteen years in office, Netanyahu became Israel's longest serving prime minister, taking the accolade from the country's founding father, David Ben-Gurion.

Mohammed bin Salman arrived on the scene only relatively recently: he entered government in 2015 and was formally appointed as crown prince in 2017. But he too is a transformational figure. In the modern era, the leadership of Saudi Arabia has never before been so closely identified with a single, charismatic individual. The new Saudi strong-man has swept away the old system of collective royal leadership, based around seniority, consensus and a parceling out of portfolios among princes. By 2018, as his biographer Ben Hubbard explains: "MBS had destroyed that (traditional) system, extending his control over the military, the oil industry, the intelligence services, the police and the National Guard."[1]

The centralization of power and the identification of leader and nation – both at home and abroad – is a characteristic of the Age of the Strongman. Bibi and MBS are strongly nationalistic leaders, with a powerful streak of paranoia about the outside world. Their shared antipathy towards Iran and eagerness to work with the Trump administration remade the geopolitics of the Middle East between 2016 and 2020.

Despite the similarities in their strategic aims and temperaments, the political and even physical environments in which Saudi and Israeli leaders operate are distinctly different. The opulence of the living conditions of Saudi royalty is unrivaled. Among the baubles that Mohammed bin Salman has bought for himself is a chateau outside Paris, costing $300 million.[2] Visitors received by the crown prince in Riyadh are often awestruck by the regal splendor of his surroundings – as they are intended to be.

By comparison, the prime minister's working quarters in Jerusalem are distinctly spartan. When I visited Netanyahu there in 2013, his office was in an unattractive but well-guarded block, at the top of a flight of stone stairs. The room he worked in was not particularly large or grand. The only hint of high living was the fat cigar the Israeli prime minister puffed on, as he held forth on global politics from the comfort of his office sofa.

Netanyahu's taste for cigars and pink champagne was eventually to feature in a much-delayed corruption trial that threatened to end his political career and even put him in prison. By contrast, MBS operates in a climate of complete impunity – and has detained and even murdered his political opponents.

But Bibi and MBS were brought together by a common enemy and a common friend. The enemy was Iran and the friend was Jared Kushner, Donald Trump's son-in-law.

Netanyahu has spent much of the last twenty years issuing dark warnings about the dangers of a nuclear Iran. Fear of Iranian influence led MBS to take Saudi Arabia to war in Yemen and to blockade neighboring Qatar.

As soon as Trump became president, it became clear that he intended to treat his family – in particular his daughter Ivanka and her husband,

Jared – as his most trusted advisers. This dynastic approach to government struck many in the Washington establishment as peculiar and inappropriate – but it was second nature to the Saudi royal family. In their different contexts, both Kushner and MBS were princelings: extremely rich men in their thirties, who owed their position in life to their families. Early in Trump's term in office, the two men were introduced by business associates of Trump and they quickly hit it off.[3] The frequent exchange of WhatsApp messages and emojis between MBS and Kushner was a source of both fascination and concern to the American intelligence community.

The generation game played out slightly differently with Netanyahu. The Israeli prime minister was a close friend of Kushner's father, the real-estate developer Charles Kushner, and once stayed with the family in New Jersey in the 1980s, with the young Jared giving up his bed to the up-and-coming Israeli politician.[4]

For Jared Kushner, an Orthodox Jew with a long-standing commitment to Israel, the Middle East was a natural area of interest. In the summer of 2020, he was able to use the shared Saudi–Israeli fear of Iran to broker a historic diplomatic breakthrough; the establishment of diplomatic ties between Israel and the United Arab Emirates. The UAE is a small, wealthy federation that is closely allied to the Saudis. Direct flights were established between Dubai, Abu Dhabi and Tel Aviv, and for the first time, courtesy of MBS, Israeli planes were given the right to fly over Saudi Arabia. The hope and expectation in Israel was that once King Salman died and MBS succeeded him, Saudi Arabia itself would establish diplomatic ties with Israel, effectively ending the Arab boycott of Israel that had begun with the establishment of the new state in 1948.

The UAE deal was a badly needed political triumph for Netanyahu. By 2020, he was clinging on in office after three successive indecisive elections, and he was also facing trial on corruption and fraud charges. Now he had a new peace treaty to boast of, which would expand the horizons for Israeli tourists and business people. The UAE–Israel deal was also a bitter blow to the Palestinians because it had been agreed without Netanyahu making any movement towards the "two-state solution" that had long been mooted as the ultimate solution to the Israeli–Palestinian conflict. Instead, the Palestinian cause, which had been so central to both Arab and global politics for decades, appeared to have been sidelined. In the aftermath of the agreement, Anshel Pfeffer, Netanyahu's biographer, speculated to me that the Palestinians might end up like the Tibetans – a downtrodden group, whose land was occupied, but whose fate was increasingly ignored by the outside world.[5]

While this outcome looked potentially tragic for the Palestinians, it was a triumph for Netanyahu's stubborn resistance to international pressure to agree to a proper Palestinian state. During the Obama administration, Bibi had endorsed the idea of a two-state solution. When I met him in his office in 2013, I asked if he was just humoring Obama by committing himself to a two-state solution. Netanyahu smiled and replied, "Well, obviously I'm doing that." But the Israeli prime minister had then set out the conventional argument for why Israel needed to agree to a Palestinian state. The danger, he argued, was that if Israel incorporated 2.7 million Palestinians on the West Bank into the state of Israel, then the government might end up having to choose between being a Jewish state and being a democracy, since Jews would be perilously close to losing their majority status in the land of Israel.*

Even at the time, it struck me that there was something formulaic about Netanyahu's recitation of the case for a two-state solution. His heart was clearly not in it. Indeed, throughout his political career, he had resisted the conventional liberal view of what Israel needed to do to secure its future. This view – pushed in different ways by figures as diverse as Bill Clinton, Tony Blair and former Israeli prime ministers, such as Ehud Barak and Shimon Peres – was that to secure international acceptance and peace with its Arab neighbors, Israel had first to make peace with Palestinians.

Netanyahu had never really accepted this argument. Instead he and his Likud Party had formed an alliance with Israel's powerful settler movement, which regarded the West Bank not as the site of a future Palestinian state but as an essential part of the land of Israel, which should eventually be incorporated into the state itself. How exactly the Palestinians would fare under this scenario was never fully spelled out. Some far-right Israeli radicals hoped for their expulsion into a

---

* As of 2020, Israel's population is roughly 8.8 million, of whom roughly 20 percent are Israeli Arabs.

neighboring Arab state, such as Jordan. Others toyed with the idea of giving the Palestinians the right to self-government in areas that were little more than glorified local councils – a political solution that was sometimes likened to apartheid South Africa, where the government had attempted to give Black South Africans the right to vote only in powerless "Bantustans."

Rather than seeing a two-state solution as the route to regional harmony, the so-called "inside-out" route to peace, Netanyahu had argued for the "outside-in" solution, in which peace with Israel's Arab neighbors would be achieved first, and the Palestinian issue dealt with later by a strengthened Israel.

The Israeli prime minister's harsh form of Zionism was deeply rooted in his own family history. Born in Tel Aviv in 1949, Benjamin Netanyahu is the son of Benzion Netanyahu, a right-wing Israeli intellectual who himself had been born in Warsaw, before moving to Palestine in 1924, at a time when it was under British rule. Even in his teens, Benzion Netanyahu was, in the words of Anshel Pfeffer, "a member of the one [Zionist] political faction that had decided not to take the Arab claims to the land into consideration."[6] The Revisionist Zionism that the Netanyahu family embraced was built around the political philosophy of one man, Ze'ev Jabotinsky, who rejected the socialism of Israel's founding father, David Ben-Gurion, and instead embraced a much more militarized form of nationalism that saw conflict with the Arab population as inevitable. Ben-Gurion regarded Jabotinsky as a fascist, and for almost the first thirty years of Israel's existence from 1948 onwards, Israeli politics were dominated by Ben-Gurion's Labour Party. It was only in 1977 that the Likud Party, led by followers of Jabotinsky, won power for the first time. And Likud was the party that Benjamin Netanyahu would go on to lead.[7]

The division between Labour and Likud was not just about ideology but also class and background. Labour was led by Eastern European exiles from an Ashkenazi background, who came from the left and were regarded as the intellectual and social elite of the new Israeli state. Likud, by contrast, drew much of its support from Sephardic Jews who had been expelled or emigrated from the Arab nations, and later from immigrants who arrived from Russia after the collapse of the Soviet Union. It was the outsiders' party, railing against the complacent, liberal elite. In that sense, the politics of Likud and Netanyahu anticipated the populist politics of Donald Trump and Brexit by decades.

Netanyahu's rejection of some of the core ideas of the founding fathers of the Israeli state also echoes the politics of Modi in India and Erdoğan in Turkey. Just as Netanyahu comes from a tradition that rejects many of the relatively liberal ideas of Israel's founding father, Ben-Gurion, in favor of a harder-edged, more populist and right-wing nationalism, so Modi and Erdoğan have pushed back against the ideas of Nehru and Atatürk.

But the strongest cultural influence on Benjamin Netanyahu himself was the United States. With Benzion Netanyahu unable to find an academic post in Israel, the family moved to the US. Between the ages of eight and ten Bibi lived in New York and he then spent much of his adolescence in Philadelphia. He took undergraduate and graduate degrees, in architecture and then management, in the US, studying at the Massachusetts Institute of Technology before taking a job as a management consultant with the Boston Consulting Group. As a result, Netanyahu is steeped in American culture, understands the United States political scene perfectly, and has been an extremely adept operator there. Many of his closest advisers, such as Dore Gold and Yoram Hazony, are native English speakers and Netanyahu's staff meetings were often conducted in English.

It took a family tragedy, however, to catapult the Netanyahu family from obscurity to national prominence. That was the death of Bibi's older brother, Jonathan (Yoni), in 1976, while leading a successful commando raid to free Jewish hostages held by Palestinian and German militants at Entebbe airport in Uganda. The "Raid on Entebbe" became the subject of three full-length feature films and turned Yoni into a posthumous national hero. His articulate brother, Bibi, who had also served in the Israeli military, quickly became hot property, courted by Israel's leading politicians, including Shimon Peres, whom Netanyahu would one day defeat in the contest to be prime minister.

Netanyahu's talents as an English-speaking advocate for Israel saw him appointed to the high-profile position of ambassador to the UN from 1984 to 1988. On his return to Israel, he joined the right-wing Likud Party. By 1993 he was party leader, and in 1996, at the age of forty-six, he became Israel's youngest ever prime minister. Although he lost power in 1999, he returned to office a decade later, winning election again in 2009. From then on, he won a series of election victories, usually by narrow margins that required painful periods of coalition-building, to keep him in the prime minister's office. The longer Netanyahu stayed in power, the more he was able to play the role of Israel's elder statesman and international face. Likud campaign posters for 2020 featured photos of Netanyahu standing next to Modi, Trump and Putin under the slogan "A Different League."

Netanyahu eventually lost office in 2021, after yet another deadlocked election. But his political longevity had allowed him to outlast Western leaders, whom he regarded as naively liberal on the Palestinian question, such as Bill Clinton, Barack Obama and David Cameron. In the post-Obama years, Netanyahu was able to take advantage of the rise of a new generation of nationalist-populist leaders – from Washington to Delhi, from Budapest to Brasilia – who ardently admire the Jewish state. This change in the international political atmosphere created new breathing space for a country that has long feared international isolation and trade boycotts.

The single most important change for the Israelis was the election of Trump in 2016. The new US president relied heavily on the support of white evangelical voters who were both more numerous than Jews and often more ardent in their support for Israel. (American Jews still tended to vote disproportionately for the Democrats.) As president, Trump delivered on a long list of Israeli objectives that once seemed like distant fantasies. In 2018, he moved the US embassy from Tel Aviv to Jerusalem and pulled out of the Iran nuclear accord, negotiated by Obama. The following year, America recognized Israeli sovereignty over the Golan Heights which had been seized from Syria during the Six Day War of 1967. Netanyahu sounded almost incredulous as he received this gift in the White House.

The ties between Trump and Netanyahu were not just diplomatic and familial: they were also ideological. As Trump's advisers struggled to turn their boss's instincts and tweets into coherent ideas, one of the thinkers they turned to was Netanyahu's favorite court philosopher, Yoram Hazony. A former aide to Netanyahu who remains a close confidant, Hazony hit the intellectual big time with his 2018 book, *The Virtue of Nationalism.*[8] Officials in the Trump White House who had worked on the president's national security strategy cited Hazony to me as a major influence on their thinking. Wes Mitchell, who served as the president's Assistant Secretary of State for Europe, suggested to EU diplomats that they should read Hazony if they wanted to understand the Trump administration's thinking.

European diplomats who made the effort were rather disconcerted by what they found. Hazony was frank in his contempt for the EU, which he characterized as a stalking horse for a new form of German imperialism. For Hazony, the only true foundation of political order and human liberty is the nation, based around a shared language, culture and religion. All successful nations, Hazony argues, need to be organized around a group "whose cultural dominance is plain and unquestioned and against which resistance appears to be futile."[9]

It is not hard to understand the appeal of that notion to white Trump supporters, worried by demographic projections which showed that, by the 2040s, whites would make up less than 50 percent of the US population. The notion that a nation has to be built around a dominant ethnic or cultural group, central to nineteenth-century nationalism, is also fervently espoused by Hungary's Viktor Orbán, who held meetings with Hazony and also cites him as an intellectual influence.

The prime minister of Hungary, a champion of "illiberal democracy," visited Jerusalem in 2018. This visit was controversial in Israel because Orbán had run an election campaign replete with anti-Semitic imagery, portraying the financier George Soros as a rich, evil puppet master, intent on flooding Hungary with refugees. But Soros was also loathed by Netanyahu, for his support of the Palestinians and Israeli human-rights organizations.

There are indeed clear ideological affinities between the Israeli and Hungarian leaders.[10] They are both ethnic nationalists who believe in "Israel for the Jews" and "Hungary for the Hungarians." The fact that Orbán's nationalism has more than a whiff of anti-Semitism about it is not especially shocking to Netanyahu, whose brand of Zionism has always assumed that the outside world is inherently anti-Semitic. In the months after Trump's election, Israeli officials worked hard to build bridges between Orbán and the White House.

For the Israeli leader, making a tactical alliance with a figure like Orbán is justified if it helps Israel. And Central European nationalists were indeed useful when the Czechs, Hungarians and Romanians vetoed an EU condemnation of America's embassy move to Jerusalem.

The Romanian prime minister even suggested that his own government might move its embassy to Jerusalem. These days, Europe's far right is much more preoccupied by Muslims than Jews and its Islamophobia often translates into support for Israel. Despite its anti-Semitic roots, France's National Front under Marine Le Pen has become a strongly pro-Israel party.

A shared suspicion of Islam also helped Netanyahu to create close ties with Narendra Modi, who in 2017 became the first Indian prime minister to visit Israel since the state's foundation. Some BJP loyalists see Israel's ferocious response to Palestinian violence as a model for India, in its struggle with terrorists based in Pakistan. In fact, Israel has sold billions of dollars' worth of weaponry to India – some of which was used on a bombing raid on Pakistan in 2019.

A trip to Israel swiftly became almost a compulsory stop for the new generation of strongman leaders, who reveled in defying liberal opinion. In September 2018, Rodrigo Duterte, the leader of the Philippines, came to Jerusalem and told Netanyahu, "We have the same passion for human beings"[11] – a double-edged compliment, given Duterte's frequent and vocal support for the deployment of death squads.

By 2019, Jair Bolsonaro was installed as president of Brazil. Even more than Trump, Bolsonaro relied heavily on evangelical voters and stressed his love for the state of Israel. Netanyahu was guest of honor at Bolsonaro's inauguration and the Brazilian was feted on a state visit to Israel a few months later. Having the largest country in Latin America as an ally was a breakthrough for Israel because the "Global South" of developing nations had traditionally been solid in its support for the Palestinians. For Bolsonaro, embracing Israel was a way of simultaneously appealing to evangelicals and the Trump White House, while sticking a finger in the eye of his enemies on the liberal left. Almost a decade earlier, his great political rival, President Luiz Inácio Lula da Silva (always referred to as "Lula"), had visited the West Bank and announced: "I dream of an independent and free Palestine."

Israel's calling card with Xi's China is technology. Wang Qishan, China's vice president, visited an Israeli tech fair in October 2018. At a time when American tech firms were getting warier of working with China, Israel was an attractive alternative. A Chinese firm now also owns and operates the port of Haifa, which is the main base for the Israeli navy and also a frequent port of call for the US Sixth Fleet.[12]

This growing closeness between Israel and China was one of the few complaints that the Trump administration had to make about Netanyahu's Israel.

Netanyahu regards these new relationships as a great achievement and dismisses liberal scruples about palling up with the likes of Duterte, Bolsonaro and Orbán. As Avi Gil, once Israel's top diplomat, has noted, "A world order that assigns less weight to human and democratic rights will exert less pressure on Israel."[13] However, even in terms of pure realpolitik, Bibi's diplomacy carries substantial risks for Israel. The most damaging charge made against Israel by its critics is that the Jewish state's claim to be a beacon of democracy is undermined by its treatment of the Palestinians. By allying with a new generation of populist-nationalists – many of whom have dubious democratic credentials – Israel further weakens its claim to be a champion of democracy.

But for Netanyahu, the benefits of cozying up to the world's strongman leaders powerfully outweighed the risk of lost support in progressive circles in the West. Visits from the likes of Orbán, Duterte, Bolsonaro and Modi were helpful. But the strongman leader who has the greatest power to improve Israeli security and prosperity is the one close by – MBS.

A political neophyte, MBS has big ambitions to remake the Middle East. At the urging of Kushner, Trump made Saudi Arabia his first foreign visit as president in May 2017. While this was a huge and much-cherished compliment to the Saudis, it also yielded direct practical benefits for Riyadh. Trump's willingness to rip up President Obama's peace deal with Iran was much more important to the Saudis than any lingering offense stemming from the Muslim-baiting of Trump's 2016 election campaign. Trump received several standing ovations during his Riyadh speech, in which he offered the absolute monarchy a "partnership, based on shared interests and values."

Formally speaking, MBS was not the leader of Saudi Arabia. That title belonged to his father, King Salman. But by the time Trump visited in mid-2017, there was little doubt that it was the 31-year-old Prince Mohammed who was the power behind the throne. He was the minister whom foreign leaders sought out for discussions. He was the man who set out the vision of a new Saudi Arabia to international business people and journalists.

It was an extraordinary rise. As recently as 2015, MBS had simply been a "prince among thousands of princes"[14] in the Saudi royal family. His ascent to power was down to a mixture of chance and personal ruthlessness. MBS's father, King Salman, was the twenty-fifth son of King Abdulaziz (Ibn Saud), the first monarch of Saudi Arabia. MBS himself was just the sixth son of Salman. As Ben Hubbard puts it: "As the sixth son of the twenty-fifth son of the founding king, there was little reason to expect that he would rise to prominence."[15] But the deaths of two of Salman's older brothers, and Salman's own successful record as governor of Riyadh, saw him named by King Abdullah as the new crown prince of Saudi Arabia in 2012. MBS was suddenly much closer to real power. When King Salman duly ascended to the throne in 2015, he appointed his favorite son, Prince Mohammed, as defense minister.

Within two months of his appointment, MBS had demonstrated his ruthlessness. In March 2015, the Saudi air force launched a series of bombing raids on neighboring Yemen in an effort to drive out the Iran-linked Houthi rebels who had taken control of the Yemeni capital. This was a startling move. The Saudi kingdom had long been a massive purchaser of armaments but it had never seemed very keen on actually using them. MBS's belief that he could win an easy victory in Yemen proved misplaced. The Saudis got bogged down in the conflict and their indiscriminate bombing saw the kingdom accused of war crimes.

But the prince's bellicose and impulsive decision to go to war in Yemen did little immediate damage to his reputation in the West. Instead, like Erdoğan before him, MBS was hailed as the great hope for a reformed Middle East. In an influential column, written in November 2015, the *New York Times*'s Thomas Friedman portrayed MBS as a reforming whirlwind, "on a mission to transform how Saudi Arabia has been governed." After an audience with MBS, Friedman was impressed by the prince's professed determination to wean the kingdom off dependence on oil and to introduce social reforms. "Since Mohammed arrived," he enthused, "big decisions that took two years to make now happen in two weeks."[16] Returning for another evening with MBS in 2017, when complaints about human-rights violations were mounting, Friedman was still impressed. He argued that "The most significant reform process underway anywhere in the Middle East today is in Saudi Arabia." It was true, he acknowledged, that just a few weeks earlier, MBS had "arrested scores of Saudi princes and businessmen." But, he added, "Perfect is not on the menu here. Someone had to do this job – wrench Saudi Arabia into the twenty-first century."[17]

To be fair, Friedman was far from alone in being impressed by MBS. Prince Mohammed was adept at forging contacts with Western opinion-formers, dazzling them with a mixture of determination, wealth and the sense that he was taking them into his confidence. One Washington power broker would occasionally show me the chummy text messages he had got from MBS. Journalists would compare notes on the opulence of the surroundings in which the crown prince had received them.

Meanwhile, Western management consultants flocked to Riyadh in search of lucrative contracts to help deliver MBS's economic reform program – known as Vision 2030. Investment bankers salivated at the prospect of bringing the national oil company, Saudi Aramco, to market: it promised to be the biggest initial public offering in history. Weapons manufacturers, influential in the Trump White House, remained fixated on Saudi Arabia, the world's largest importer of armaments.

Friends of Israel were delighted that Saudi Arabia's new ruler didn't seem to care much about the Palestinians and instead saw Israel primarily as an ally against Iran. Even human-rights activists applauded some of MBS's reforms, such as the long-overdue decision to allow women to drive, something which had required the prince to rein in the power of the much-feared religious police.

Yet, there were also skeptics in the West. As one senior British official put it to me, "My question is whether MBS is more like Lee Kuan Yew or Saddam Hussein." In other words, was the Saudi prince a wise if authoritarian reformer, like Lee who had modernized Singapore? Or was he a ruthless out-of-control dictator like Saddam?

The paradox was that under MBS, social freedoms were expanding against the backdrop of a reign of terror. The crown prince was genuinely determined to widen the possibilities open to Saudi youth. Unusually for a Saudi royal, he understood the importance of public opinion and social media. An imposing figure, who is over six foot tall, MBS employed experts to burnish his image on Twitter by portraying the crown prince as a modernizer and a nationalist.[18] As MBS himself often observed, two-thirds of his country's population of

34 million was under thirty. Society was loosened up, making it easier for the young to find entertainment, launch businesses, mingle and travel.

But at the same time, MBS showed a growing intolerance for opposition and dissent – even within his own family. One extraordinary discordant note was struck early after his ascent to power, when Western intelligence officials received reports that the prince had put his own mother under house arrest. (It was speculated that MBS wanted to prevent her influencing his father, the king.) Initially, King Salman had made his favorite son only second in line to succeed him. Ahead of MBS was his cousin, MBN, Prince Mohammed bin Nayef. But in June 2017, MBN was detained, held incommunicado and forced to abdicate his position. A video of him swearing allegiance to MBS was circulated on social media, before the former crown prince was taken off and put under house arrest in a palace in Jeddah.[19]

There were also mass arrests of dissidents and critics of MBS. Only sycophantic approval of the new crown prince was safe. One independent journalist who was forced to flee the country wrote a column for the *Washington Post*, headlined "Saudi Arabia wasn't always this oppressive. Now it's unbearable." In it he complained of "fear, intimidation, arrests and public shaming of intellectuals."[20]

The author of that article was Jamal Khashoggi. Just over a year later, he was dead, murdered in the Saudi consulate in Istanbul. The gruesome assassination of Khashoggi – whose body was dismembered with a bone saw – inflicted huge damage on MBS's international reputation. The Saudis had initially suggested that he had mysteriously disappeared; then that he had been accidentally killed in a rogue kidnapping operation. But few people with any real knowledge of Saudi Arabia doubted that this was an operation that had been personally ordered by a vengeful MBS. That was certainly the conclusion of the CIA, in a report that was rapidly leaked (and later published in full by the Biden administration).[21]

The murder of Khashoggi put an end to laudatory profiles of MBS in the Western press. But it did not finish the crown prince's business and diplomatic relationship with the West. In the immediate aftermath of the killing, many prominent Western businessmen had pulled out of a glitzy investment conference dubbed "Davos in the desert." But when I asked one CEO when he thought he and his colleagues would return to Saudi Arabia, he smiled and replied, "Just as soon as it's off the front pages."

President Trump's reaction was similarly pragmatic. "It could very well be that the Crown Prince had knowledge of this tragic event – maybe he did, maybe he didn't . . . The United States intends to remain a steadfast partner of Saudi Arabia to ensure the interests of our country."[22] Trump was not alone in his amoral pragmatism. In November 2020, Saudi Arabia had the honor of hosting the G20 summit of the world's most powerful countries. Covid-19 meant that the summit had to be held virtually. Nonetheless, human-rights activists mounted a campaign to get world leaders to boycott the event because of MBS's participation. But the boycott call was ignored – allowing Saudi Arabia's de facto leader to give the closing address, before an audience that included such liberal stalwarts as Angela Merkel of Germany and Justin Trudeau of Canada. In truth, the G20 summit already involved other leaders well known for human-rights abuses – President Xi of China, President Erdoğan of Turkey and President Putin of Russia.

The reality is that MBS is not an aberration in the Age of the Strongman. On the contrary, in his ruthless drive to centralize power, his cultivation of a cult of personality and his willingness to commit murder, he is very much in tune with the spirit of the age.

10 Bolsonaro, Amlo and the return of the Latin American caudillo (2018)

"Brazil faces a moral and political crisis." Fernando Henrique Cardoso sounded detached and analytical in São Paulo in August 2017. But he was describing the potential destruction of his life's work. A former professor of sociology, Cardoso served as president of Brazil from 1995 to 2002 – consolidating the country's democracy, reforming its economy and laying the foundations for an economic boom. The optimism of the post-Cardoso years was captured by a famous *Economist* cover in 2009, which showed the statue of Christ the Redeemer in Rio, soaring into space like a rocket, under the headline "Brazil takes off." But Cardoso, now eighty-six, was watching his country crash back to earth.

Battered by political mismanagement and a slump in the prices of key exports, such as iron ore and soya beans, the Brazilian economy had shrunk by almost 8 percent in the previous two years. President Dilma Rousseff had been impeached and removed from office in 2016 and some 40 percent of members of Congress were under investigation for corruption. Many of Brazil's most powerful businessmen and politicians had been sent to prison, as part of an anti-corruption drive known as *Lava Jato* (Car Wash). Polls showed that only 13 percent of Brazilians still had faith in their country's democracy.

With ordinary Brazilians suffering and the political class disgraced, the conditions were ripe for the rise of a populist, anti-system politician. When I met Cardoso in São Paulo, early opinion polls for the 2018 presidential election were already showing Jair Bolsonaro, a far-right congressman, in second place. First elected to parliament in

Brazil in 1990, the former army captain had made little impression in politics for more than twenty-five years. But in an atmosphere of political and economic crisis, Bolsonaro was suddenly the name on everybody's lips. His promise to get tough on criminals – both in Congress and in Brazil's crime-ridden slums – was hitting home. Like Donald Trump in the US and Rodrigo Duterte in the Philippines, Bolsonaro had built a huge personal following through social media and used shocking rhetoric to make himself stand out. He had declared that if he saw two men kissing in the street, he would assault them. He had defended the use of torture by the military, proclaiming defiantly that most Brazilians agreed with him. Voting to impeach President Rousseff in 2016, he had even dedicated his vote to Colonel Brilhante Ustra, who had run a notorious torture squad during Brazil's years of military dictatorship from 1965 to 1985.

A year out from the election, most of the members of the Brazilian elite whom I met in August 2017 were still not willing to believe that a man they regarded as crude, stupid and violent could really make it all the way to the presidential palace. "Most pundits see Mr Bolsonaro as too extreme to win," I wrote afterwards. "But the reassurances I received in well-appointed offices reminded me uncomfortably of conversations in Washington in 2015, when a Trump victory was deemed inconceivable."[1]

That foreboding was justified. On October 28, 2018, Bolsonaro swept to a crushing victory in the Brazilian presidential election, aided by the fact that the most charismatic left-wing politician in the country, former President Lula, had been disqualified from running against him, after being imprisoned on corruption charges.

Bolsonaro's victory had a continental, indeed global significance. Until the early 1980s, Latin America had been dominated by authoritarian leaders; in 1978, there were just three democracies in the whole of the continent. The political landscape was pockmarked with military juntas and dictators such as Chile's Augusto Pinochet or Argentina's Jorge Videla. But by the beginning of the 1990s, democracy had triumphed across most of the continent. The transition to democracy in Brazil in 1985, which ended more than twenty years of military rule, was a particularly significant moment because of the country's size and role as a regional leader. With a population of over 200 million, Brazil is the seventh most populous country in the world, and the largest in Latin America; roughly one in two South Americans is Brazilian.

During the Cardoso and Lula presidencies, Brazil was widely celebrated as a nation that had successfully embraced globalization and democracy and left the dark days of authoritarianism behind it. Cardoso became a friend and confidant of Bill Clinton, whose "third way" philosophy of combining orthodox economics with social liberalism he emulated in Brazil. Lula, a former trade-union leader from a humble background, had built on Cardoso's economic reforms and begun to tackle Brazil's notorious inequality through social reforms – including a guaranteed income for poorer families, linked to school attendance, known as the *bolsa familia* – which attracted global praise. Just as Cardoso, a multilingual technocrat, had been perfectly in tune with Clinton, so Lula, the social reformer and community organizer, was a perfect fit with the Obama presidency. Indeed President Obama had publicly embraced his Brazilian counterpart, proclaiming, "I love this guy."

With the election of Bolsonaro, Brazilian politics had once again tracked political trends in the US. Like Trump, Bolsonaro was a compulsive tweeter and had adopted many of the US president's slogans, denouncing "fake news," "globalism," "political correctness" and the liberal elite. In the Brazilian context, an impatience with political correctness translated into contempt for the environmentalists and international NGOs who, Bolsonaro argued, were holding back the country's development, particularly by opposing development of the Amazon. At a time of mounting concern about global warming, Bolsonaro's eagerness to allow more of the rainforest to be chopped down horrified the world's environmentalists, although it was met with indifference in the Trump White House.

Like Trump, Bolsonaro treated politics as a family business. His son, Eduardo, was swiftly given an important role in the administration and dispatched to the White House to discuss geopolitics with Jared Kushner, Trump's son-in-law. When I returned to Brazil early in the new administration in 2019, I was told by a prominent economist that Bolsonaro was "just like Trump, only stupider." Since the US president was not famed for his intellect, I was a little surprised. But then I was reminded that Trump, at least, had built and led a major business. Bolsonaro, by contrast, had never risen above the rank of army captain.

Even members of the president's own administration did not bother to hide their contempt for their boss. When one of my *FT* colleagues asked a cabinet minister about one of Bolsonaro's stranger statements on the economy, he was informed bluntly: "The president talks a lot of shit."

As with Trump, the fact that intellectuals held Bolsonaro in contempt did not deter the president's supporters – on the contrary, he had a rapport with small-town and rural Brazil, whose values were more conservative than big cities like Rio. Bolsonaro, unlike Trump, had risen from genuinely humble origins. Born in 1955, he grew up in Eldorado Paulista, a town of 15,000 people, surrounded by farmland – 150 miles from São Paulo, Brazil's commercial capital. The son of an unlicensed dentist, Bolsonaro grew up poor with two brothers and three sisters. As a young man, he was fascinated by the police and the military. When he was fifteen, his small town had been the scene of a shoot-out between police and left-wing guerrillas, which had thrilled the young Bolsonaro and made him determined to join the forces of law and order. In 1973, he had passed the exams to get into military academy – a genuine achievement that undermines the idea, beloved of his opponents, that Bolsonaro is a moron.[2]

In the army, he campaigned for higher wages and better conditions for soldiers. Once he had moved into politics in the 1990s, he was noted as an outspoken supporter of the military. In an era when most Brazilian politicians were eager to embrace democracy, his open nostalgia for the years of military rule seemed eccentric and out of tune with the times.

But as his biographer Richard Lapper suggests, Bolsonaro's deep social conservatism was actually more in tune with the attitudes of many ordinary Brazilians than Brazil's urban elite may have realized. An opinion poll taken in 2020 suggested that 61 percent of Brazilians supported President Bolsonaro's plan to open new schools run by the military, and majorities opposed both gay marriage and abortion.[3] As with Trump and Duterte, Bolsonaro had cut through with the public, by denouncing "political correctness" and promising simple solutions and tough-sounding remedies.

In the 2018 presidential election, Bolsonaro put together a distinctively Brazilian populist coalition, described by Lapper as "beef, bible and bullets." The beef was the powerful agricultural and ranching interests attracted by Bolsonaro's promise to do away with the environmental restrictions that restrained their expansion. The bible was the 30 percent of Brazilians who, like Bolsonaro, had embraced evangelical Christianity. The bullets represented Brazil's powerful gun lobby.

Many of Brazil's middle class voted for Bolsonaro out of fear of crime or disgust at corruption. And while the academics I met were usually contemptuous of Bolsonaro, many working people I spoke to – shopkeepers, tour guides, office workers – seemed more indulgent. They saw Bolsonaro as an outsider, bravely battling a corrupt system and they respected his physical courage. On the campaign trail in 2018, he had been stabbed in the back and gravely wounded, only surviving after complex surgery. When I saw him speak in person for the first time, in Davos in 2019, I wondered why he had not taken off his coat throughout his brief period onstage. The answer, I was told by one of his staffers, was that the president was still wearing a colostomy bag, as part of his recovery from surgery.

As with Trump in the US, much of Brazil's big business was prepared to swallow its distaste for Bolsonaro in return for promises of less red tape and lower taxes. They were also encouraged by the fact that the president appointed prominent liberal economists to key positions in his administration. At the start of his political career, Bolsonaro had been an advocate of state control of the economy – he had even once suggested that Cardoso deserved to be shot, for selling off state assets. But he campaigned for the presidency as an economic liberal, arguing for privatization and tax cuts. Some of his supporters in business argued that his more outrageous remarks were simply designed to gain attention and to dramatize an issue. They were comments that – as was once said of Donald Trump – were "meant to be taken seriously, but not literally."

It soon became clear that the Bolsonaro government was an uneasy coalition between liberal economists and right-wing culture warriors, who railed against "cultural Marxism." International businessmen and bankers were impressed by Paulo Guedes, a Chicago University-trained economist who was appointed as economy minister, with a mandate to reform the country's heavily indebted pension system and to carry out large-scale privatizations. But sitting around the cabinet table with Guedes was Ernesto Araújo, the foreign minister, who argued that

climate change was "dogma," promoted by "globalists" intent on subverting democracy and serving China. Araújo even appeared to suggest
that Covid-19 was part of a Communist plot to expand state control,
stating that "Coronavirus is making us wake up once more to the communist nightmare."[4]

Some of the culture warriors in the new government proved too
peculiar even for Bolsonaro. In early 2020, Roberto Alvim, his culture
minister, gave a speech in which he proclaimed that "Brazilian art in
the next decade will be heroic and national." Unfortunately, it turned
out that parts of the speech appeared to have been plagiarized from an
address by Hitler's propaganda minister, Joseph Goebbels. Bolsonaro
was forced to sack his culture minister.[5] The Alvim affair was, on one
level, ludicrous. But the suggestion that government officials in Brazil,
or elsewhere in Latin America, had sympathies with fascism also had a
distinctly sinister echo in a continent which, within living memory, had
been the host to a clutch of brutal military regimes, many of whom
had espoused far-right ideologies.

Between 1962 and 1966 alone, there had been nine military coups
across Latin America, including Argentina and Brazil – a demonstration
of the contagious nature of political trends across the region. The Cold
War was raging and most of the generals who took power cited the
need to resist Communist influence – exemplified by Castro's Cuba.
The military regimes that sprouted across the continent ruled with dif-
fering levels of brutality. The worst regimes, such as those in Argentina
and Chile, became notorious for the "disappearance" of thousands of
political dissidents, as well as widespread torture. In Argentina, up to
30,000 may have been killed in the "dirty war" between 1976 and 1982.
By contrast, Brazil's National Truth Commission, set up in 2012, clearly
identified "only" 434 dissidents who had "disappeared" or been murdered by Brazil's military rulers. But the commission also suggests that
thousands of indigenous people may have been killed, and brutal torture of dissidents was also common.[6] Bolsonaro, however, argues that
the military's "tough" measures were justified by low crime rates and
economic development.

Latin America's transition from military regimes to democratic
forms of government took place largely in the 1980s, even before the
fall of the Berlin Wall. The most important trigger was the continent's
Latin American debt crisis of 1982. That year, as Michael Reid puts

it, "the dictatorships buckled under the opprobrium of economic failure . . . Rather than risk their professional cohesion, Latin America's armies sat down with the civilian populations and negotiated a return to the barracks."[7] At the time, the move away from autocracy in Latin America came just after the return of democracy to Spain and Portugal – and foreshadowed events in the rest of the world. In Eastern Europe, pressures were growing within Soviet bloc countries, such as Poland, and in Southeast Asia, Ferdinand Marcos was felled by a "people power" revolution in the Philippines in 1986. The previous year, José Sarney had become Brazil's first civilian president since the 1960s, and the country played an important part in the regional and global trend away from authoritarianism and towards liberal democracy.

With the emergence of Bolsonaro in 2018, Brazil was once again part of a global political shift – but this time away from liberal internationalism and towards strongman populist rule. Although the president looked back to the era of military rule in Brazil with open nostalgia, this was not a straightforward reprise of the Latin American authoritarianism of the 1960s and 70s. It was, instead, a distinctly twenty-first-century style of populism, which owed more to Donald Trump than to the generals who had once ruled Brazil. Unlike the generals, Bolsonaro was elected and he faced a lively opposition and an independent media and courts. Many of the Brazilian leader's catchphrases were borrowed straight from Trump, such as his talk of "fake news" and a "deep state." Bolsonaro also had a Trump-like taste for conspiracy theories, often suggesting, for example, that environmental activists were the tool of foreign powers, who wanted to take over the Amazon and steal Brazil's precious resources. While Trump was Bolsonaro's personal role model, the Brazilian leader also had political soul mates in Europe and Asia. His emphasis on crime and on middle-class fears and insecurities bore a strong resemblance to Duterte's approach in the Philippines, as did his adept use of social media. At his presidential swearing-in ceremony in 2019, Bolsonaro's two main foreign guests of honor were Viktor Orbán of Hungary and Benjamin Netanyahu of Israel.

For students of populism, Latin America is fertile ground since it is a political style that has a long and checkered history across the continent. Michael Reid argues that populism has two main characteristics, both of which have a distinct contemporary relevance. First of all, it is a "brand of politics in which a strong, charismatic leader purports to be a savior, blurring the distinction between leader, government, party and state, and ignoring the need for the restraint of executive power through checks and balances. Second, populism has often involved redistribution of income and/or wealth in an unsustainable fashion."[8] As Reid points out, the distinction between "right" and "left," which is traditionally so fundamental to Western politics, is not always helpful when analyzing populism. Juan Perón, the archetypal Latin American populist, who served three terms as president of Argentina between 1946 and 1974, emerged from the military, protected Nazi war criminals and was clearly influenced by fascism – but he also became a hero to many on the left because of his self-proclaimed efforts to eliminate poverty and his espousal of statist economics.

In contemporary Latin America, populists associated with the right, such as Jair Bolsonaro, have competed with left populists such as Venezuela's Hugo Chávez, Evo Morales of Bolivia, and Andrés Manuel López Obrador, who was elected president of Mexico in 2018. The main similarity of the left and right populists is that they all claim to be representing the people against the elite – and they all promise simple solutions to complex problems.

Just as Bolsonaro formed an ideological alliance with Trump and other right-wing populists such as Orbán and Netanyahu, so Latin America's left-wing strongmen have also attracted praise and attention from political admirers overseas. In the 1960s and 70s, it was Fidel Castro's Cuba that attracted political pilgrims from around the West. By the 2000s, it was Hugo Chávez's Venezuela that had become the chic cause for the radical left. Jeremy Corbyn, who led Britain's Labour Party to two electoral defeats during his disastrous period as leader, once described Chávez as "an inspiration to all of us fighting back against austerity and neoliberal economics."[9]

Chávez first tried to seize power in Venezuela in a coup in 1992 but then won a democratic election in 1998. Over the next decade, he followed a textbook pattern of strongman rule: he packed the Supreme Court, altered the electoral system in his favor, encouraged a cult of personality via rambling and bombastic appearances on television, and denounced independent critics as tools of hostile foreign powers. For a while, Venezuela's huge oil reserves kept the economy afloat. Where Castro's Cuba had attempted to win favor by dispatching doctors overseas – as well as soldiers to Africa in the 1970s – Chávez liked to give gifts of oil to foreign friends from Bolivia to New York City. In 2007, Ken Livingstone, the socialist mayor of London, announced that he was able to cut bus fares courtesy of fuel subsidies from Chávez's Venezuela.

At the time, some argued that Chávez's gift was inappropriate, given that an estimated one-third of Venezuelan households were still believed to be living in poverty.[10] But Chávez had also embarked on a war on poverty at home – subsidising food, pouring money into education and literacy programs, and nationalizing key industries. These programs burnished his international reputation as a progressive. But they were financed by a rising oil price and the accumulation of debt. Chávez's rule was also closely associated with corruption, cronyism, and intimidation of the press and political opponents.

When Chávez died of cancer in 2013, the oil price was turning and the bills were coming in. Under Nicolas Maduro, his less charismatic successor, Venezuela plunged into poverty and social breakdown, a process that the Venezuelan government blamed on US sanctions, but whose roots began at home.[11] By 2018 over 80 percent of Venezuelan households were living in poverty and millions had fled the country. On a visit to northern Brazil the following year, I frequently came across Venezuelan refugees begging by the side of the road – a tragic and humiliating fate for the citizens of a country that had once been regarded as one of the most successful states in Latin America.

The disastrous economic record of Venezuela under Chávez and Maduro cast a shadow over much of the Latin American left. In his election campaign, Bolsonaro lost no opportunity to try to tie Lula and his Workers' Party to the Chávez catastrophe. But it was in Mexico, not Brazil, that another left-wing populist took power. Andrés Manuel López Obrador, known universally as Amlo, was inaugurated as president of the country in December 2018 – a month before Bolsonaro – after a landslide election victory, which placed him 31 percentage points ahead of his nearest rival. In Mexico, as in Brazil, the election of a charismatic populist was widely seen as a repudiation of the country's governing elite.

The fact that both Brazil and Mexico were now governed by populist leaders had a much broader regional significance. Brazil and Mexico are the two most populous countries in Latin America. They are both members of the G20 group of leading nations and they see each other as rivals for regional leadership. While Bolsonaro rails against "cultural Marxists," Amlo's chosen foes are "neoliberals." Bolsonaro was an army officer, whereas Amlo spent many years as a community organizer. But despite these differences, the two leaders also have certain similarities. Both won power against a background of widespread disillusionment with corruption, crime and violence. Both are populists, who claim a direct connection with the people.[12] Both are nationalists and avowedly religious.

One important difference is that whereas Bolsonaro seems content to largely subcontract the management of the economy to professors and technocrats, Amlo has taken charge personally, as part of a war on poverty that has strong echoes of both Lula in Brazil and Chávez in Venezuela. Amlo's chosen policies have included a program of scholarships for the underprivileged, an increase in the minimum wage and the cancellation of major infrastructure projects that he regarded as wasteful and tainted by corruption. Unusually for a left-wing populist, Amlo is also a strong believer in the control of public spending.

Some of Amlo's first moves demonstrated a populist's impatience with independent institutions: a Supreme Court judge was forced out, as was Mexico's energy regulator, who had complained that his agency was being staffed with unqualified cronies. The number of contracts awarded without a bidding process was also an ominous sign.[13] Amlo's proposal to stage a referendum on whether to put all his predecessors as president on trial for corruption combined populism with the strongman's urge to imprison his political opponents.

The Mexican president started most days in office with a 7:00 a.m. press conference. Showing a Castro-like fondness for the sound of his own voice, Amlo would often hold forth for two hours with a rambling discourse that frequently involved personal attacks on journalists, businessmen or environmentalists who had displeased him. But while the Mexican intelligentsia rolled their eyes at this daily ritual, Amlo maintained considerable support among the population as a whole. Ordinary Mexicans were particularly impressed that he had cut his own salary in half. A year into his presidency, his popularity ratings were high.

Yet Amlo's reforms were not crowned with economic success. In 2019, his first full year in office, the economy grew at its slowest rate for a decade. To be fair to the Mexican president, he faced very unfavorable conditions, including a trade war with the US and a plunging oil price, but the signs were ominous.

With their economies struggling, Mexico and Brazil were both in a weakened state when they were hit by the coronavirus. True to their populist instincts, Bolsonaro and Amlo reacted in similar ways. The Brazilian leader claimed that Covid-19 was not much more than a case of the sniffles. The Mexican president brandished a six-leaf clover, which he claimed would protect him against the virus. He also advised his fellow countrymen to keep going to fiestas and to visit restaurants. Amlo's refusal to take the pandemic seriously meant that he did little to bolster Mexico's frail health system or to put into place a spending plan to stimulate the economy.

Both countries were soon among the worst-affected in the world by Covid-19. By the end of 2020, Brazil had recorded the second-highest number of deaths in the world, after the US. Mexico, the tenth most populous country in the world, was in third place globally for recorded Covid-19 deaths. In both countries, it was easy to blame these high mortality rates on the Trump-like insouciance of their political leaders. The initial take of many experts was that the terrible toll taken by the pandemic was exposing the flaws of populism and so would weaken the grip of strongman leaders like Bolsonaro and Amlo. Ian Bremmer, the head of the influential Eurasia consultancy, wrote in April 2020: "Which major country now faces the world's worst political mess? Which head of state finds himself in the deepest trouble? There is a good case to be made for Brazil and its president."[14] I weighed in myself with a column headlined "Jair Bolsonaro's populism is leading Brazil to disaster."[15] By the middle of 2020, with Covid-19 out of control, there was speculation that Bolsonaro might be impeached.

But the high death rates in Brazil and Mexico did not immediately destroy the political standing of either Bolsonaro or Amlo. In economies where the majority of the population have very little by way of savings, many people were grateful to be spared a lockdown. In Brazil, Bolsonaro's popularity was also bolstered by emergency cash handouts to the poor. The long-term economic, health and social consequences of the pandemic will play out over many years. But the similarities between the initial responses of Bolsonaro and Amlo demonstrated that right and left populism are often underpinned by the same instincts.

The Mexican and Brazilian leaders' responses to the defeat of Donald Trump were also revealingly similar. Bolsonaro kept up his display of loyalty to Trump, long after most other fellow travelers had accepted the reality of the president's defeat. On January 7, the day after a pro-Trump mob stormed the US Congress, Bolsonaro echoed their complaints about the US election, telling supporters, "There were people who voted two, three, four times. Dead people voted. It was a free-for-all. Nobody can deny that."[16] For some Brazilian analysts these remarks were not just unwise but ominous. Bolsonaro supporters too have often made allegations about voter fraud in Brazil, focusing on poor areas with large Black populations. With the Brazilian leader himself facing a presidential election in 2022, some feared that he was once again preparing to imitate the Trump playbook.

Bolsonaro's dismay at the removal of his ideological soul mate from the White House was predictable. Amlo's reluctance to acknowledge Trump's defeat was more surprising. As a Mexican and a leftist, Amlo had no obvious reason to feel any affection for a president who had labeled Mexican migrants to the United States rapists and criminals. When running for election, Amlo had indeed called Trump a neo-fascist. But as Mexican leader, he struck up an unlikely friendship with the populist to the north. In part, this was simple pragmatism. All Mexican leaders have to try to get on with the US president. But Amlo and Trump also appeared to see something they liked in each other. They were both populist leaders who had declared war on their countries' political and media establishments. They had both been harsh critics of NAFTA, the North American Free Trade Agreement – demonstrating that the populist right and the populist left are also linked by a shared suspicion of free trade and liberal economics. The two presidents' first meeting at the White House in 2020, which was also Amlo's first trip overseas after nineteen months in office, was regarded as a success by both sides.

The sense that there was a bond between Amlo and Trump was strengthened by the Mexican president's surprising response to Trump's electoral defeat. Both pragmatism and principle should have inclined Amlo to swiftly acknowledge the reality that Trump had lost and that Joe Biden was now the legitimate president. But along with the leaders of Russia and Brazil, Amlo dragged his feet, insisting on Trump's right to dispute the election result. The Mexican leader's reaction probably reflected his own personal political history: Amlo had twice unsuccessfully run for president. In 2006, he had narrowly lost the election to Felipe Calderón. Rather than accepting the result, he had cried fraud and organized mass sit-ins in Mexico City's central square. His response to electoral defeats in 2006 and 2012 was quite similar to Trump's reaction to defeat in 2020.

Since Brazilian and Mexican politics have often shadowed developments in the US, it is natural to speculate that Trump's defeat might also anticipate a shift in ideological tides in Latin America's two largest countries. In the aftermath of the US election, Bolsonaro was certainly more isolated internationally. With Covid-19 taking a heavy toll in lives, the economy slumping and Lula back on the political scene, Bolsonaro was clearly preparing the ground to dispute the result of the presidential election of 2022 by making Trump-style claims of voter fraud. The danger is that Brazil's institutions – in particular, the army – may not be as robust as their American equivalents in the defense of democracy and the rule of law.

Elsewhere in Latin America, the populist tide may still be rising. Amlo's term in office runs until 2024 and there is already speculation that, emulating the likes of Putin and Xi, he may seek to amend the constitution to extend his stay in office. The Mexican president's cult of personality and domination of the political scene was captured by the title of a well-received book about him: *El país de un solo hombre* (The Country of One Man).[17]

Meanwhile, several Latin American leaders with more technocratic and establishment credentials paid a heavy political price during the pandemic.

The South American countries that were strictest in trying to enforce lockdowns were often led by presidents educated at elite American universities, such as Chile's Sebastián Piñera (Harvard), Colombia's Ivan Duque (Georgetown) and Peru's Francisco Sagasti (Penn). But the countries that locked down got scant reward for their prudence. The economic shocks in the most heavily locked-down countries were worse than in laxer Brazil. In Peru by the end of 2020, half the urban population was unemployed.[18] Under those circumstances, it was little surprise that Pedro Castillo, a left-wing populist, whose party had praised Hugo Chávez, won the Peruvian presidential election in 2021.[19] With major elections looming across the continent, there are good grounds to fear that the next couple of years could see a surge in victories for populist leaders, from both the right and the left.

As we have seen, in the 1980s, Latin America set the trend for the democratic wave which would sweep away autocracies across the globe. If other countries in the region now follow Brazil and Mexico in turning towards charismatic, strongman-style leadership, the demonstration effect could be felt well beyond South and Central America. Africa, which also experienced a democratic wave in the 1990s, is another continent that is grappling anew with the dangers and temptations of strongman rule.

11 Abiy Ahmed and democratic disillusionment in Africa (2019)

The Age of the Strongman has involved a recurrent pattern. A charismatic new leader emerges somewhere in the world. He is portrayed in the Western media as a liberal reformer. Western politicians and institutions weigh in with encouraging comments and offers of assistance. Then, as time passes, awkward facts emerge. The liberal reformer becomes increasingly authoritarian. Disillusionment sets in.

Since 2000, this pattern has played out with Putin, Erdoğan, Xi, Modi and Orbán. But the emergence of strongman leaders all over the world does not seem to have defeated the West's urge to find new liberal heroes to embrace. On the contrary, it may have made Western opinion-formers even more eager to find champions of liberal democracy in a world in which strongman authoritarianism seems to be on the march.

From 2018 to 2020, the whole cycle – from enthusiasm to despair – played out in the global reaction to Abiy Ahmed, who became leader of Africa's second-most populous nation, Ethiopia, in April 2018. In his first hundred days in office, Abiy moved to liberalize Ethiopia's political system – lifting a state of emergency, releasing thousands of political prisoners, inviting opposition groups to return from exile and encouraging media freedom. He also moved swiftly to end hostilities with neighboring Eritrea, traveling to the Eritrean capital, Asmara, and making concessions to settle a long-standing territorial dispute. The governing Ethiopian People's Revolutionary Democratic Front was rebranded too, as the more presentable Prosperity Party.[1]

A rite of passage for new leaders seeking to cut a figure on the world stage is a visit to the World Economic Forum in Davos, where I watched from a few yards away as the new Ethiopian prime minister made his debut in January 2019. It was hard not to be impressed by this good-looking, confident forty-two-year-old with his outspoken liberal principles. The audience broke out into spontaneous applause when he announced that there were no longer any journalists in prison in Ethiopia and that 50 percent of his cabinet were women.

In his Davos address, Abiy took direct aim at the idea that the strongman model was the route to development, telling his audience: "We believe it is not possible to sustain growth without embracing democracy . . . We see democracy and development as interlinked." This was just what the Davos crowd wanted to hear and the questioning was gentle and credulous. Borge Brende, the WEF's moderator, told the audience that within months of taking power, Abiy had persuaded his fellow citizens to subordinate their ethnic identities to a common Ethiopian identity. Turning to Abiy, he asked admiringly: "How did you do that?" Abiy replied, disarmingly, that it was easy to make peace: "Sit together with people, put egos aside."[2]

Later that year, Abiy Ahmed was awarded the Nobel Peace Prize – doubtless to the chagrin of Donald Trump, who had made little secret of his belief that he would be a worthy recipient for the award. The Nobel Prize citation commended Abiy for making peace with Eritrea and praised his democratic reforms "that gave many citizens hope for a better life."

From the beginning, however, some experienced observers of Ethiopia were skeptical of the Abiy phenomenon. As early as September 2018, Michela Wrong argued that far from being the antidote to the strongman model, Abiy might actually be just another strongman in the making. "He is garnering hyperbolic comparisons to the likes of Mahatma Gandhi, Mandela and Mikhail Gorbachev," she wrote. "The better parallels are with populist contemporaries such as Donald Trump, Vladimir Putin and Recep Tayyip Erdoğan, who use jingoistic appeals to nationalism to truncate or, in some cases, supplant domestic political debate."[3] Wrong had noticed Abiy's strident Ethiopian nationalism, and its potential to reopen regional conflicts.

At first glance, Abiy's background made him almost perfectly positioned to bridge the country's ethnic and religious divides: his mother was Christian and Amhara, his father Muslim and Oromo. He even speaks Tigrinya, the language of the Tigrayans, the ethnic group that had dominated government for many years before Abiy came to power. His avowed goal as prime minister was to create a stronger national identity, by eschewing the old model of ethnic federalism.

Ethnic tensions had already been smoldering in the years before Abiy's accession to power, with mass protests from the Oromo, Ethiopia's largest ethnic group, against the Tigrayan domination of the national government. Installed as prime minister, Abiy purged many prominent Tigrayans from senior positions in the army, security forces and government. The Tigrayan People's Liberation Front left the government and senior figures in the party returned to their home region. Some Oromo nationalists still took to the streets to protest that Abiy had not done enough to shift the balance of power and privilege in their favor. But it was his challenge to the traditional domination of the Tigrayans that led to war.

In late 2020, Abiy accused Tigrayan leaders of defying central authority by holding unauthorized elections in their home region. The Ethiopian armed forces launched a bombing campaign and a ground offensive to repress the Tigrayan rebellion. Both sides accused each other of atrocities against civilians amid reports of 50,000 refugees fleeing the area and 1.3 million people needing emergency assistance.[4]

In the new atmosphere of war and conflict, Abiy abandoned his political liberalism. Journalists and opposition politicians were arrested and there were reports of the state use of torture. After just three years in power, Abiy's reputation as a standard-bearer for liberal values was now severely tarnished. This repeated a global pattern in the Age of the Strongman. But it is also a particularly familiar story in Africa, where many leaders hailed as liberation heroes in the aftermath of decolonization later turned into authoritarian despots.

Well before the rise of Putin, Xi, Modi and Trump, many African countries had had bitter experiences of strongman rule. The year before seeing Abiy speak in Davos, I had witnessed the economic effects of authoritarianism gone wrong in Zimbabwe. Crossing the border into a country that is firmly under the thumb of a strongman leader can be simultaneously tense and tedious. So it had proved at the Zimbabwe–Botswana frontier in February 2018. As a border guard disappeared with my passport, I was left with plenty of time to study the large portrait on the wall of Zimbabwe's new president, Emmerson Mnangagwa. He had been sworn into office just a couple of months earlier, as the successor to Robert Mugabe, who had ruled the country since independence in 1980.

At the time, there were still those who hoped that Mnangagwa would rescue Zimbabwe from the sorry political and economic situation bequeathed by Mugabe. But Mnangagwa's nickname, "the crocodile" – bestowed on him during his period as Mugabe's intelligence chief and defense minister – suggested those hopes might be in vain. (As a Russian dissident once put it to me, discussing former members of the Soviet Communist Party who had repackaged themselves as democrats: "Somebody cannot be a bastard all their life, and then suddenly not a bastard.")

Eventually the border guard reappeared and handed back my passport with a slightly sardonic smile. Clambering into my car, I asked the driver to take me to a bank, so that I could draw out some cash. He laughed and replied: "I can take you to the bank, but there won't be any money there." After a period of hyperinflation under Mugabe, the Zimbabwean dollar had been withdrawn from use. Instead Zimbabweans were using foreign currencies – mainly US dollars and South African rand – and there was a severe money shortage. Even in Victoria Falls, a major tourist destination, the local bank was shuttered, with a crowd of despondent-looking people sitting nearby hoping that some cash might eventually arrive. The only local currency available was vast-denomination notes for figures like a billion Zimbabwe dollars. Relics of the Mugabe era of hyperinflation, they were now worthless curios and sold to tourists for a US dollar each by street hawkers.

The whole scene was a reminder of the perils of strongman rule. When Mugabe had come to power in 1980, he was a liberation hero – a former guerrilla fighter, who had helped to negotiate an end to white-minority rule in Rhodesia. An intelligent and articulate man, Mugabe seemed the right kind of leader to guide his country to a more prosperous, democratic and equal future. Zimbabwe itself, with a well-educated population and a flourishing agricultural sector, seemed well placed to prosper in this new era. But the reality proved sadly different. Within a few years of coming to power, Mugabe had launched a vicious campaign against his political opponents and their supporters. A North Korean–trained army unit – the notorious "Fifth

Brigade" – was unleashed on the region of Matabeleland, and was responsible for massacres and human-rights abuses. In the decades that followed, Mugabe's rule became synonymous with despotism, corruption and economic destruction.

Mnangagwa, Mugabe's former aide, failed to break this sorry pattern. Initially, there were cautious hopes that he might give his country a fresh start. In April 2018, the new Zimbabwean leader was welcomed to the Commonwealth Heads of Government meeting in London, where he had a cordial meeting with Boris Johnson, who was then the UK foreign secretary. But only a few months later, Zimbabwean security forces were gunning down protesters in the capital, Harare. After further bloody repression in 2019, the UK imposed sanctions on members of the Zimbabwean leader's inner circle.[5]

The liberation hero who turns into a despotic strongman ruler is an all-too-familiar figure in the history of post-colonial Africa. Others who fit the bill included Mobutu Sese Seko of the Democratic Republic of Congo, Felix Houphouët-Boigny of the Ivory Coast, Hastings Banda of Malawi and Isaias Afwerki of Eritrea.[6] But not all African liberation heroes have followed the dismal pattern. In South Africa, Nelson Mandela's release from prison, his extraordinary magnanimity towards his former oppressors and his rise to the presidency of post-apartheid South Africa broke the stereotype of the liberation leader who somehow never gave up power and turned into a despot. Unlike Mugabe or Mobutu, Mandela retired from office peacefully, stepping aside in 1999 for his former colleague from the African National Congress, Thabo Mbeki. Post-apartheid South Africa now became a magnet for desperate Zimbabweans fleeing Mugabe.

Yet even in South Africa things took a turn for the worse. The presidency of Jacob Zuma from 2009 to 2018 was associated with massive corruption, economic stagnation and talk of "state capture," even state failure. Zuma's vast compound near the eastern town of Nkandla built with state funds featured an amphitheater, swimming pool, livestock pens and a reception center.[7] When this palatial expansion to his homestead was uncovered, the pool was defended as a "fire pool" from which emergency services would draw water. All of this was revealed, discussed and savagely parodied in the South African press and by the political opposition. But South Africa's free press and state institutions were too weak to stop the looting of state coffers until Zuma was finally forced out of office in 2018.

The damage he left behind was considerable, with leading companies such as Eskom, the state electricity company, effectively bankrupt. When I interviewed Cyril Ramaphosa, Zuma's successor, at a conference in London in 2019, the new president suggested that the corruption of the Zuma years could have cost South Africa the equivalent of 10 percent of ifs GDP. "It was much bigger than people could have imagined," he lamented; the cost "runs way beyond 500 billion rand" – $34 billion.[8]

In 2021, Zuma was finally brought to justice and sentenced to fifteen months in prison for contempt of court, for refusing to attend a judicial inquiry into corruption during his period in office. It was proof that the rule of law still worked in South Africa and that the country's institutions were capable of fighting back against strongman rule. But South Africa paid a heavy price. Encouraged by Zuma's political allies, rioters and looters took to the streets. With the country suffering from 32 percent unemployment, many people needed little encouragement to join in ransacking and theft. Over three hundred people were killed in a week of wild disorder.

The South African riots were a reminder of the difficulties of sustaining democracy in countries suffering from deep poverty and inequality. But despite the failures of elected leaders such as Mugabe and Zuma, Africans in general prize democracy. In a poll conducted in 2019 across thirty-four countries by research network Afrobarometer, over two-thirds of those interviewed selected it as the best form of government. As in the West, though, confidence in democracy has been eroding. Around half of those polled in the Afrobarometer survey said they were "dissatisfied" with democracy, up from a quarter twenty years earlier.[9]

The fact that liberation heroes could lead their countries into despotism and that democratically elected presidents have looted public finances has led some Africans and outside observers to take another look at the strongman model. In some countries, strongman leaders have been associated with the restoration of peace and with rapid economic development. The two examples most often cited are Paul Kagame of Rwanda and Meles Zenawi, Ethiopia's leader from 1995 until his death in 2012, six years before Abiy Ahmed came to power.

Kagame is perhaps Africa's best-known autocrat. Although he has now led his nation as president or de facto leader for nearing three decades, he has developed a large group of foreign admirers. For Bill Clinton, he numbers among "the greatest leaders of our time." Tony Blair has named him a "visionary." Former UN Secretary General Bank Ki-moon has pointed to Rwanda as a model for other African nations to emulate.[10]

At first glance, it is hard to deny the scale of Kagame's achievements. Growth under his leadership has averaged around 8 percent per year. Kagame's critics have suggested that the growth figures have been artificially boosted. But other, more easily verified, development indicators have also risen. Life expectancy is about sixty-nine, the same as sub-Saharan Africa's greatest success story, Botswana. International business people rate Rwanda as an efficient place to work and invest.[11]

Kagame's fans are especially impressed by the sense of order that pervades the nation, given its horrendous history of genocide. In 1994 up to one million Tutsis and Hutu moderates were hacked to death by extremist members of the ethnic Hutu majority. Kagame, who formally became president in 2000, made healing Rwanda's ethnic rifts the central theme of his leadership. His regime, though dominated by Tutsis, publicly frowns on ethnic distinctions, and Rwanda's national anthem now declares that "our common culture identifies us, our single language unifies us." Kagame has remarked that his own DNA reveals he has Hutu blood.[12]

In Kagame's Rwanda, villages are decorated with carefully planted flower beds, and inhabitants are told to wear shoes. Before Covid-19, tourism was flourishing. Kagame has also avoided some of the more obvious self-indulgences of strongman rule. He discourages an overt cult of personality, and as a military man turned technocrat, he has an international reputation for taking governance very seriously.

These advances, however, have come at a cost in political freedom. Kagame's grip over Rwanda is total: he claimed 98.7 percent of the vote in 2017, and the constitution has been amended to allow him to stay in power until 2034. Even more sinister is the fact that dissidents and opposition figures have often wound up dead in odd circumstances, such as Rwanda's former spymaster Patrick Karegeya, who was found drugged and strangled in a South African hotel room in 2013. When asked about Karegeya's demise, Kagame denied responsibility but declared, "I actually wish Rwanda did it. I really wish it."[13] A recent hostile biography of the president blames him squarely for the murder of Karegeya, and argues that the Rwandan leader is also linked to a string of killings of his regime's critics, both at home and abroad.[14]

Human Rights Watch reported that exiled Rwandan journalist Charles Ingabire was murdered following numerous threats and a failed first attack.[15] Kagame's critics have been pursued through the courts as well. In September 2020, the internationally famed business-man Paul Rusesabagina, who saved over a thousand Rwandans during the genocide – a story told in the film *Hotel Rwanda* – was arrested and charged with being "the founder, leader, sponsor and member of vio-lent, armed, extremist terror outfits . . . operating out of various places in the region and abroad."[16]

For many years, Kagame's Western backers have been prepared to largely overlook all this. Bill Clinton, still haunted by his administra-tion's lack of action during the Rwandan genocide, has said: "I suppose I do make more allowances for a government that produces as much progress as this one." Indeed, the US has often protected Kagame, for example by pushing for the replacement of a prosecutor for the Inter-national Criminal Tribunal for Rwanda who had strayed too close to implicating Kagame in brutal Tutsi reprisals against Hutu refugees.[17] Samantha Power, appointed as head of USAID by the Biden adminis-tration, is also a noted admirer of Kagame.

The Rwandan leader is not the only example of "developmental authoritarianism," supported by the West. A similar dynamic played out in Ethiopia before the Abiy Ahmed period. From 1995 to 2012, the East African nation was under the tight control of Prime Minis-ter Meles Zenawi. His repressive instincts were also often excused because of his record of economic development and his techno-cratic approach to government: he gave erudite interviews to the Western press on everything from telecoms privatization to the pro-cessing of commodities. No one could doubt that Zenawi had vision when he outlined Ethiopia's future, planning to nurture its domestic industries much as the "Asian Tigers" of South Korea and Taiwan had done.[18]

As in Rwanda, Ethiopia's growth figures were impressive. From 2002 to 2012, GDP grew at over 10 percent, double the average rate of other sub-Saharan nations. Under Zenawi, extreme poverty fell by 15 percent.

Fifteen thousand village health clinics were built and Ethiopia's rudimentary road system saw visible improvement. Life expectancy was said to have increased by an astonishing twenty-five years, from forty to around sixty-five.[19]

Zenawi's ability to talk policy in a way that enchanted Western onlookers was only one part of his appeal. In stabilizing Ethiopia and in pursuing policies that were friendly to the US, Zenawi also served the West's larger strategic purposes. On the other hand, Ethiopia's size, economic growth and strategic position in the Horn of Africa has also attracted considerable Chinese investment and diplomatic interest. China funded the construction of a new headquarters for the African Union that opened in Addis Ababa, the Ethiopian capital, in 2012. But Zenawi also kept onside with Washington, allowing the US to station drones in Ethiopia and cooperating in joint anti-terrorism exercises in Somalia.

Much like Kagame, Zenawi presented himself as the acceptable face of strongman rule. President Obama's national security adviser, Susan Rice, spoke on his death in 2012 of his "world-class mind," declaring, "He wasn't just brilliant. He wasn't just a relentless negotiator and a formidable debater. He wasn't just a thirsty consumer of knowledge. He was uncommonly wise."[20]

But as in Rwanda, the trade-off was repression. In the 2010 elections, two years before his death, Zenawi claimed an absurd vote share of 99.6 percent. After the 2005 elections, around two hundred protesters were shot by security forces. Teachers' unions and human-rights organizations were dissolved, and opposition parties outlawed. Zenawi also ensured the continued political dominance of Tigrayans, who represent around 6 percent of the population. Though relying on a sort of ethnic federalism to keep Ethiopia together, there was no question as to which group was on top.[21] Perhaps it was an awareness of the uncomfortable compromises involved in the West's embrace of Zenawi that partially accounted for the ecstatic reception of the more outwardly liberal Abiy Ahmed.

If even in the wealthy and powerful United States, identity-based politics has become a powerful enough force to threaten the country's long-established democratic structures, it is perhaps not surprising that African countries such as Ethiopia, Rwanda and Zimbabwe – all of which have powerful ethnic divisions that have caused wars – should struggle to establish pluralist democracies. Go to Beijing and you are likely to be told that only naive Americans and Europeans believe that liberal democracy is the appropriate system for Africa, where poverty remains endemic and state structures weak. The bleak view in China is that most African countries will need some sort of strongman to hold their nations together. They simply have to hope that they get a Kagame or a Zenawi rather than a Mugabe or a Zuma.

By most measures, democracy across the continent has been in gentle decline over the past decade – a development that Nic Cheeseman of the University of Birmingham describes as "democratic difficulties rather than democratic collapse."[22] In the 1990s, after the end of the Cold War, many African nations and leaders moved towards democracy and the number of countries counted as democracies rose. But as China's influence increases, the ideological winds blowing into the continent are coming from a different direction. In 2007, the value of Chinese trade with Africa stood at around $148 billion. The US managed $39 billion. For obvious reasons, Beijing has no interest in making aid or trade conditional on democratic governance, so there is less pressure for political reform. At certain points, China has even actively protected its autocratic friends, for example by pressuring the International Criminal Court to refrain from prosecuting Omar al-Bashir of Sudan.[23]

China does more than just enable dictators – it also gives them tools to tighten their grip on power. For years, the Chinese Communist Party has invited African politicians to its own training programs. While some of the curriculum taught appears innocuous, such as Chinese traditional culture and economic development strategies, much of it is more insidious. Participants are taught to produce effective propaganda, manage opposition and monitor dissent. Senior ANC officials from South Africa, including fifty-six from its National Executive Committee, took part in these programs between 2008 and 2012. Ethiopian administrators have sent delegations since 1994.[24]

Even newer nations such as South Sudan have been drawn into China's orbit, which has bestowed thousands of scholarships on its students. The repercussions for political culture could be distinctly illiberal. "In 10 years' time, one of [these students] will be the leader of South Sudan," remarked Samson Wasara, the vice chancellor of South Sudan's University of Bahr el Ghazal. "When you go to China they will not be talking about democracy."[25]

China has also helped with technology. In 2014, the Chinese telecoms company ZTE provided Ethiopia with the infrastructure to tap into its citizens' communications. In Tanzania, Deputy Minister for Transport and Communications Edwin Ngonyani declared in 2007 at an event cohosted by the Cyberspace Administration of China that "Our Chinese friends have managed to block such media [internet sites such as Google] in their country and replaced them with their home-grown sites that are safe, constructive and popular. We aren't there yet, but while we are still using these platforms we should guard against their misuse."

Nowhere has China's export of totalitarian tech been more evident than in Zimbabwe. In 2018, it adopted plans to install facial recognition systems in its cities and public transport hubs with the help of Guangzhou tech company CloudWalk. While ostensibly a crime-fighting initiative, activists are concerned. Zimbabwean journalist Garikai Dzoma predicts that "African autocrats . . . will no doubt use it to enhance their political positions by hounding opponents." Zimbabwe's plans may in turn strengthen China's already extraordinary surveillance capacities – CloudWalk's system will allow China to expand its own facial recognition database by integrating faces with non-Han features.[26]

China's willingness to provide financial support for Zimbabwe makes it much easier for Mnangagwa to resist Western pressure for political liberalization. During his period in office, work began on a new six-story parliament building in Harare, with China footing the $140 million bill.[27] The payoff of such spending for Beijing became apparent when Zimbabwe, along with fifteen other African countries, signed off on a letter to the UN Human Rights Council lauding Beijing's "remarkable achievements in the field of human rights" and rebranding its internment camps for Uighurs as "vocational education and training centers."[28]

Other authoritarian nations are also paving the way for African strongmen. While countries like the US often turn a blind eye to the misdeeds of allies, Russia dispenses with any pretence of concern. When Guinea's President Alpha Conde declared he would seek an unconstitutional third term, the country's Russian ambassador remarked that "Constitutions aren't dogma, the Bible, or the Koran. Constitutions adapt to reality, it's not realities that adapt to constitutions."[29] Russia, much like China, has also been directly involved in propping up dictatorships. In the Central African Republic, a Russian citizen was even appointed to the position of national security adviser.

In the Trump era, America's own support for democracy in Africa dropped away markedly. When the Democratic Republic of Congo held elections in January 2019, the US did nothing to condemn the massive fraud which pushed Felix Tshisekedi to the presidency. Instead, it fully endorsed the results. Mvemba Phezo Dizolele, from the Center for Strategic and International Studies, has characterized the move as a dispiriting reversal: "The U.S. did a lot to get Congo where it got in terms of elections, but then the U.S. at the last minute washed its hands of it."[30]

The Biden administration signaled early on that it intended to return to a more traditional American approach. Shortly after President Biden was sworn into office, Jake Sullivan, the new national security adviser, expressed his unease about the conflict unleashed by Abiy Ahmed, warning against the "risk of violence against civilians, including potential war crimes, in the fighting around Mekelle in Ethiopia."[31] Abiy was undeterred by American criticism or by the threat of famine in Tigray and continued to prosecute his war. In July 2021, he won a landslide victory in parliamentary elections that the US described as "significantly flawed." But with China still easily the largest investor in Ethiopia, criticism from Washington is relatively easily brushed off.

It was not just the Americans or the Chinese who had reason to be following events in Ethiopia with deep interest. It is Europe that is likely to be most directly affected by the success or failure of African governments. That is because of the extraordinary population boom taking place on the Africa continent. Projections by the United Nations and other organizations suggest that the population of Africa is likely to double between 2020 and 2050, as the continent adds an extra 1.2 billion people.[32]

The combination of poverty, climate change and bad government – plus proximity – means that many young Africans may head to Europe in the hope of a better life. Roughly half a million Africans applied for asylum there in the three years from 2015 to 2017. Many of them were fleeing despotic countries such as Ethiopia's neighbor Eritrea, where Isaias Afwerki had instituted a policy of compulsory, open-ended military service for young men.

These migration pressures on Europe are likely to increase in the coming decades. And as we have seen, the fear of the cultural and economic impact of migration is perhaps the most powerful force fueling populist, strongman nationalism on the European continent. Finding convincing answers to those fears may be the most urgent dilemma facing European liberals in the coming years.

12 Merkel, Macron and Europe's struggle against the strongmen (2020)

Throughout the Age of the Strongman, liberal internationalists have looked for champions of democracy around the world: political leaders who can hold back the tide of populist nationalism. Various figures have been held up as advocates of liberal values, including Jacinda Ardern of New Zealand and Justin Trudeau of Canada. During the Trump years, attention focused in particular on the leaders of the European Union's two most powerful nations – Angela Merkel of Germany and Emmanuel Macron of France.

After the twin shocks of Brexit and the US presidential election in 2016, the political establishment in France looked very vulnerable. François Hollande, the incumbent president, was so unpopular that he did not even attempt to run for re-election in 2017. In the eighteen months before the vote, France was hit by the worst terror attacks in its history. Simultaneous assaults by Islamists in Paris in November 2015 killed 131 people. The following summer, a further eighty-six people were murdered by a truck that deliberately ploughed into crowds celebrating Bastille Day in Nice. The conditions seemed ripe for a far-right victory.

With Hollande standing down, the presidential election of 2017 was contested by two insurgent candidates. The far-right National Front was represented by Marine Le Pen. Running against her in the second and final round of voting was Emmanuel Macron, the young standard-bearer of a new party, En Marche.

I had met Macron at a breakfast at the French Embassy in London in

2015, when he was France's economy minister – an economic liberal in the soft-left government of Hollande. It was clear that the diplomats hosting the event adored Macron. He was from their world: pro-EU and pro-market, a former banker, highly educated and capable of speaking at length on abstruse subjects (he had written his student thesis on Hegel and Machiavelli). Over coffee and croissants, switching easily between French and English, he outlined his plans for freeing up the French economy, promising a cut in the wealth tax and breaks for entrepreneurs. The overall impression made by the young minister was that he was capable, charismatic and perhaps a little cocky.

During the election campaign, Macron's youth – he was thirty-nine at the time of the presidential vote – and the fact that he headed a new party allowed him to channel some of the anti-establishment rage that had driven both Brexit and the election of Trump. Macron presented himself as the candidate of radical change. His book, published a year before the election, was called *Revolution*. But in most respects Macron was a product of the traditional French elite par excellence, educated at the country's most traditional and exclusive institutions and a reliable standard-bearer of the establishment's worldview. Nonetheless, when Macron declared his candidacy, it looked like a long shot. But he got lucky. François Fillon, the leading candidate on the French right and the favorite for the presidency at the beginning of 2017, was unexpectedly hit by a corruption and expenses scandal. With Fillon eliminated in the first round, Macron became the candidate of all those who opposed the far right.

The stakes in the French election were truly global. Marine Le Pen was threatening to pull France out of the European single currency and flirting with leaving the EU itself – by promising a British-style referendum on Frexit. That could well have spelled the end of the European Union. The EU could survive Brexit, but Frexit would be another matter. French politicians and thinkers had designed the original European Coal and Steel Community, the forerunner to the EU, in the 1950s. France had pushed hard for the creation of the euro in the 1980s, and the country's withdrawal might cause the currency to collapse. If Le Pen won, the European project would be in grave danger. That would suit both Vladimir Putin and Donald Trump just fine, and many Brexiters in the UK would also feel vindicated.

In the months before the election, many of my French friends were palpably nervous. Some were even discussing emigration in the event that the far-right won the presidency. But Le Pen put in a disastrous debate performance (she later claimed to have been suffering from a splitting headache), and after that Macron cruised fairly easily to victory. In fact, his position as the anti-extremist candidate was always a strong basis for victory. As in Germany – and unlike the US – the French far right still struggles with a stigma dating back to the Second World War. In May 2017, Macron won comfortably, with 66.1 percent in the second round of voting.

The political and social themes that Macron championed in his 2017 campaign positioned him as the social and ideological antithesis of strongman politics. Leaders like Putin, Xi, Trump, Modi, Bolsonaro and Erdoğan are all nationalists; Macron, by contrast, is a defiant "globalist." His view, as he told his biographer Sophie Pedder, is that "The new political split is between those who are afraid of globalisation, and those who see globalisation as an opportunity, or at least as a framework for policy that tries to offer progress for all."[1] The core voters for Macron's En Marche were educated, middle-class liberals – the kind of people whose American and British counterparts had voted for Hillary Clinton or Remain. The white, working-class voters from "left-behind" areas in France, whose British and American equivalents had voted Trump or Leave, were the bedrock of support for Marine Le Pen. Later they formed the basis for the *gilets jaunes* street protests, which rocked France in 2018 and 2019 and were provoked by Macron's effort to raise fuel taxes.

For Macron, increasing fuel tax was an environmental imperative. While the Western strongmen, such as Trump and Bolsonaro, have tended to scoff at climate change and to be suspicious of experts, Macron is a technocrat who has made his sponsorship of the Paris climate accords central to his politics. Rejecting the nostalgic nationalism of many of the new strongmen, Macron's politics is determinedly futurist in tone. As he self-confidently proclaimed: "What our country needs is to rediscover a taste for the future, rather than a morbid fascination with an uncertain past."[2]

If Macron's politics and outlook defied the strongman model, that was even more true of the French president's key political partner in Europe, the German chancellor Angela Merkel. Her deliberative, low-key style was a stark contrast to the macho posturing of leaders like

Putin, Trump, Bolsonaro and Erdoğan and helped to earn Merkel the nickname of *Mutti* (Mummy).

While the US president reveled in the gaudy surroundings of his branded clubs and towers, Merkel lived modestly with her husband in a third-floor apartment in central Berlin. One summer's day in 2020, out of curiosity, I walked over to her street, which overlooked the Spree River towards Berlin's Museum Island. The only visible sign that I was standing outside the chancellor's residence was a police car and a small guard post in front of the handsome apartment building.

In the aftermath of Trump's victory in 2016, Merkel was hailed in some quarters as the true leader of the free world.[3] Her close aides insisted that the accolade embarrassed her, but the German leader evidently chose to become the spokesperson for traditional liberal values. When offering Donald Trump a partnership, she pointedly made it clear that this was to be based on "freedom, respect for the law and the dignity of man, independent of origin."

Merkel had grown up in East Germany, the daughter of a Lutheran pastor. She was a star pupil, who won prizes for her mastery of the Russian language – a skill that would later come in handy when speaking to Vladimir Putin (although the Russian president also speaks German, a legacy of his period as a spy in East Germany). Born in 1954, she was thirty-five by the time the Berlin Wall fell. That night in November 1989, rather than rushing to the Brandenburg Gate like many Berliners, Merkel went to the sauna and then for a beer with a friend.[4] In the East, Merkel had pursued a successful career as a scientist, receiving a doctorate in quantum chemistry in 1986. She had also kept well clear of East German politics. It was only after the fall of communism that she entered politics as a protégé of Helmut Kohl, the chancellor who had brought about German unification. After rising through the ranks of the Christian Democratic Union, she became chancellor herself in 2005 – the first Easterner and the first woman to lead the country.

By 2015, when the refugee crisis struck Europe, Merkel was already Europe's most important political figure. She had shaped and controlled the EU's response to the euro crisis and as a result had been vilified in Southern Europe as the face of uncaring German conservatism. But nobody doubted her grasp of the issues. Tim Geithner, the US treasury secretary, remarked after the global financial crisis that Merkel was the only world leader he had dealt with who was "numerate."[5]

It was the refugee crisis, and the election of Trump a year later, that turned Merkel into something of an icon for beleaguered Western liberals. Her choice not to close Germany's borders to the millions of refugees bottled up in Eastern Europe was a bold move for a chancellor famed for her wait-and-see caution. At a crucial moment, Merkel decided to suspend Germany's application of the Dublin convention, which stated that refugees had to apply for asylum in the first safe country they reached. On the chancellor's say-so, Syrians and others could leave Hungary and enter Germany. It was a decision deeply rooted in German history and in Merkel's own personal story as a woman who had grown up behind the Berlin Wall. While Trump rode to power on the slogan "Build the Wall," Merkel became famous for a rather different three-word phrase: *"Wir schaffen das"* ("We can do this") – her response to the challenge of assimilating more than a million mainly Muslim refugees into German society.

While her actions made her a heroine to liberals, she became a villain in the eyes of many right-wing populists. To them, the German chancellor was the epitome of lofty "globalism," willing to disrupt the stability and future of her own country so as to look good in the eyes of the liberal intelligentsia. After the terrorist attacks in France in 2015 and 2016, the populist right in the US and Europe became even more insistent in arguing that Merkel had been criminally naive to allow a huge influx of Muslims, mainly from war-torn Syria, to enter Europe.

Merkel's ideological foes hoped the German chancellor would pay a heavy political price for her stance on refugees. In the September 2017 federal elections in Germany, the atmosphere at Merkel's election rallies was often ugly. One of her aides told me sorrowfully that the barracking of the chancellor was so loud and aggressive, particularly in eastern Germany, that she often could not make herself heard above the abuse. The election result was a serious blow to the chancellor. The CDU's share of the vote fell by eight points to 33 percent. To form a government, Merkel had to once again go into coalition with the center-left Social Democrats (SPD), who themselves had suffered their worst result since the Second World War.

The center ground in German politics was shrinking. The largest opposition party in the German parliament was now the far-right

Alternative for Germany (AfD), described by Sigmar Gabriel, Germany's foreign minister, as little more than neo-Nazis. The actual picture was more nuanced, although still troubling. The party had been founded in 2013, by conservative economists angry about Germany's role in bailing out Greece during the euro crisis. But, particularly after the refugee crisis, it had become a more conventional anti-immigration and xenophobic party. A radical wing within the AfD was also flirting with neo-Nazi themes. One prominent figure, Björn Höcke, decried the Holocaust memorial in Berlin as a "monument of shame" and demanded a re-evaluation of Germany's attitude to its past. Höcke was also accused of making veiled references to speeches by Hitler and Goebbels in his own orations.[6] Despite this, in parts of the country, especially former East Germany, the party was getting 25 percent of the vote.

For all the outward calm in Berlin, both the domestic and the international situation became increasingly threatening to the German establishment. The German security services placed the AfD under surveillance, as a potential threat to democracy. But as one senior government figure put it to me: "When the far right is at 5 percent we can ask the police to keep an eye on them. When they are at 25 percent in eastern Germany, they are the police."

During the twentieth century, no city felt the deadly allure and disastrous consequences of strongman leadership more than Berlin. When Hitler finally committed suicide in his bunker, his capital city lay in ruins around him. For the current German elite, therefore, nationalism in any form remains highly suspect. As Thomas Bagger, a leading German intellectual and the diplomatic adviser to the country's president, Frank-Walter Steinmeier, put it to me: "France and Britain can always fall back on the nation-state. That is much harder for Germany."

As Bagger saw it, after 1989 Germany had embraced a version of Francis Fukuyama's "end of history" thesis, with its comforting belief in the triumph of liberal democracy and internationalism. After the fall of the wall, Bagger argued, "We felt that we were on the right side of history for once, and it felt pretty good." A nationalist strongman such as Vladimir Putin was treated with a degree of condescension. Merkel saw him as a figure from the nineteenth century, struggling to cope with the modern world. Firm in the belief that they understood the direction of history and understood the formula for success in the twenty-first century, Germany's leaders felt that, in Bagger's phrase, politics was now little more than the "administration of the inevitable."[7]

From 2014 to 2017, a series of shocks forced Merkel and the German establishment to abandon this complacency. The conflict in Ukraine and the Putin government's annexation of Crimea in 2014 signaled the return of Russia as a military threat. The Germans did not have the visceral fear of Russia felt in Poland or the Baltic states, but nor could they feel detached from the situation in Ukraine, like the Italians or the French – Berlin, after all, had been laid waste by Russian troops in 1945.

Shock followed shock: after Crimea in 2014, the following year saw the peak of the refugee crisis, and 2016 was the year of Brexit and Trump. The future of the EU, the bedrock of German foreign policy, was thrown into question. So was the support of the US, the traditional guarantor of German security. While previous American presidents from Kennedy to Reagan to Obama had given high-profile speeches in Berlin, Trump chose to make his first major address in Europe in Poland. His antagonism towards Merkel was both ideological and personal. As one of Trump's senior aides told me: "I've been in the room together with the two of them and it's ugly. She's like the professor and he's the kid who hasn't done his homework."

With Trump in the White House and Britain heading out of the EU, the election of Macron as president of France in 2017 was greeted with delight and relief in Berlin. The new French president made a powerful and symbolic gesture on the night of his victory, choosing to take to the stage to the sound of "Ode to Joy," the anthem of the European Union, rather than "La Marseillaise," the French anthem. It was a clear rejection of the resurgent forces of nationalism around the world.

Macron's victory was a blessing for Merkel – but it was also a challenge. While the new French president's warm embrace of the EU was profoundly welcome to Germany, his specific proposals were regarded with suspicion by the Merkel government. Macron was enthusiastic about the issuance of common European debt and the creation of a European finance ministry, both of which were widely regarded in Berlin as little more than sophisticated attempts to get the thrifty Germans to subsidize the spendthrift French.* Macron's passion for "European sovereignty" and his suggestion that NATO was increasingly "brain-dead" were also greeted with irritation by the German government,[8] which continued to view the alliance as fundamental to Western security. Visiting Berlin towards the end of 2019, I found German officials fuming about the French president's tendency to shoot from the hip. One even suggested that Macron was turning into a more intellectual version of Trump, making policy on the hoof, in ways that left his officials floundering to catch up and to explain their boss's latest pronouncements.

It took Covid-19 to warm up the sometimes chilly relationship between Merkel and Macron. In its first stages, the coronavirus hit Southern Europe hardest, in particular Italy and Spain. The Northern Europeans' initial reluctance to offer generous financial assistance to the South threatened to create another crisis of solidarity within the EU. Matteo Salvini, Italy's populist standard-bearer, fumed that once again selfish Germans were leaving Italians to suffer alone. Some predicted that Covid-19 could even blow up the EU.

Faced with such threats to the European project, Merkel acted. As in the refugee crisis of 2015, the German chancellor abandoned her habitual caution and made a bold gesture. In March 2020, Merkel endorsed the idea that the EU should – as Macron had long pleaded – issue common debt on the financial markets to fund joint projects. It was sold as a one-off project to fund Covid relief. But the details mattered less than the significance of the gesture. In Berlin, Paris and Brussels, it was generally agreed that a Rubicon had been crossed: the common currency was now going to be backed by commonly issued debt. In the long run, Macron envisioned the development of a deep EU bond market that could rival the US Treasury market as a safe asset for the world's investors. That in turn could allow the euro eventually to create an alternative to the dollar as the world's major reserve currency. Since the US dollar is the source of so much of America's global power, the internationalization of the euro would be a major

---

* This was a common suspicion in Northern Europe. In 2018 I moderated a discussion between Mark Rutte, the Dutch prime minister, and Bruno Le Maire, Macron's economy minister, in which the Dutchman repeatedly pointed out that France had not run a balanced budget since the 1970s.

step on the road to Macron's goal of *"Europe puissance"* – Europe as a world power.

When Merkel took this potentially momentous decision in 2020, she was nearing the end of her political career. She had been in office since 2005, but unlike the world's strongman leaders, she did not aspire to stay in office forever, and instead announced that she would step down as chancellor in 2021. But she was leaving at a time of her choosing and the announcement was made at a moment when her ratings were once again at near-record highs. By forging an agreement with Turkey, Merkel had managed to stem the flow of refugees. It was a pragmatic, slightly dirty deal that arguably replicated some of the controls on freedom of movement demanded by the likes of Orbán without fully acknowledging it. Nonetheless, the sense of crisis in Germany had diminished and the far right had begun to squabble among itself. The defeat of Donald Trump in November 2020 also meant that Merkel had outlasted her adversary in Washington.

If global politics followed the arc of a simple morality tale, a triumphant Merkel would have retired with the future of liberal democracy secure in Europe and strongman politics in retreat around the world. But reality is inevitably more complicated. Merkel and other European leaders are well aware that the Biden presidency could simply be an interlude in the US – before the return of Donald Trump, or a similar figure, in the 2024 presidential election. Within the EU itself, Viktor Orbán and Jaroslaw Kaczynski have established illiberal, populist governments in Hungary and Poland that have threatened some of the basic elements of a democratic state, such as the independence of the courts and the media.

In some ways, Macron had been a successful French president. His demand for much deeper EU integration was eventually met with a positive response in Berlin. And although his domestic political opponents accused him of being remote and haughty, Macron's poll ratings were consistently stronger than those of François Hollande.

The French president has also avoided major political and personal scandals at home. But he was unsurprisingly unable to meet the hopes of dynamic change and renewal that he had excited in 2017 – or to change France's profound sense of pessimism. The *gilets jaunes* protests and continuing acts of domestic terrorism – including the beheading of Samuel Paty, a teacher, by Islamists in 2020 – fed the domestic sense of insecurity. A Harris poll taken in April 2021 showed that 84 percent of French people agreed that "violence in France is getting worse, day by day," 73 percent agreed that French society was collapsing and 45 percent claimed to believe there would soon be a civil war.[9]

Macron and his aides were well aware that many of the social and economic conditions that have fueled the rise of the populist right elsewhere in the West are also deeply embedded in France. In a moment of frankness, the French president admitted to a BBC interviewer that had France held a referendum on leaving the EU, like Britain, it too would "probably" have voted to leave.[10] The country suffers from high unemployment and deindustrialization. Decades of immigration have changed its demographic makeup and France now has the highest Muslim population of any EU country. The conspiracy theory that a globalist elite is planning to flood the West with non-white immigrants is popular in France. Renaud Camus's *Le Grand Remplacement*, the French book detailing the alleged plot, has become a foundational text for white nationalists across the West. Antidemocratic sentiment is also not far from the surface in France. In 2021, a letter from a group of retired generals that flirted with the idea of a military coup was praised by Le Pen – with polls suggesting 49 percent of people agreed that the army needed to intervene to guarantee law and order in France.

In response to the persistent challenge from the far right, Macron moved to the right himself, positioning himself as France's champion in a war against radical Islam. In foreign policy, Macron's France found itself clashing increasingly with Erdoğan's Turkey, particularly over Libya and the eastern Mediterranean. The French president, normally outspoken in his defense of human rights, even awarded France's highest award, the Légion d'honneur, to Abdel Fattah al-Sisi, the strongman leader of Egypt, who had clashed repeatedly with Erdoğan but also brutally repressed the Muslim Brotherhood.

At home, Macron's administration brought forward new laws to combat Islamist "separatism" and to protect secular and republican values. The proposals included bans on the issuance of "virginity certificates" for women and on separate sessions for men and women at public swimming pools. On issues of security and social values, some of Macron's ministers adopted a rhetoric that was hard to distinguish from that of the far right. Gerald Darmanin, the hard-line interior minister, described Islamism as a "Trojan horse containing a fragmentation bomb that is targeting our society."[11] As Macron moved to the right, ahead of the 2022 presidential election, so Le Pen moved to the left by softening policies that had frightened off some voters in 2017, such as her opposition to the euro and her hints about Frexit.

Nonetheless, the differences between Le Pen and Macron remained stark. While condemning Islamism, Macron refused to cross the line into Orbán-like hostility towards migration and refugees. He also remained fervently committed to the idea of strengthening the EU and reforming, rather than reversing, globalization.

The ideological cleavage between Le Pen and Macron is typical of the wider international politics in the Age of the Strongman. As Le Pen herself put it, "We no longer have a left-right split, but one between nationalism and globalism. In this confrontation we have every chance of coming to power at a time across the world when the ideas we promote – control of immigration, economic patriotism, rational and reasonable protectionism – are increasingly powerful."[12] Le Pen identifies with an international trend that has produced strongman nationalist leaders all over the world. She has targeted many of the same easily caricatured enemies already identified by the likes of Donald Trump: illegal migrants, snobbish elites, "fake news" media and rootless globalists.

The global battle of ideas is waged not just by politicians but also by intellectuals, philanthropists and the institutions they finance. For many strongman leaders, one adversary in particular epitomizes the globalist forces that they claim to be battling against: the billionaire financier and philanthropist George Soros. Le Pen has claimed that Soros is the enemy of France, demanding, "We must lead a reconquest of the freedom of our country against this billionaire . . . He commits crimes against nation-states."[13] The prominent position of George Soros in the demonology of nationalist populists says a lot about the ideological battles of the Age of the Strongman – arguments that will continue to frame politics in France, Europe and the wider world over the coming decade.

13 George Soros, Steve Bannon and the battle of ideas

Strongman leaders require enemies. And many of the world's nationalist strongmen have chosen to denounce the same bogeyman. As a billionaire Jewish philanthropist, with pronounced liberal views, George Soros has been turned into the epitome of "globalism." Like Emmanuel Goldstein in Orwell's *Nineteen Eighty-Four*, he is denounced as the hidden power behind every outrage or conspiracy against the common man.

In 2017, I took an audit of the various alleged crimes and conspiracies with which Soros's name had been linked. A couple of hours of research revealed that, over the course of a few months, the eighty-seven-year-old had been accused of faking a chemical attack in Syria, funding anti-Trump marches in Washington, coming up with a "Soros Plan" to flood Hungary with refugees, forcing a change of government in Macedonia, undermining the Israeli prime minister and getting several key White House aides sacked.

A few weeks later, after writing a column headlined, "Soros hatred is a global sickness," I received an unexpected invitation to dine with the man himself at his house in central London.[1] It was a pleasant, if slightly peculiar, occasion. First of all, no mention was made of my column either in the invitation or during the meal. Instead, his aides told me that Soros wanted to discuss the prospects for democracy in China. And indeed that was almost the sole subject of our conversation. At one point, Soros asked me how long I thought it would take for the Chinese Communist Party to lose its grip on power. The truthful answer to this is that I have no idea but I ventured a guess at thirty years. "That's a pity," he replied, "I'd hoped to be alive to see it."

Inevitably, the real Soros is very different from the Bond-villain version that stalks the dreams and conspiracy theories of the far right. Although his intellectual and campaigning energy appeared undimmed, he was hard of hearing and a little frail. To combat his increasing deafness, Soros wore headphones at the dinner table and guests had to speak into a microphone. Nonetheless, he told me that he was intending to play tennis the following morning. Most strikingly, he appeared unconcerned – even mildly amused – by the vilification and threats that were directed at him from all corners of the world.

In the years since our dinner, the fashion for seeing "Soros" behind everything has intensified. He was accused by President Trump of funding illegal migration into the United States and by Trump supporters of being behind impeachment proceedings and the "theft" of the 2020 presidential election. On other occasions, he has been denounced by political leaders in Malaysia, Poland, Romania, Turkey and Brazil, all of whom claim that the billionaire philanthropist is plotting against them.

In the 1990s, Soros was in tune with the spirit of the age, as he used the billions he had made in finance to support the transition to democracy in post-Communist Europe and elsewhere. But now the global political climate has changed and liberal ideas are in retreat. For a new generation of nationalists Soros has become the perfect villain. He is an internationalist in an age of nationalism. He is a supporter of individual not collective rights. He is the fifty-sixth richest man in America, according to the 2020 Forbes rich list, which calculated that he was worth $8.6 billion.[2] (His fortune would be considerably larger, had he not also given away $32 billion since 1984.)[3] The fact that Soros is Jewish taps into anti-Semitic sentiments – making it easier to cast him in the role of the shadowy and manipulative international financier, once reserved for the Rothschilds.

Soros's commitment to liberal individualism and minority rights is a product of his own extraordinary life story. Born in Hungary in 1930, he was thirteen years old when the Nazis invaded the country. His father, Tivador, was a lawyer and author who edited a literary magazine in the international language, Esperanto, beloved by believers in a global community. When the Nazis arrived in 1944, George's life was saved by his father's prescient decision to equip his son with false papers and send him to the countryside to live with a provincial official, posing as his godson. Living this double life, Soros was even taken by his guardian on trips to take inventories of confiscated Jewish property (an episode that was later used by his enemies to smear him as a Nazi collaborator).*

When the Nazi regime gave way to Soviet occupation after the war, Soros found his way to London at the age of seventeen where he worked as a waiter and in other menial jobs before becoming a student at the London School of Economics. Here he fell under the spell of Karl Popper. The Austrian-born philosopher's seminal work, *The Open Society and Its Enemies*, was a vigorous defense of liberalism and democracy, profoundly influenced by his own experiences of the tragedies that had befallen Central Europe. Soros later wrote that when he first read Popper's book, "It struck me with the force of revelation . . . I had direct experience of what Popper called closed societies, where the enforcement of the dogma of the one-party state leads to repression and totalitarianism." By contrast, Popper was championing an open society that "tries to build a government that allows people with different interests and ideas to live together in peace."[4] The philosopher's principles of tolerance, rationalist skepticism and empiricism profoundly influenced Soros. His charitable foundation is called the Open Society Foundations, as a tribute to his intellectual mentor.

Popper's insistence on the fallibility of human knowledge also helped to shape Soros's approach to finance. After getting his degree at the LSE, Soros worked at a number of odd jobs, including as a shop assistant, before in 1953 he was taken on by Singer and Friedlander, an investment bank in London. In 1956, he moved to the US to work on Wall Street, eventually setting up his own firm, Soros Fund Management, in 1970. Applying Popper's insights to financial markets, Soros questioned the conventional idea that markets are rational. He searched for irrationality in market behavior and proved to be an extremely astute investor. By the 1980s, he was a billionaire.

Approaching his fiftieth birthday, Soros began to look for a new purpose in life. He found this through a form of political philanthropy, using his enormous fortune to help fund the causes of liberalism, democracy and an open society. Early grants were made to help Black students in apartheid South Africa. And, as the Communist world gradually began to open up in the 1980s, Soros looked for windows

---

* Since he was a child in hiding, the accusation is absurd and distasteful.

into the Soviet bloc and in China, mainly through investments in education and in support for civil society organizations.

When the Berlin Wall came down, he was ideally placed – with the money, local knowledge and the underlying vision – to support nascent democratic institutions. In 1991, he set up the Central European University, initially in Prague, before transferring it to his native Hungary. In another typical initiative, he transferred $100 million to fund the salaries of unemployed Soviet scientists and to pay for scientific journals to reach the former USSR. As Soros later observed, "We had history on our side in the early years. It was at the time when open societies were very successful and gaining ground."[5]

For Soros, the term "open society" was "shorthand for a society in which the rule of law prevails as opposed to rule by a single individual and where the role of the state is to protect human rights and individual freedom. In my personal view, an open society should pay special attention to those who suffer from discrimination or social exclusion and those who can't defend themselves." At the same time, Soros remained an astute and influential player in the markets. In 1992, he gained the reputation as "the man who broke the Bank of England," after his hedge fund placed huge bets against the pound sterling, eventually helping to force Britain out of the European Exchange Rate Mechanism (ERM) on September 16, the day that became known in the UK as "Black Wednesday." Soros was reputed to have made over $1 billion from his successful speculation against the pound. The British government under John Major was humiliated and never really recovered its poise.[6]

Soros's role on Black Wednesday made him internationally famous and did a great deal to create his mystique. Initially, this seemed to be a largely positive development. Soros's newfound fame opened doors for him and the Open Society Institute. Most of the post–Black Wednesday recriminations in the UK were directed at the Major government, rather than the financier who had outwitted them. Indeed, if anything, Soros was rather admired for the audacity and insight of his financial speculation.

But elsewhere, Soros's wealth, his global reach, political views and Jewish heritage began to make him an object of suspicion. The first time I came across a conspiracy theory centered on Soros was during the Asian financial crisis in 1997, when Mahathir Mohamad, the prime minister of Malaysia, accused the investor of trying to wreck his country's finances.[7] At the time, this did not seem like the harbinger of a global trend. After all, Soros was a well-known currency trader, famous for his role in Black Wednesday, while Mahathir was a well-known anti-Semite.

By the early 2000s, however, Soros was beginning to crop up regularly in the discourse of the American far right. In 2007, he was denounced on Fox News as the "Dr. Evil of the whole world of left-wing foundations."[8] The origins of Soros hatred in the US may date back to his opposition to the Iraq war and his efforts to prevent the re-election of George W. Bush in 2004. Soros's financial aid to liberal causes in the US, such as voter registration drives for minorities, further enraged the Republican right; as did his support for international institutions, such as the UN.

With the advent of the Trump administration, anti-Soros propaganda moved into the American mainstream. The president himself was happy to indulge in conspiracy-mongering aimed at Soros. During the bitter congressional fight around the confirmation of Brett Kavanaugh to the Supreme Court in September 2018, Trump tweeted that anti-Kavanaugh demonstrators were "paid professionals" and their signs were "paid for by Soros and others."

For the nationalists in the Trump administration, Soros was the epitome of the "globalism" that they were pledged to destroy. At times, they explicitly linked their enemies – inside and outside the administration – to George Soros. When America First nationalists became worried that General H. R. McMaster, national security adviser to President Trump in 2017–18, was purging their allies in the White House, they set up a website called "McMaster leaks," which featured a cartoon of McMaster being manipulated by puppet masters labeled "Soros" and "Rothschilds." Fiona Hill, who served as director for Europe and Russia in the Trump NSC, was accused of being a "Soros mole" by Roger Stone, the president's longtime friend and adviser, because she had once worked with Soros's Open Society Foundations. In Congressional testimony during the first impeachment proceedings against the president, in November 2019, Hill compared the attacks on Soros to "The Protocols of the Elders of Zion," one of the longest-running anti-Semitic conspiracy theories in history, arguing that "The trope against Mr. George Soros was also created for political purposes." For Hill, the attacks were an "absolute outrage."[9]

Inevitably, Trump supporters accused Soros of orchestrating the impeachment of the president. Rudy Giuliani, the president's lawyer who had played a key role in trying to force the Ukrainian government to investigate Joe Biden's family, told *New York* magazine that Soros had "controlled" the US ambassador to Ukraine – who had refused to cooperate with Giuliani . When it was put to Giuliani that he was dabbling in anti-Semitic conspiracy theories, he accused Soros of being anti-Israel and added: "Soros is hardly a Jew. I'm more of a Jew than Soros is. I probably know more about – he doesn't go to church, he doesn't go to religion – synagogue."[10]

This tendency to see the financier as at the heart of a globalist conspiracy to subvert the nation also crossed over to the United Kingdom, courtesy of Trump's friend Nigel Farage, who incorporated attacks on Soros into his political rhetoric, claiming at one point that Soros "in many ways is the biggest danger to the entire western world," and that he was seeking "to undermine democracy and to fundamentally change the makeup, demographically, of the whole European continent."[11] From the godfather of British Euroskepticism, the anti-Soros rhetoric spread into the ruling Conservative Party, which was leading the charge for Brexit. Boris Johnson's party was forced to launch an investigation into one of its own MPs, Sally-Ann Hart, for sharing a video suggesting that Soros controls the EU. The Brexit-supporting *Daily Telegraph* ran a splash article accusing Soros of being behind a "secret plot to thwart Brexit,"[12] referring to a fundraising dinner Soros had hosted at his London house in support of the campaign for a second referendum.

Soros conspiracy theorists in the UK and the US often defended themselves against charges of anti-Semitism by using the Giuliani defense, arguing that Soros himself could no longer be counted as Jewish because he was both a secular atheist and a critic of Israel. Some of the more obtuse members of the Conservative and Republican parties may perhaps be unaware of the historical baggage attached to the language they use. But the deliberate use of anti-Semitism in anti-Soros campaigns was much harder to ignore when it cropped up in Central Europe, the heartland of the Holocaust, and in particular in Soros's own birthplace, Hungary. In the 2017 Hungarian election, Viktor Orbán, the country's prime minister, had plastered the country with posters featuring a grinning Mr. Soros and demanding "Don't let Soros have the last laugh" – a reference to an alleged plan by Soros to flood Hungary with refugees. The philanthropist was demonized as a root-less financier, intent on the destruction of the Hungarian nation.

There is clearly an echo-chamber element to the anti-Soros cam-paigns around the world, as far-right groups pick up on the same conspiracy theories. But some strongman leaders have more concrete reasons to fear Soros's Open Society Foundations, which fund civil-society organizations that promote education, a free press, minority rights and anti-corruption initiatives. The Russian government was particularly angered by Soros's support for pro-democracy forces that played a role in the Rose Revolution in Georgia in 2004, which Mos-cow regarded as an attack on its domination of the former Soviet territory.[13] In 2015, the Putin government forced the Open Society Foundations out of Russia, since it was no longer willing to tolerate their support for organizations such as Memorial, which promoted research into the Soviet terror and Stalin's gulags.

Soros's activities have also made him a target in Israel, where the obvious anti-Semitism of anti-Soros campaigns around the world mat-tered less to the Netanyahu government than Soros's support for Palestinian rights, liberal Israeli think tanks and other causes unpopu-lar on the Israeli right. Yair Netanyahu, the prime minister's son, has denounced Soros on Twitter as "the number 1 anti Israeli and anti Jew-ish world actor."[14] He even republished a cartoon of Mr. Soros dangling the world in front of a reptilian creature – the kind of image that his father would denounce as anti-Semitic in another context.

Soros conspiracy theories do not just provide strongman leaders with a convenient bogeyman and some easy rhetoric. In some places, they have been used as a means to persecute individuals and organiza-tions that stand in the way of incipient dictatorship. Perhaps the worst single example came with the imprisonment of Osman Kavala, a lib-eral Turkish businessman, who had once been a board member of Soros's Open Society Foundations. Kavala was jailed by the Erdoğan government, with the Turkish president explicitly accusing Kavala of being part of a Soros-led conspiracy against the Turkish state. "Who is behind him?" Erdoğan asked rhetorically. "The famous Hungarian Jew, George Soros. This is a man who was assigned to divide nations and to shatter them – he has so much money."[15]

Seemingly not content with accumulating enemies across the West,

Russia and the Middle East, in his later years Soros has increasingly turned his attention to China, which he correctly identified as the most dangerous single enemy to the values of an open society. Shortly after I had met him in London, in January 2019 Soros gave a speech in Davos, in which he outlined his concerns: "China isn't the only authoritarian regime in the world, but it's undoubtedly the wealthiest, strongest and most developed in machine learning and artificial intelligence. This makes Xi Jinping the most dangerous opponent of those who believe in the concept of open society."[16]

Soros had long been interested in China. He first introduced his philanthropy to the country in the mid-1980s, allying himself with economists and policy-makers linked to the reformist premier, Zhao Ziyang, who lost power just before the Tiananmen Square massacre of 1989. But in the post-Tiananmen period, Soros had found himself squeezed out of the country, anticipating the backlashes against his "political philanthropy" that were to come later in Russia, Hungary and even the US.

The vilification of George Soros has a significance that extends well beyond his personal story or the role that he plays as a bogeyman for the far right. It is part of a backlash against liberalism that has uncomfortable echoes of the Europe of the 1930s. In his influential history of the Holocaust, Saul Friedländer sees the rise of Nazism and the desire to exterminate the Jews as part of a "crisis of liberalism in continental Europe." He points out that "Throughout Europe, the Jews were identified with liberalism and often with the revolutionary brand of socialism." As a result the nationalist right "targeted the Jews as representatives of the worldviews they fought and, more often than not, tagged them as the instigators and carriers of these worldviews." As Hitler saw it, "the Jew strove to destroy the nations by spreading racial pollution, undermining the structures of the state . . . [and] achieving the disintegration of the vital core of all the nations in which he lived."[17] Those ideas sound uncomfortably similar to some of the accusations hurled at George Soros and supposed "globalists" today.

Soros has never made much of the obvious anti-Semitism behind the attacks on him, or the death threats and attempts on his life, which included a bomb posted to his home in New York. At times, however, he has admitted that some of the accusations hurled at him "hurt me tremendously."[18] But his associate Michael Vachon is probably accurate when he says that Soros is also proud of the enemies he has made, adding, "He doesn't delight in it, or waste time on it either."[19]

Soros is by no means a saint of course and can be capricious and entitled. While market purists believe that financial speculation serves a valuable purpose, many economists would disagree, and even Soros himself has expressed doubts about the social and economic impact of the globalized financial markets in which he has made his fortune. But born in Europe just as democracy was collapsing in the first half of the twentieth century, he had been fortunate enough to escape totalitarianism and to be able to play an active part in the resurgence of democracy and open societies in Europe and around the world. Yet as Soros approaches the end of his life, he himself has become the focus for the fury of the political forces of nationalist authoritarianism and strongman politics that he spent so many years battling. Ideas that had once seemed vanquished or confined to the fringes of politics have staged a resurgence in the Age of the Strongman.

In the 1930s and 40s, the United States was a bulwark of liberal democracy and the values of an open society. But in the twenty-first century, illiberal, nationalist and anti-democratic ideas have taken hold on the American right and begun to flow back from the US into Europe. Just as Soros has sought to encourage liberalism around the world, so Steve Bannon, Donald Trump's campaign manager in 2016, has also taken his ideological battle across the Atlantic. Bannon, like Soros, sees himself as engaged in an international battle of ideas that must be fought in Europe – as well as the United States.

In mid-May 2019 I woke up in a hotel room in Berlin, reached over for my phone, and idly began to check my emails. The first message I saw came from an unexpected sender – Bannon. It read: "Brilliant analysis in today's paper. Would love to connect to share more of the western hawks' perspective."

The *FT* column Bannon was responding to discussed Western policy to China. I had argued that America and China were both revisionist powers. China wanted to displace America as the world's leading political power, but to do so it needed to maintain the current global economic system. The US was determined to remain the world's pre-eminent political power, but to do that, hawks in the Trump administration had decided to unpick the current global economic system. I assumed that it was the implied criticism of "globalism" that had attracted Bannon's attention.[20]

Receiving praise from a man widely reviled as a racist, or even a fascist, was not an entirely comfortable feeling. Nor could I be sure that the email was, in fact, from Steve Bannon. Still, I was intrigued. So I replied politely, saying that I would be pleased to meet Mr. Bannon when I was next in America but that I was currently in Germany. A reply came back: it turned out that Bannon too was in Germany and was on a train heading to Berlin, after spending time in the "hinterland," where he had been conferring with the German far-right party Alternative für Deutschland (AfD).

We arranged to meet later that evening at the Hotel Adlon. A colleague in London, to whom I mentioned my upcoming rendezvous, texted me to say that he disapproved – "Would you have interviewed Goebbels?" he asked. The lobby of the Hotel Adlon seemed like a good place to contemplate that question. As the smartest hotel in Berlin, it had played host to many prominent Nazis, including Goebbels himself. But my answer to that question was that, as a journalist, I would have certainly wanted to meet the Nazi propaganda chief – or even Hitler himself.

After a few minutes, Bannon's security man – a squat, muscular, shaven-headed Brit – approached and took me up to a suite on the hotel's third floor. The man christened "sloppy Steve" by Donald Trump was wearing jeans and a T-shirt, and sipping a glass of water. His manner was businesslike, but affable. I told him that the other congratulatory email I had got that morning had been from Professor Jeffrey Sachs, an ardent critic of Trump and an admirer of China. Bannon laughed. "You've really got the ideological bases covered."

As his email had suggested, Bannon was much keener to talk about China than about culture wars or white nationalism. On his coffee table was a heavily underlined copy of that day's *Financial Times*, as well as a book called *Unrestricted Warfare: China's Master Plan to Destroy America*, which he urged me to read.[21] Bannon – like Soros – was clearly preoccupied by the political and ideological threat posed by a rising China.

Repackaging history, perhaps for my benefit, Bannon argued that the key messages of Trump's successful election campaign in 2016 had been "economic nationalism" and the need to confront China, rather than immigration or white nationalism. When I pressed him about his association with the German far right, he claimed that he had been urging the AfD to put less stress on its anti-immigration message and instead to campaign on economic nationalism. This seemed like an odd piece of advice, given that Germany – unlike the US – enjoyed a massive trade surplus and had a flourishing manufacturing sector. But Bannon insisted to me that Germany had failed to understand the economic threat it was facing from China. "If the Germans don't do anything," he claimed, "in a decade's time, the *Mittelstand* will be devastated."*

Nonetheless Bannon was not disavowing the "culture wars." He proudly claimed coauthorship, with the White House aide Stephen Miller, of "the last interesting speech Trump made," which had been given in Warsaw as a deliberate gesture to Trump's ideological allies in the Polish government. In his speech, Trump had redefined the idea of the West. Rather than portraying the US and its allies as the champions of freedom and of universal values, he had presented a view of the West "based on bonds of culture, faith and tradition" – bonds that were far from universal. "We write symphonies. We pursue innovation. We celebrate our ancient heroes, embrace our timeless traditions and customs," Trump had declared. As in his inaugural address, the president struck an apocalyptic note in Warsaw, claiming that "The fundamental question of our time is whether the West has the will to survive."[22] To me, it seemed obvious that Trump and Bannon's efforts to undermine the EU would weaken the West in any future struggle with China. But Bannon disagreed: "I love Europe, just not the EU. To me, people like Orbán, Farage and Salvini are heroes. The United States needs Europe – but as an ally, not as a protectorate."

One threat that Orbán, Farage, Salvini and Trump had all focused on was mass immigration, particularly from the Muslim world, which was treated as a menace to "our timeless traditions and customs." Indeed, if China was the external enemy, I had little doubt that Bannon, Miller and Trump regarded non-white immigrants as the internal foe. Why else would Bannon have described Tommy Robinson, a

---

* The *Mittelstand* are the small and medium-sized industrial firms that are often held to be the key to German economic and exporting prowess.

far-right anti-immigration activist in Britain, as "the backbone of the country"?[23] Breitbart, the "news" service that Bannon had run, also specialized in inflammatory stories about immigration and racial issues.

After our meeting in Berlin, I followed stories about Bannon's international movements and connections with greater interest. A few months later, he popped up in Paris, speaking favorably of the anti-establishment *gilets jaunes* street protests, while putting himself up at the Hotel Bristol. (Populism was evidently no bar to staying at the most luxurious hotels.) On a visit to Tokyo, I was told that Bannon had just been in town, mixing with some of the hard-line nationalists in Shinzo Abe's ruling party. In Brazil I was told that Bannon was close to Olavo de Carvalho, Bolsonaro's intellectual guru. In Milan, Bannon had celebrated the electoral success of the anti-immigration Northern League, led by Salvini, who himself is a great admirer of Vladimir Putin.

Elsewhere, I came across an account of a long meeting that Bannon had had in Rome with Alexander Dugin, one of Putin's favorite ideologues.[24] Dugin seemed to be another ubiquitous figure in this network of far-right thinkers. He was close to Konstantin Malofeev, a billionaire Russian nationalist I met in Moscow in the summer of 2019. Malofeev, in turn, was close to Salvini and the Northern League. In Shanghai, that same year, I discovered that Eric Li, a Chinese nationalist I knew well, had hosted Dugin as a visiting fellow at Fudan University's China Institute.

Tracing all these connections was fascinating and gave me an insight into how conspiracy theories are formed. It was tempting to see something inherently sinister in all these transnational links between far-right and nationalist thinkers of different stripes. But that, of course, was not so different from what the far right projected onto the "globalist" left. They had noticed that George Soros had funded projects involving various thinkers they disliked. Some of these people might have worked for Tony Blair or Bill Clinton or a major media organization. X knew Y and both were funded by Z – before long, a grand conspiracy was in play.

In reality, with both the far right and the globalist left, I felt that simpler and rather more ramshackle dynamics were at work. People interested in nationalist and anti-liberal ideas were intrigued to meet each other; they might exchange ideas, trade connections and even provide each other with funding. But that did not mean they were part of an organized network that tied together a global movement. Indeed, some of these thinkers clearly held incompatible views. Bannon's central mission was to block the rise of China and preserve the US as the sole superpower. Dugin detested the US and wanted to build a special relationship between Russia and China. Li was clearly intrigued by Trump but as a Chinese nationalist could hardly embrace Bannon's ideas.

It was also possible to overemphasize the influence of these people. Bannon, after all, had been sacked from the Trump White House in August 2017. Many Russia experts doubted that Putin really took Dugin seriously, pointing out that he had been fired from his job at Moscow State University in 2014. And while Eric Li's profile in the West was high because of his fluent English, he seemed to be on the margins of power within China itself.

Nonetheless, these people did – and do – matter. They have helped to create the intellectual backdrop against which the strongmen operate, providing some of the key ideas, arguments and slogans that underpin populist nationalism. And, while there are clearly significant differences between these thinkers, there are also certain recurring themes that are common to their discourse. Crucially they include anti-liberalism and anti-globalism. Many of them are passionate opponents of both feminism and the advancement of LGBT+ rights, which they portray as a "politically correct" attack on the natural order. Hatred for liberalism and globalism is also linked to a veneration of the nation state. Universal values are rejected because they supposedly threaten the distinctiveness of particular cultures and civilizations; that, in turn, often shades into racism and an emphasis on ethnic purity. Since the preservation of a particular civilization is paramount, democracy is only valuable to the extent that it furthers this goal. It can and must be discarded if it fails to protect the chosen civilization and its values. Not all of these ideas are held by all of the thinkers who promote strongman politics but they are recurring themes that crop up on different continents.

My attempt to understand the global backlash against liberalism led me to the thinking of a man who taught just a few hundred yards down the Unter den Linden from the Adlon Hotel, where I had met Steve Bannon. Carl Schmitt was a member of the Nazi Party and based at Berlin University (now Humboldt University) from 1933 to 1945. He has been described as the "crown jurist of the Third Reich" and for decades after the defeat of Nazism, his ideas were widely regarded as beyond the pale. But in recent years, there has been a global revival of interest in Schmitt's work. Chinese legal scholars, Russian nationalists, thinkers of the far right in the US and Europe are all drawing upon the work of the premier legal theorist of Nazi Germany. These far-right thinkers have provided much of the intellectual energy, justifying the actions of strongman leaders like Xi, Putin and Trump.

Jan-Werner Müller, a Princeton professor and expert on populism, describes Schmitt as "the [twentieth] century's most brilliant enemy of liberalism."[25] Despite his Nazi past, Schmitt's thinking has re-entered the academic mainstream in recent years. As Müller puts it: "When I started to write about Schmitt in the mid-1990s, I was told that one could only write about him as a historical figure – i.e. since he had been a Nazi, one could not take him seriously as a thinker." But since then, "in many ways his thought has been normalized." In 2017, Oxford University Press published *The Oxford Handbook of Carl Schmitt*, whose blurb notes that "Despite Schmitt's rabid anti-Semitism . . . the appeal of his trenchant critiques of amongst other things . . . representative democracy and international law . . . is undiminished." Schmitt is now to be found on the reading lists of political philosophy courses taught at Cambridge, Harvard and Beijing universities.

Schmitt's hostility to parliamentary democracy and his support for the power of an authoritarian leader to decide the law led him to embrace Nazism. He issued a legal opinion justifying Hitler's suspension of democracy and assumption of emergency powers after the Reichstag fire in 1933. And when the Nazis murdered hundreds of their enemies in the "Night of the Long Knives" the following year, Schmitt wrote a notorious essay justifying the killings entitled "The Führer Protects the Law." He called for the expulsion of Jewish academics from Germany and convened a conference on purging German law of Jewish influence.

Despite this, contemporary anti-liberals find much to admire in the work of Schmitt. He scorned ideas such as the separation of powers and universal human rights and argued instead that the distinction between "friend" and "enemy" is fundamental to politics: "Tell me who your enemy is and I will tell you who you are." To Schmitt, liberal talk of the brotherhood of man was nonsense. "Whoever invokes human-ity wants to deceive" is perhaps his most famous dictum.[26] For far-right thinkers emphasizing national self-interest over universal human rights, Schmitt's assault on liberal universalism is seductive.

While liberals are concerned with the establishment of the rule of law, Schmitt was more interested in how the rule of law can be sus-pended through the declaration of a state of emergency. As he wrote: "Sovereign is he who decides on the exception." This argument has a particular resonance in modern Germany, where the AfD insists that Angela Merkel should have suspended international law on refugees, rather than allowing over one million migrants to enter Germany in 2015 and 2016. Indeed, the Trump administration also considered declaring a limited state of emergency, in response to the alleged threat to America's southern border posed by illegal migrants and refugees. Contemporary Turkey and Egypt provide further examples of how the declaration of a state of emergency has led to the suspen-sion of legal rights, to devastating effect.

But, perhaps surprisingly, it is in China where the Schmitt revival seems to have gone furthest and been most influential. As Lin Laifan, a law professor at Tsinghua University in Beijing, put it in 2016: "Carl Schmitt is really famous in today's China. Many political theorists, phi-losophers and legal scholars . . . find his thinking very persuasive and very profound."[27]

The man regarded as the "pre-eminent representative of Schmitt's thought"[28] in China is Jiang Shigong, director of the Center for Politics and Law at Beijing University. Jiang has also served as a senior Chinese official in Hong Kong and as an important exponent and elaborator of Xi Jinping thought. He has enthusiastically adopted Schmitt's friend–enemy distinction. "Between friends and enemies," he has written, "there is no question of freedom, only violence and subjugation."[29] Jiang also argues, in Schmittian mode, that "The crucial questions in politics are not questions of right or wrong, but of obedience and disobedience."[30]

This line of thinking underpins President Xi's decisive rejection of the liberal tradition in Chinese politics. At the time when Xi assumed power, Chinese liberals had been pressing for China to move towards the rule of law, involving the separation of powers and the establish-ment of an independent judiciary; the American liberal philosopher

John Rawls, was much cited. But Xi has decisively rejected these ideas. As he stated categorically in 2018: "China must never follow the path of western constitutionalism, separation of powers or judicial independence."[31]

It was a conversation with Eric Li of Fudan University that first alerted me to the vogue for Carl Schmitt among authoritarian thinkers in China and around the world. Li mentioned to me that he had persuaded Alexander Dugin to become a senior fellow at Fudan's China Institute. "Isn't Dugin a fascist?" I asked, trying to sound curious rather than aggressive. "No," replied Li. "But he's very into the thought of Carl Schmitt." "What does that mean?" I asked. "Everything is political," was Li's enigmatic reply. What it meant, I came to realize, was that the philosophical justification for strongman authoritarian rule rested on the idea that there could be no such thing as truly independent institutions or even an objective truth. Everything is political. In an essay entitled "Carl Schmitt's Five Lessons for Russia," Dugin approvingly quoted the Nazi thinker's dictums of "Politics above all else" and "Let there always be enemies." While Putin's attitude to Dugin seems to be fairly equivocal, Dugin himself is an unabashed celebrant of the cult of the strongman leader. "Putin is everywhere," he has written. "Putin is everything. Putin is absolute and Putin is indispensable."[32]

As a believer in the importance of the Eurasian land mass to Russian destiny, Dugin also latches on to Schmitt's importance of "great spaces," "large geopolitical entities, each of which should be governed by a flexible super-state." Ironically, this was a doctrine used to justify the Nazi invasion of Russia, in the search for *Lebensraum*. But Dugin finds in Schmitt not only a moral justification for great land empires but "a clear understanding of the enemy facing Europe, Russia and Asia that is the United States of America along with its island ally, England." In Beijing, Jiang Shigong is also increasingly interested in Schmitt's idea of "great spaces." Now that the Chinese elite is embracing the idea of China displacing the US as the world's leading power, the Schmittian concept of building a land empire across Eurasia is of new relevance. And as rivalry over control of the South China Sea increases, Schmitt's hostility to the maritime powers of the anglophone world – with their (allegedly) self-serving ideas of international law – is also attracting attention.

Far-right thinkers in the US and Europe are also drawn to Schmitt's ideas. Richard Spencer, the American white supremacist who coined the term "alt-right," has cited Schmitt, along with Nietzsche, as an inspiration. He was filmed in November 2016, celebrating the election of a new president with a shout of "Hail Trump!" His Russian ex-wife has translated Alexander Dugin's works into English.

Schmitt's friend–enemy distinction and his insistence that supposedly "independent" institutions, such as courts and universities, are in fact part of the political order has also had a strong influence on Jair Bolsonaro's intellectual guru, Olavo de Carvalho, who has been hailed by Steve Bannon as "one of the great conservative intellectuals in the world."[33] A former astrologist and self-educated philosopher given to railing against "cultural Marxism," Carvalho has used Schmitt's writings to justify the argument that even the teaching of the theory of evolution should be seen as a question of politics rather than science.[34] For Carvalho, politics is above all a ruthless, Schmittian battle between friend and enemy. Political struggle, he has written, "is not about destroying ideas, but destroying the careers and the power of people. You have to be direct and to act without respect."[35] It is this kind of thinking which secured him the seat of honor next to President Bolsonaro at a dinner at the Brazilian Embassy in Washington DC in 2019. The person seated on the other side of Bolsonaro was Steve Bannon.

Bannon himself is known to be an admirer of Julius Evola, an Italian fascist thinker, who corresponded with Schmitt. But had Trump's former campaign manager ever read Schmitt himself? That was a question I discussed over breakfast one morning in 2019 with Peter Wittig, the former German ambassador in Washington, who was then serving in London. He was pretty sure that Bannon had come across Schmitt's ideas. "In fact, I gave him some of Schmitt's work to read. I thought he would be interested." The ambassador paused and looked a little pained. "Perhaps that was a mistake."

In reality, Bannon is an intellectual magpie, picking up and using ideas that serve his personal and political purposes. A certain merging of the personal and the political in Bannon's life became evident when he was arrested in 2019 aboard the yacht of Guo Wengui (also known as Miles Kwok), a Chinese billionaire in exile in the US who is a fierce critic of Xi Jinping. Guo, it turned out, was a business partner and generous funder of Bannon – which might have partially explained Bannon's ability to stay at the Hotel Adlon and no doubt added some extra passion to his anti-China advocacy. The charge laid against Bannon when he was arrested was that he had misappropriated money from "We Build the Wall," a fundraising drive to construct President Trump's promised wall along the Mexican–American border. All this made it tempting to dismiss Bannon as no more than a grifter – a man promoting populist ideas to line his own pockets. But whatever the truth of the embezzlement charges laid against him, Bannon is also a genuine ideologue who, through his association with Donald Trump, has changed the world.

When the Trump presidency reached its *Götterdämmerung* moment in the storming of the Capitol on January 6, 2021, Bannon was back on the scene. In the days of desperation that followed his electoral defeat, Trump had consulted his former adviser several times on how to respond. Through his podcast and other media outlets, Bannon had promoted the idea that the election had been stolen and urged demonstrators to descend on Washington.

The efforts to overturn the election and to trash the institutions of US democracy were very much in the spirit of both Steve Bannon and Carl Schmitt. It was the kind of politics in which the world was rigidly divided between friend and enemy, and where the only political imperative was to triumph over your foe. And indeed, as a strongman leader, Trump had tried to reach for the tools recommended by Schmitt: the declaration of an emergency and the suspension of the normal operation of the law.

The failure of the pro-Trump insurrection that January day in 2021 was a profound relief to supporters of liberal democracy in the United States and around the world. But alongside the hope, there is doubt. The US itself is deeply divided and the Republican Party remains in thrall to Donald Trump. America's global power is diminishing. And many of the other major powers in the world – China, Russia, India, Turkey, Saudi Arabia – are run by strongman leaders. Can the Biden administration really turn the tide?

Epilogue: Biden in the Age of the Strongman

On 20 January 1961, John F. Kennedy, America's youngest ever president, gave his inaugural address from the steps of the Capitol. Exactly sixty years later Joe Biden, America's oldest ever president, was sworn in at the same place.

Kennedy used the magisterial backdrop of Congress to proclaim that the "torch has passed to a new generation." America was prepared to "pay any price, bear any burden" to ensure the "survival and success of liberty" around the world. For Biden, the background of the Capitol had a more sinister edge. He was speaking just two weeks after Congress had been stormed by a riotous mob of Trump supporters, intent on overturning the result of the presidential election. Biden was a representative of an older generation that had almost seen the torch of liberty extinguished in the US itself. "We have learned again that democracy is precious," he proclaimed. "Democracy is fragile. And at this hour, my friends, democracy has prevailed." In a brief passage addressed to "those beyond our borders," the new president promised: "America has been tested and we have come out stronger for it. We will repair our alliances and engage with the world once again."

The failure of democracy in the United States would have been a cataclysmic global event. The last fifteen years have seen the most sustained decline in political freedom around the world since the 1930s. But throughout the 1930s, the two most powerful countries in the world, the United States and Britain, remained liberal democracies. If Trump and his supporters had succeeded in thwarting a democratic election, America's traditional role as "leader of the free world" would have ended. The two most powerful countries of the current era, the

United States and China, would both have been in the grip of authoritarian nationalism.

Trump's defeat in 2020 does not mean that the danger has passed. The Biden administration is fighting strongman politics on two fronts. At home, it faces the threat of a Republican Party that is still dominated by Trump. Overseas, Biden is dealing with increasingly assertive strongman leaders in China and Russia. Some of the allies that he will look to in order to push back against Xi Jinping and Vladimir Putin – including India, Poland and the Philippines – have themselves embraced forms of strongman leadership. As in the Cold War, this may compromise America's ability to draw clear lines between a free and unfree world.

These domestic and foreign challenges are linked. America will not be able to defend freedom overseas if it cannot save its own democracy. On the other hand, if America's domestic turmoil consumes most of the energy of the Biden administration, the US will have less time and fewer resources to devote to supporting political liberty elsewhere in the world. And there is no plausible alternative to America that could play that role. Germany, France or the EU as a whole don't have the political structures, military power or diplomatic reflexes to step in and replace the US as a global champion for political freedom. The "Anglosphere" of English-speaking allies of the US – including Britain, Australia, Canada and New Zealand – looks to Washington for leadership. When Biden chose to withdraw US troops from Afghanistan in the summer of 2021 – precipitating the collapse of the Kabul government – some of America's European allies were aghast. But they swiftly concluded that they could not sustain their own presence in Afghanistan without US support. The allies had no option but to follow Washington's lead.

In his first press conference as president, Biden defined his own task clearly: "This is a battle between the utility of democracies in the twenty-first century and autocracies. We've got to prove that democracy works."[1]

For the Biden administration, the struggle to prove that democracy works has to begin at home. It is a formidable task. Biden's victory in the 2020 presidential election was clear, but not crushing. He barely enjoys a governing majority in Congress. And there is little sign of the Republican Party repudiating Trump. Even before the 2020 vote, more than half of Republicans agreed that "the traditional American way of life is disappearing so fast that we may have to use force to save it."[2] After the election, some 77 percent of Republican voters agreed with Trump's contention that there has been "major fraud" in the vote. Following the storming of Congress, Trump's approval rating among Republicans dipped only very slightly; while that of Mitch McConnell, the leader of the Senate Republicans, who had voted to approve Biden's election, plummeted.[3] Observing these trends, Michael Gerson, a former speechwriter for President George W. Bush, concluded that most of the Republican Party had essentially given up on democracy, in favor of the preservation of a "White Christian America of its imagination," which it believed to be "on the verge of destruction."[4] A month into the Biden administration, 61 percent of Republican voters said that Trump's endorsement would be more likely to make them vote for a candidate; almost half agreed that Trump had been "called by God to lead."[5] The Trump cult even extended to his wider family. Looking ahead to who would run for the Republicans in the 2024 presidential election, Mark Meadows, Trump's former chief of staff, predicted: "I can tell you, the people that are at the top of that list, all of them have Trump as their last name."[6]

Biden's efforts to weaken the dangerous lure of Trumpism got off to a strong start, with the passage of a $1.9 trillion stimulus package, which provided direct financial benefits to millions of Americans. But the chaotic withdrawal from Afghanistan over the summer of 2021 marked the end of the president's brief honeymoon. A resurgence of inflation, the migrant crisis on America's southern border and infighting within the Democratic Party further punctured Biden's popularity. When I visited Washington in October 2021, the president's ratings were hovering around 40 percent, and 60 percent of voters believed that America was on the wrong track. After the wildness of the Trump years, my meetings in the White House and the State Department were reassuringly normal. But the officials whom I spoke to already seemed haunted by the fear that Biden might fail – and the dread of what a second Trump presidency might mean for America and the world. The issues that most motivate Trump's base – immigration and identity politics – remain intensely controversial. And Biden himself will be eighty-two by the time of the next election. His vice president is Kamala Harris – a Black woman. Any prospect of a Harris presidency would further stoke the fears and energy of the Republican Party base.

The watching world knows that the forces Trump represents are still powerful in the US. There is a strong chance that Biden may simply represent a four-year interlude, before those forces return to power. As the political scientist Jonathan Kirshner puts it: "The world cannot unsee the Trump presidency . . . From this point forward, countries around the globe will have to calculate their interests and expectations with the understanding that the Trump administration is the sort of thing that the US political system can plausibly produce."[7] But it is not just the lurking shadow of Donald Trump that will inhibit Biden's ability to reassert global American leadership. The world has reason to question whether the US, as a nation, still has the energy and means to fight for liberal democracy around the globe.

The Biden team has talked repeatedly about running a foreign policy for the American middle class.[8] In other words, all foreign policy commitments would be scrutinized to see whether they deliver benefits for ordinary Americans. The likely product of that kind of approach is a more modest and cautious approach to the world.

Biden's advisers know that the American people are profoundly weary of foreign wars, so are cautious about deploying force abroad. The desperate scenes as the Americans pulled out of Afghanistan, while the Taliban regained control of the country, sent a much more powerful signal than any number of presidential proclamations that "America is back."

The Kennedy "bear any burden" approach was the product of a world in which the power of the American economy was unrivaled. But the Biden administration took office at a time when China was already the world's largest manufacturing and trading power. At the end of 2019, 128 of 190 countries in the world traded more with China than with the US. The lure of Chinese trade and investment is a potent diplomatic and political force across Asia, Africa and Latin America. By contrast, protectionism is still on the rise in the US. The Democrats are unlikely to sign many (or any) new trade deals overseas – making it harder to counter Chinese economic influence.

All of these factors place limits on Biden's declared ambition to restore American global leadership. Nonetheless, the defeat of Donald Trump and the arrival of Biden in the White House changed the global political climate. All of the strongman leaders discussed in this book have had to adapt to the new situation.

For Vladimir Putin, Biden's election looked like bad news. Trump had always shied away from criticizing or confronting the Russian leader. Better still, from the Kremlin's point of view, Trump was openly skeptical of America's alliance system. A second Trump term could have spelled the end of NATO, which would have been a geopolitical triumph for the Kremlin. By contrast, Joe Biden is committed to NATO and has a long history of wariness of Russia. A week before the 2020 presidential election, he had stated: "The biggest threat to America right now . . . is Russia."[9] Shortly after his inauguration, Biden was asked on television if he regarded Putin as a "killer." His reply, "I do," caused outrage in the Kremlin – and led to the temporary withdrawal of the Russian ambassador to Washington.

The return of an American president who was prepared to confront Putin on questions of democracy and human rights coincided with an intensification of domestic repression in Russia. The jailing of Alexei Navalny in February 2021 came less than a month after Biden's inauguration. It led to mass demonstrations in Moscow and other cities which were met with police violence and mass arrests. For many Russia analysts this seemed to mark a new phase in Putin's long rule. As Andrei Kolesnikov of the Carnegie Moscow Center put it: "Maybe he was always brutal, but now he has decided to be brutal freely, openly and without restrictions."[10]

Many Russian liberals were initially invigorated and inspired by Navalny's resistance. They took heart from the bravery of his speech in the dock, when he argued that his own imprisonment was "not a demonstration of [Putin's] strength, but of weakness," and scoffed that Putin would be remembered by history as "Vladimir the underpants poisoner." But with the passage of time, liberal exhilaration at Navalny's show of defiance gave way to depression. The bleak truth was that Navalny had been sent away to a penal colony; and Putin was still in the Kremlin. In the Age of the Strongman, it is getting harder to preserve the faith that truth, bravery and popular protest will ultimately triumph over authoritarian rule. From Belarus to Venezuela, from Russia to Hong Kong, the contemporary evidence often seems to point the other way.

After dealing with Navalny, Putin once again focused on his external enemies. In July 2021, the Russian leader published a long essay, "On the Historical Unity of Russians and Ukrainians," which portrayed Ukrainian independence as a historical aberration, exploited by Russia's enemies. The implied threat became more real with a buildup of Russian troops on the Ukrainian border, which led the Biden administration to warn publicly of a possible Russian invasion of its western neighbor.

A similar combination of domestic repression and external aggression emerged in Xi Jinping's China during the first year of the Biden presidency. Leading Hong Kong activists like Joshua Wong and Jimmy Lai were sent to prison and virtually the entire leadership of the pro-democracy movement was put on trial for subversion. China also passed a new election law for Hong Kong in March 2021, closing off any possibility of further advances for the democracy movement, by setting up a pro-Beijing committee to vet all electoral candidates for "patriotic" sentiment.[11] Throughout 2021 Chinese air-force exercises around Taiwan became increasingly frequent and threatening.

When it came to China, Biden continued the confrontational policies adopted by Trump. He promised that "on my watch" China would not "become the leading country in the world . . . the most powerful country."[12] But whereas Trump saw the rivalry above all in economic terms, Biden added a more explicitly ideological edge. For him, the contest between the US and China is the centerpiece of the battle between autocracy and democracy, which he believes will define the twenty-first century.

As vice president in the Obama administration, Biden had spent many hours in direct meetings with Xi. He liked to say that the Chinese leader "does not have a democratic bone in his body." The first meeting between Tony Blinken, the new US Secretary of State, and Yang Jiechi, China's top foreign policy official, swiftly descended into public acrimony. Blinken opened up by condemning China's actions over Hong Kong, Xinjiang and Taiwan, and its cyberattacks and "economic coercion" of American allies. In response, Yang accused the US of being an imperial power, beset by racism at home, and remarked scornfully: "The US does not have the qualification to say it wants to speak to China from a position of strength."[13] China's mocking references to American weakness were not simply for public consumption. The fact that the US had suffered 800,000 deaths from Covid-19 by the winter of 2021 – compared to an official death toll of less than 5,000 in China – was treated in Beijing as a vindication of the Chinese system and a confirmation of American decadence.

These early encounters with the Biden administration probably also strengthened Xi's long-held assumption that the US is a hostile power, intent on regime change in China. The argument that China is under siege from hostile foreign forces will be used to bolster the case for prolonging Xi's leadership beyond the normal ten years, a move that is likely to be formalized at the next Communist Party congress in the winter of 2022. The Chinese statement issued after the Yang–Blinken meeting emphasized the "core status" of Xi's leadership, adding that he "enjoys the wholehearted support of 1.4 billion people." While this sounds improbable, there is little sign that China's beleaguered liberals have any immediate chance of pushing back against the entrenchment of strongman rule in Beijing.

The Biden administration's effort to put democracy and human rights back at the center of foreign policy was an unwelcome development for Xi Jinping and Vladimir Putin. But for other strongman leaders, the situation is more ambiguous. Figures like Narendra Modi, Mohammed bin Salman, Recep Tayyip Erdoğan and Jair Bolsonaro all have reason to be wary of America's renewed emphasis on human rights. On the other hand, as potential US allies in a new cold war with China and Russia, these leaders all have grounds to hope that Washington will avoid confronting them about their own domestic political arrangements. Even then, allying with America is not a straightforward choice. All US allies, including the strongmen, have to consider how much faith to put in Biden's promises of renewed American leadership, set against the apparently inexorable rise of China and the aggression of Russia.

The centrality of India to America's efforts to contain Chinese power gave Narendra Modi particularly good reason to hope that the Biden administration will gloss over the erosion of democracy in India. The first overseas trip made by Biden's defense secretary, Lloyd Austin, included a stop in Delhi. The importance of India to Washington's efforts to counter Beijing was underlined in September 2021, when Biden hosted the first ever summit meeting of the leaders of "the Quad" – the US, India, Japan and Australia. The Quad is widely seen as an informal alliance, pulling together the major powers in the Indo-Pacific, to counter China.

But the increasing authoritarianism of Modi's India has not gone unnoticed in Washington. When a key member of Biden's foreign-policy team listed his concerns to me in October 2021, he spontaneously mentioned the erosion of democracy in India. I expressed surprise, saying that I had assumed that the strategic importance of India would incline the US to turn a blind eye. My interlocutor replied that "In my experience if you turn a blind eye to something, you often get a nasty surprise."

But Western criticism and pressure is unlikely to weaken Modi. Indeed it could even strengthen his position with his Hindu nationalist base. Like Putin and Xi, the Indian leader is digging in for the long term.

One strongman ally of the US who had reason to fear an immediate backlash after the defeat of Trump was Mohammed bin Salman of Saudi Arabia. The murder of Jamal Khashoggi, the humanitarian catastrophe in Yemen and MBS's special relationship with the Trump White House made the Saudi strongman a deeply suspect figure for the Biden team. Within weeks of coming to office, the Biden administration withdrew American support for the war in Yemen and agreed to release the CIA report on Khashoggi's killing. MBS and the Saudis had to adjust fast. Peace moves in Yemen were announced and the Saudi blockade of Qatar was lifted.

But the adjustments were not all one way. Faced with a struggle for influence in the Middle East with Russia and China, the Biden administration could not afford an antagonistic relationship with Saudi Arabia. Saudi intelligence remained a crucial resource in the struggle against terrorism, and MBS controls the country's intelligence agencies. For all the hopeful talk in Washington of sidelining the crown prince, the reality is that MBS is still likely to succeed King Salman as the head of state and may then stay in power for decades. Western companies remain eager for Saudi business. For all those reasons, the Biden team decided that it could not risk a full-scale break with MBS and resisted pressure to sanction him for his role in the Khashoggi killing.

In June 2021, Benjamin Netanyahu lost power in Israel after twelve uninterrupted years in office – and numerous inconclusive elections. When opposition politicians finally succeeded in putting together a governing coalition, Netanyahu's response to his loss of power was strongly reminiscent of Trump. He declared that he had been the victim of "the greatest electoral fraud in the history of the country" and of a conspiracy by the Israeli "deep state," which he argued was behind his prosecution for corruption. But in Israel, as in the US six months earlier, the country's institutions held firm. Netanyahu lost office and his corruption trial continued.

The American and Israeli political crises came within six months of each other and demonstrated something important about the struggle against strongman leadership. Leaders with autocratic instincts can come to power anywhere in the world. The difference between the strongmen who manage to prolong their rule indefinitely and those who can be forced from office or held to account by the law is very often the strength of a country's institutions. In the US and Israel, national institutions passed the test.

The coalition government that replaced Netanyahu stretched from the left of the Israeli political spectrum to the far right. It even included Ra'am, an Islamist party linked to the Muslim Brotherhood – the first Arab-Israeli party to serve in a government of the Jewish state. The sole unifying principle for the coalition partners was a shared determination to get Netanyahu out of power. Even so, the new government could only muster a parliamentary majority of one. Netanyahu, although on trial for corruption, remained outwardly confident that he would soon return to the prime minister's office.

The Israeli experience points to a number of lessons and questions for countries with strongman rulers that are still fortunate enough to hold competitive elections. Are the opposition forces sufficiently motivated to unite against the strongman? Are the country's institutions still strong enough to ensure a free election? Will the strongman step down if he loses power? These dilemmas will play out in the coming years in a number of countries that will hold significant votes in 2022 and 2023, including Hungary, the Philippines, Brazil and Turkey.

In the aftermath of Trump's defeat, Viktor Orbán of Hungary became an even firmer favorite of the populist right in the US. In the summer of 2021, Tucker Carlson, the most prominent pro-Trump anchor on Fox News, moved his entire show to Budapest for a week, in a bid to showcase Orbán's Hungary as a model for America. Interviewing Orbán, Carlson praised his policies on culture and migration and claimed that he had met many Americans who had moved to Budapest for political reasons, "because they want to be around people who agree with them, who agree with you."[14] Out of favor in official circles in Washington and Brussels, Orbán also looked to Moscow and

Beijing. In the same year that the Central European University was finally forced out of Budapest, China's Fudan University opened a new campus in the Hungarian capital.

With the departure of Angela Merkel from power at the end of 2021, Orbán became the longest serving leader in the EU. But the Hungarian leader's period in power could come to a close in 2022, when he faces a potentially close election. In anticipation of the poll, six opposition parties used a primary process to unite around a single candidate – Peter Marki-Zay, a small-town mayor. As in Israel, the urge to get a strongman out of power had produced an unlikely coalition, bringing together the liberal left and the nationalist right. Accepting the opposition nomination, Marki-Zay pointedly announced: "We will always stand besides homosexuals, like we support Jews or gypsies." He also pledged that Hungarians would be "faithful citizens of the EU."[15] The Hungarian opposition, however, face an uphill battle. Orbán has a strong base of support. And, in more than a decade in power, he has changed Hungarian electoral law in his favor and systematically neutered the media. If he loses in a close election, Orbán might well follow a Trumpian playbook and refuse to accept the result.

Jair Bolsonaro in Brazil is another of Trump's former allies who faces a difficult election in 2022. The court-ordered release from prison of his old rival, former president Lula, ensured that Bolsonaro will face a formidable opponent in the presidential poll. A year out from the election, with both inflation and unemployment in double digits, Bolsonaro's disapproval ratings were at 65 percent. But if he loses in October 2022, the Brazilian strongman is likely to emulate Trump by refusing to accept the result and instead attempting to subvert democracy. Ahead of the vote, he repeatedly insisted that the election was likely to be rigged. At one rally, Bolsonaro told cheering supporters that "I have only three possible fates: arrest, death or victory."[16] In this atmosphere, there was open discussion in the Brazilian and international media of the possibility of a military coup or civil unrest if and when Bolsonaro refused to accept defeat. Brazil's institutions – including the courts and the army – may soon be put to a severe test.

Turkey, under President Erdoğan, is threatened by a similar scenario ahead of a presidential election scheduled for 2023. By then, Erdoğan will have completed twenty years in power. But his increasing authoritarianism and economic incompetence have led to a backlash. As in Hungary and Israel, a heterogenous opposition coalition has come together, dedicated to ousting the strongman from power. With inflation running at 20 percent and the Turkish lira halving in value in 2021, the opposition – described by the *Financial Times* as "an improbable alliance of nationalists, Kurds, leftists, rightwingers, secularists and religious conservatives"[17] – has good reason to hope for victory in the next parliamentary and presidential elections. But if Erdoğan or his AK Party lose at the ballot box in 2023, there is absolutely no guarantee that the Turkish strongman would relinquish power or that the Turkish state would be able to force him out.

In the Philippines, by contrast, Rodrigo Duterte surprised some of his critics by not insisting on changes to the constitution that would allow him to stay on for a second term, after elections in May 2022. The Filipino strongman's preferred option was to be succeded by his daughter, Sara. But Sara disappointed her father by instead choosing to run as the vice presidential running mate of Bongbong Marcos, the son of the former Filipino dictator, Ferdinand Marcos. For Filipino liberals, the departure of Duterte is a welcome prospect, but the apparent merger between the Marcos and Duterte dynasties is alarming – particularly since Bongbong is intent on rewriting history to portray the Marcos dictatorship as a golden era of progress and stability.

It is possible that by the end of 2023, Orbán, Bolsonaro, Duterte and Erdoğan will all have lost power. But while some strongman rulers may fall, others could rise. In France, the early stages of the presidential election of 2022 saw Emmanuel Macron facing strong challenges from two far-right candidates – Marine Le Pen and Eric Zemmour, a former journalist. The Zemmour campaign, in particular, embraced all the familiar themes of a would-be strongman ruler: a lament about national decline, a promise to make France great again, a pledge to halt all immigration, a condemnation of "Islamo-leftism" and "crazy gender thought."

Across the channel, some British conservatives flirted energetically with both Le Pen and Zemmour. For hard-line Brexiters, the defeat of Macron would be a welcome blow to the hated EU. Boris Johnson, however, cannot afford to openly embrace strongman candidates or anti-democratic forces in Europe, since that would swiftly open a rift with the Biden White House. The fact that Biden had called Boris Johnson a "physical and emotional clone" of Trump created some nervousness in the British government. So did the new American president's self-proclaimed Irish identity, which could become significant at a time when tensions in Northern Ireland are rising as a result of Brexit. But Britain, like Israel and Poland, is too important and traditional an American ally for the US to alienate without very good reason. The British, in turn, quickly signaled their willingness to adapt to Washington's increasing rivalry with Beijing. The signing of a new defense pact between Australia, Britain and the US – known as Aukus – underlined the point.

At home, however, Johnson continued to flirt with the strongman style – in particular, by attacking independent institutions that constrain a prime minister's power. Angered by the UK Supreme Court's ruling that his suspension of parliament had been illegal, the Johnson government brought forward legislation to curtail the judiciary's power to overrule government decisions. Even Conservative lawyers were outraged. Edward Garnier, who had served as attorney general in the Cameron government, protested that "This government seems to forget that, like all of us, it too is subject to the law . . . This is a country under the rule of law and not under a dictatorship."[18]

The robustness of Britain's institutions meant that Johnson's instinctive rule-breaking and cronyism led to a backlash. Efforts to change parliament's anti-corruption rules to benefit a friend of Johnson's created an outcry in the media and had to be withdrawn. Revelations about parties in Downing Street that had broken the government's own pandemic regulations led to investigations and resignations. By the end of 2021, the polls suggested that a majority of the British public had concluded that Johnson is unfit for the job of prime minister.

Johnson's travails fit a pattern for many of the populist nationalists who have come to power around the world over the past decade. Leaders like Erdoğan, Modi, Trump, Bolsonaro, Johnson and Duterte have often proved much better at campaigning than running a country. They are superb at building a personal following – but they lack the technocratic skills and patience to govern effectively.

These flaws suggest that the strongman style of government may contain the seeds of its own destruction. And that raises a crucial question: is strongman rule still the rising trend in world affairs—or has it peaked?

When a powerful new political or ideological trend emerges, it is always tempting to believe that it will continue to gather force long into the future. After the Russian Revolution, many Communists came to believe that the collapse of capitalism globally was inevitable. During the 1930s, it was fashionable to believe that liberal democracy was in terminal decline all over the world. And after the end of the Cold War, Francis Fukuyama famously proclaimed the "end of history," arguing that ideological competition had ended and that liberal democracy was the only viable system left.

In reality, history often has been more cyclical than linear. Political trends have risen and fallen. Past precedent suggests that the Age of the Strongman will also come to an end, at some point. But it could last as long as thirty years.

All efforts at historical periodization are slightly artificial. But it is possible to identify two distinct eras in postwar politics, both of which lasted roughly thirty years. The period from 1945 to 1975, known as *les trentes glorieuses* in France, was identified with strong economic growth across the West, alongside the construction of welfare states and Keynesian demand-management, all played out against the international backdrop of the Cold War.

By the mid-1970s, this model had run into trouble in the Anglo-American world, with Britain suffering from "stagflation" and President Jimmy Carter diagnosing a national "malaise" in the US. A new era (often termed neoliberal by its critics) began in 1979 with the election of Margaret Thatcher in Britain, followed by that of Ronald Reagan in the US in 1980. In retrospect, this was also part of a global shift. In 1978, Deng Xiaoping came to power in China and initiated a policy of market-based "reform and opening." The Communist bloc in Europe began to crack with the formation of the Solidarity trade union in Poland in September 1980. The foundations of a globalized capitalist economy were emerging.

This "neoliberal era" also lasted roughly thirty years until it was discredited by the global financial crisis of 2008. In its aftermath, the West appeared weakened and strongman leaders such as Putin and

Erdoğan became more willing to challenge Western power and political norms. With the elevation of Xi Jinping to the leadership of China in 2012, the Age of the Strongman was truly launched.

It is significant that, unlike the previous two cycles described, the Age of the Strongman started outside the West. Indeed, most Western intellectuals assumed, complacently, that the US was immune to the strongman style of politics. The election of Trump in 2016 disproved this decisively. Britain's vote for Brexit in the same year demonstrated that the UK was also prey to nostalgic nationalism and populism. With the Anglo-American heartland of liberal democracy in disarray, advocates of the strongman style of politics were empowered across the world.

The two previous epochs in postwar history had followed a similar arc. A new ideology emerged, achieved some initial successes, and so gained fresh prestige and attracted new followers. A sense of ideological momentum then created a demand for the original ideas behind the movement to be pushed further and faster. And that led to overreach, eventually created a backlash and the demand for a new approach. A good example of ideological overreach is the way in which the Reaganite demand for lower taxes and less red tape eventually led to the excessive deregulation of finance that culminated in the financial crisis of 2008. On a geopolitical level, the Western elite's intoxication with globalization led to the rapid incorporation of China into the world economy. But now that country's growing wealth and power has sparked a backlash against globalization.

If the latest era follows a similar pattern, then the strongman style is well into the emulation phase of the cycle. After 2016, it became standard practice for leaders like Bolsonaro, Orbán, Putin and even Netanyahu to use Trumpian language and tactics: denouncing "fake news," questioning climate science and condemning "globalists."

But while the precedent of previous eras suggests that the Age of the Strongman could last as long as thirty years, there is an important qualification. For the strongmen to prosper, the populist nationalism that these leaders typically espouse needs to be validated by success. China has certainly taken this lesson on board. It has used the coronavirus pandemic to argue that the Chinese system – informed by Xi Jinping thought – has proved its superiority to Western liberalism. But beyond China's borders, incompetence seems to be catching up with some strongman rulers. Trump's mishandling of Covid-19 contributed to his defeat. Bolsonaro, Amlo and Erdoğan have all bungled both the pandemic and their national economies.

Political liberals have reason to hope that incompetence will eventually undermine support for autocratic leaders. But, unlike democrats, strongman leaders are not in the habit of yielding power gracefully when things turn sour. In the US, the margin of Trump's defeat and the strength of American institutions were enough to thwart his efforts to overturn the result of the 2020 election. But in other national contexts, strongman leaders such as Orbán, Bolsonaro and Erdoğan may prove harder to shift.

Some aspects of modern politics are strongly reminiscent of the last great crisis of liberal democracy in the 1930s. Political freedoms and democracy are once again in retreat. Protectionism is back in vogue. Liberals are losing confidence. The desire of autocratic regimes to annex parts of neighboring states or otherwise expand their territories – which lay behind so much of the troubles of the 1930s – is also creeping back into fashion. Russia's annexation of Crimea in 2014 set a dangerous precedent. China is intent on turning the South China Sea into its own territorial waters in violation of international law. Beijing is also increasingly strident in its demands for "reunification" with Taiwan.

As nationalists, strongman leaders have a tendency to look for enemies abroad if things get difficult at home. The rising tensions in the neighborhoods of China, Russia and Turkey are reminders that, in previous eras, strongman politics has been closely associated with war. In the 1930s, it took a world war to bring the era of the dictators to an end. Today, the risk of a military confrontation between the US and Russia and China, in particular, is rising. But fear of a nuclear holocaust helped to keep the peace during the Cold War (albeit with some narrow escapes). A similar terror of nuclear disaster will probably prevent a war between the major powers during the Age of the Strongman.

A bigger risk may be the threat that the decline of liberal internationalism poses to the global economy and to the environment. When the global financial crisis broke out in 2008, world leaders convened swiftly in the first ever G20 summit. Facing a common threat, the leaders of the US, China, the EU, Russia, Japan and other nations were able to overcome their political differences and work together.

But in the era of strongman politics, international cooperation is no longer in fashion – as the fractured global response to the coronavirus has illustrated. The rise of populist strongmen makes it much less likely that the world will muster an effective response to climate change. That point was underlined at the UN General Assembly meeting of 2019, when the opening speaker was President Bolsonaro of Brazil. Rather than expressing contrition or even concern about the wildfires devastating the Amazon, Bolsonaro launched into an angry diatribe against the globalists who were daring to infringe upon Brazilian sovereignty by trying to organize an international effort to save the Amazon.

By 2020, China accounted for 29 percent of global emissions of carbon dioxide – more than the US and EU combined. Without Chinese action, there will be no effective global response to climate change. But the rising antagonism between the US and China will also make it harder to achieve international agreement on global warming. Rather than becoming a spur for rival countries to work together, the increasingly ominous news about climate change could become another source of mutual recrimination between China and the US. By the time the Age of the Strongman comes to a close, irreparable damage may have been done to the environment.

In the US, the defeat of Trump may feel like a new chance for liberal democracy. In China, by contrast, the chaos and division of the 2020 presidential election is presented as further evidence of the decadence of the US system. Xi Jinping and the ideologues who surround him are increasingly prepared to assert the superiority of the "China model" over the values preached by the West.

However, a major difficulty for Beijing is that the "China model" is increasingly associated – at home and abroad – with the personality cult around Xi Jinping. Strongman rule almost invariably leads to the creation of a personality cult, because it becomes politically impossible to admit that the leader is capable of weakness or error. Since the leader can be seen to do no wrong, debate and criticism have to be shut down. Strongman rule ultimately has to rest on fear and coercion. This model of government is not just unattractive: it is also a recipe for trouble. Without open discussion and safe ways of challenging authority, governments that are in thrall to a strongman can adopt disastrous policies – and persist with them, long after a more open system would have changed course. The personality cult around Mao led China to disaster. Indeed, leader cults have rarely ended well anywhere.

The inability to tolerate criticism is not the only flaw in the strongman model. Two other characteristic (and linked) difficulties center around succession and infirmity.

In the purest form of the strongman system, where checks on the leader are effectively removed, everything comes to depend on the man at the top. His replacement – or even discussion of his eventual departure – is profoundly destabilizing. Once the strongman is gone, therefore, all sorts of interests are threatened as rivals jostle for power and scores are settled. Strongman leaders, their families and entourages have good reason to fear that there will be a reckoning, if they ever let go of power. As a result, strongmen typically cling on to power.

Some observers of Russia suspect that Vladimir Putin might quite like to retire, after more than twenty years running Russia. But if Putin were to go, the Russian legal system, which Putin has used to harass his enemies, could be turned upon his friends and family, by whoever succeeds him in the Kremlin. Leaders such as Xi and Erdoğan run similar risks. When a strongman loses power, the stability of the entire political system built around him is at risk. This compulsion to stay in office is a clear feature of the Age of the Strongman. Vladimir Putin and Recep Tayyip Erdoğan are both now approaching twenty years in office. In China, President Xi is digging in for another decade in power.

But even a strongman leader eventually becomes old and infirm. Xi, Putin and Erdoğan are now all in their late sixties. Rumors that Erdoğan is suffering from cancer are common in Turkey. Xi is overweight and a former smoker. If any of these leaders were to die or to become incapacitated, their countries would be plunged into crisis. When a strongman's health fails, the usual reaction is to cover up the problem. The leader's entourage have to stage-manage his appearances in public and find ways to govern, as the boss loses focus.

Even if their physical health holds up, decades in power can often cause a leader to succumb to megalomania or paranoia – or to lose touch with the ordinary life of the nations they lead. Democratic systems, for all their weaknesses, have institutions and laws that manage the crucial and delicate problem of succession. Durable political systems ultimately rely on institutions, not individuals. And successful societies are built on laws rather than charismatic leadership.

For all these reasons, strongman rule is an inherently flawed and unstable form of government. It will ultimately collapse in China and in most other places where it is tried. But there may be a lot of turmoil and suffering before the Age of the Strongman is finally consigned to history.

Acknowledgments

This book draws on many years of travel and work for the *Financial Times*. So my first debt of gratitude is to the *FT*, for giving me the opportunity to think and write about world politics.

I have also drawn upon the wisdom and hospitality of *FT* colleagues around the world. I would particularly like to thank Ed Luce in Washington, a great friend who has been a generous host on several occasions. In Moscow, I would like to thank Henry Foy, Max Seddon and Kathrin Hille. Kathrin was also a great help in other postings in Beijing and Taipei. I am also grateful to Laura Pitel in Turkey; to Jamil Anderlini, Nicolle Liu and Tom Mitchell in Beijing and Hong Kong; to Amy Kazmin, Victor Mallet and Jyotsna Singh in Delhi; to John Reed in Jerusalem; Simeon Kerr in Dubai; James Shotter in Warsaw; Guy Chazan and Tobias Buck in Berlin; and to Andres Schipani and Joe Leahy in São Paulo. Many colleagues in London have also been a source of help and ideas. I would particularly like to thank David Pilling, Martin Wolf, Jonathan Derbyshire, Fiona Symon and Roula Khalaf.

Dan Dombey read large sections of the book and gave me plenty of helpful feedback and encouragement. Jeremy Shapiro and Shruti Kapila were also generous enough to read parts of the manuscript in draft and to provide comments.

As will be evident to readers, this book draws upon twenty years of conversations with people all over the world. Many of them are quoted or cited in the book. Some live in countries threatened by strongman rule, so they might not thank me for thanking them by name. But I am truly grateful to everybody who has bothered to explain things to me over the years.

Most of this book was written during the Covid-19 pandemic, which brought my global travels to a sudden halt. The pandemic did,

however, have one positive side effect: it meant that four recent graduates were confined in the same house as me for many months. My
children – Natasha, Joe, Nathaniel and Adam – all chipped in with
research and ideas. Adam and Nat were particularly helpful, research-
ing the chapters on Southeast Asia and Africa, respectively. My wife,
Olivia, joined the discussions and kept everybody sane and happy during lockdown.

Finally, I'd like to thank my literary agents, James Pullen and Sarah
Chalfant at the Wylie Agency, who always provided good, friendly
advice delivered with the legendary Wylie promptness. It has once
again been a great pleasure to work with the Bodley Head and with
Stuart Williams and Jörg Hensgen in particular. Other Press, where I
have been guided by Judith Gurewich and edited by Yvonne Cárdenas,
provided the perfect home in the US.

Notes

Introduction

1 These figures are compiled by Max Roser of Oxford University's Martin School, drawing on data from the Varieties of Democracy project. See ourworldindata.org.

2 Freedom House, "Freedom in the World 2021: Democracy under siege."

3 Quoted in Mehdi Hasan, "It wasn't just Trump – every US president has gotten Putin wrong," MSNBC, June 16, 2021.

4 Brian Parkin and Rainer Buergin, "Merkel says Russia risks harm to itself with nineteenth-century ways," Bloomberg, March 13, 2014.

5 "A Turkish Success Story," *New York Times*, January 28, 2004.

6 Nicholas Kristof, "Looking for a Jump-Start in China," *New York Times*, January 5, 2013. The passage was drawn to my attention by Richard McGregor in *Xi Jinping: The Backlash* (Lowy Institute, 2019), p. 9.

7 Thomas L. Friedman, "Letter from Saudi Arabia," *New York Times*, November 25, 2015.

8 Thomas L. Friedman, "Saudi Arabia's Arab Spring At Last," *New York Times*, November 23, 2017.

9 Gideon Rachman, "India needs a jolt– and Modi is a risk worth taking," *Financial Times*, April 28, 2014.

10 Freedom House, "Freedom in the World 2020: A Leaderless Struggle for Democracy."

11 Rachel Frazin, "Biden calls Boris Johnson a physical and emotional clone of Trump," *The Hill*, December 13, 2019.

12 See Masha Gessen, "Autocracy Rules for Survival," *New York Review of Books*, November 10, 2016.

13 "'Trump Defends Putin Killing Journalists," Daily Beast, April 13, 2017.

14 Rana Mitter, "The World China Wants," *Foreign Affairs*, January 2021.

15 Ramachandra Guha, "Modi Personality Cult Runs Contrary to BJP's Own Objections to Worship of Individuals," Scroll.in, August 2, 2020.

16 Charlotte Gao, "Xi: China Must Never Adopt Constitutionalism," *The Diplomat*, February 19, 2019.

17 Reuters video, April 14, 2020.

18 Quoted in *The Economist*, "Getting off the train," February 6, 2016.

19 See Nathaniel Rachman, "The Simpleton Manifesto," *Persuasion*, October 15, 2020.

20 John Johnston, "Boris Johnson blasted over claims deep state is betraying Brexit," Politics Home, January 14, 2019.

21 Conversation with the author, Berlin, October 2019.

22 Ibid.

23 Fiona Hill, *There Is Nothing for You Here: Finding Opportunity in the 21st Century* (Mariner Books, 2021), p. 224.

24 "No job, no house, no welfare," *The Economist*, May 30, 1998.

25 See Roberto Foa, "Why strongmen win in weak states," *Journal of Democracy*, January 2021.

26 "Genocide Aside," *The Economist*, February 13, 2021.

27 Jeffrey Goldberg, "Why Obama Fears for Our Democracy," *The Atlantic*, November 2020.

28 "Can you foil the love tonight?," *The Economist*, November 19, 2020.

29 The importance of machismo to strongman leaders throughout history, such as Mussolini, Gaddhafi, Putin and others, is an important theme of Ruth Ben-Ghiat's book, *Strongmen: How They Rise, Why They Succeed, How They Fall* (Profile, 2020).

30 Conversation with the author, Moscow, August 2019.

31 Mark Easton, "Coronavirus: Social media spreading virus conspiracy theories," BBC, June 18, 2020.

1. Putin – the archetype

1 Fiona Hill and Clifford Gaddy, *Mr Putin: Operative in the Kremlin* (Brookings Institution Press, 2013). Fiona Hill went on to head the Russia desk in the Trump White House, and gave testimony during the impeachment hearings into President Trump.

2 New Year's address by Acting President Vladimir Putin, December 31, 1999, www.en.kremlin.ru.

3 Discussed in Ivan Krastev and Stephen Holmes, *The Light That Failed – A Reckoning* (Allen Lane, 2019), p. 108.

4 Quotes from Lionel Barber and Henry Foy, "Vladimir Putin says liberalism has become obsolete," *Financial Times*, June 27, 2019.

5 See Susan Glasser, "Putin the Great," *Foreign Affairs*, September/October 2019.

6 Quoted in Catherine Belton, *Putin's People – How the KGB took back Russia and then took on the West* (William Collins, 2020), pp. 26, 39–41.

7 Hill and Gaddy, p. 76.

8 Belton, p. 85.

9 Hill and Gaddy, p. 9.

10 Quoted in Belton, p. 112.

11 Ibid., p. 11. Belton also provides a fascinating account of how Putin's original sponsors in Yeltsin's circle pushed him forward – and then came to regret their decision.

12 As quoted in Anton Troianovski, "Branding Putin," *Washington Post*, July 12, 2018

13 James Ciment, "Life Expectancy of Russian Men Falls to 58," *BMJ*, August 21, 1999.

14 Interview with the author, Moscow, September 2014.

15 "Putin's Russia," Rachman Review podcast with Fyodor Lukyanov, October 9, 2019.

16 Krastev and Holmes, p. 82.

17 Conversation with the author, Moscow, 2008.

18 Quoted in Jan Matti Dollbaum, Morvan Lallouet and Ben Noble, *Navalny: Putin's Nemesis, Russia's Future* (Hurst, 2021), p. 152.

19 See Max Seddon, "Lunch with the FT: Alexei Navalny," *Financial Times*, November 22, 2019.

20 Luke Harding, "Revealed: the $2 billion offshore trail that leads to Vladimir Putin," *The Guardian*, April 3, 2016.

21 "Russian billionaire Arkady Rotenberg says 'Putin Palace' is his," BBC, January 30, 2021.

22 "Vlad's the boss: 'World's secret richest man' Vladimir Putin guards his secret billions like a mafia godfather, expert claims," *The Sun*, March 22, 2018.

23 Chris Giles, "Russia's role in producing the tax system of the future," *Financial Times*, July 29, 2019.

24 Quoted in Martin Chulov, "Can Saudi Arabia's 'great reformer' survive the death in the consulate?," *The Guardian*, October 13, 2018.

25 Quoted in Elias Isquith, "Rudy Giuliani," Salon, March 4, 2014.

26 The original interview was carried out by Alastair Campbell for *GQ* in 2014.

27 Tobias Jones, "How Matteo Salvini Became Putin's Man in Europe," *Prospect*, August 30, 2019.

28 Anne Applebaum, "The False Romance of Russia," *The Atlantic*, December 12, 2019.

29 These links are described in Belton, pp. 427–36.

30 Quoted in Troianowski, *Washington Post*.

31 Julian Borger, "Russia is a regional power showing weakness over Ukraine," *The Guardian*, March 25, 2014.

2. Erdoğan – from liberal reformer to authoritarian strongman

1 Robert Kaplan, "At the Gates of Brussels," *Atlantic*, December 2004.

2 Quoted in "To Brussels on a wing and a prayer," *The Economist*, October 9, 2004.

3 Ibid.

4 See Gideon Rachman, *Easternization* (Other Press, 2018), p. 202.

5 See Soner Cagaptay, *The New Sultan: Erdoğan and the Crisis of Modern Turkey* (IB Tauris, 2020), p. 4.

6 Quoted in Kaya Gene, "Erdoğan's Way," *Foreign Affairs*, September 2019, p. 29.

7 See Steven Cook, "How Erdoğan Made Turkey Authoritarian Again," *The Atlantic*, July 21, 2016.

8 See Aykan Erdemir and Oren Kessler, "A Turkish TV blockbuster reveals Erdoğan's conspiratorial, anti-Semitic worldview," *Washington Post*, May 15, 2017.

9 See Jenny White, "Democracy is Like a Tram," Turkey Institute, July 14, 2016.

10 Jonathan Head, "Quiet end to Turkey's college headscarf ban," BBC, December 31, 2010.

11 Gideon Rachman, "Don't Be Blind to Erdoğan's Flaws," *Financial Times*, October 10, 2011.

12 There is a vivid account of the coup attempt in Hannah Lucinda Smith, *Erdoğan Rising: The Battle for the Soul of Turkey* (William Collins, 2019), pp. 203–21.

13 See Laura Pitel, "Turkey: Gulenist crackdown," *Financial Times*, September 11, 2016.

14 See Gene, *Foreign Affairs*, p. 33.

15 Laura Pitel, "Europe's top human rights court orders Turkey to release jailed Turkish politician," *Financial Times*, December 22, 2020.

16 Matthew Wills, "The Turkish Origins of the Deep State," JSTOR Daily, April 10, 2017.

17 See the testimony of John Bolton and Fiona Hill, cited on p. 128.

18 Gideon Rachman, "Modi and Erdoğan Thrive on Divisive Identity Politics," *Financial Times*, August 10, 2020.

19 Peter Spiegel, "José Manuel Barroso: Not everything I did was right," *Financial Times*, November 4, 2014.

20 "Turkey slams EU officials in row over Netherlands campaigning," BBC, March 14, 2017.

21 Quoted in Laura Pitel, "Erdoğan's great game: soldiers, spies and Turkey's quest for power," *Financial Times*, January 12, 2021.

22 David Kirkpatrick and Carlotta Gall, "Audio Offers Gruesome Details of Jamal Khashoggi Killing," *New York Times*, October 17, 2018.

23 Laura Pitel, "Turkey Senses Growing National Challenge to Erdoğan," *Financial Times*, June 24, 2019.

24 Tweet by @SonerCagaptay on June 2, 2020.

3. Xi Jinping – China and the return of the cult of personality

1 Nicolas Berggruen and Nathan Gardels, "How the world's most powerful leader thinks," WorldPost, January 21, 2014.

2 John Simpson, "New Leader Xi Jinping Opens Door to Reform in China," *The Guardian*, August 10, 2013.

3 Frank Dikötter, *How to Be a Dictator: The Cult of Personality in the Twentieth Century* (Bloomsbury, 2019), p. 105.

4   Quoted in Chris Buckley, "Xi Jinping opens China Party Congress, his hold tighter than ever," *New York Times*, October 17, 2017.

5   Quoted in Tom Phillips, "Xi Jinping heralds new era of Chinese power at Communist Party Congress," *The Guardian*, October 18, 2017.

6   "China's Economy in Six Charts," *Harvard Business Review*, November 2013.

7   See Evan Osnos, "Born Red," *New Yorker*, March 30, 2015.

8   There is a good short account of Xi's early life in Kerry Brown, *The World According to Xi* (IB Tauris, 2018). Also see the excellent essay by Evan Osnos cited above.

9   Quoted in François Bougon, *Inside the Mind of Xi Jinping* (Hurst, 2018), p. 56.

10 See Osnos, *New Yorker*.

11 Brown, *The World According to Xi*, p. 16.

12 McGregor, *Xi Jinping: The Backlash*, p. 34.

13 Edward Wong, Neil Gough and Alexandra Stevenson, "China's Response to Stock Plunge Rattles Traders," *New York Times*, September 9, 2015.

14 "Rumors swirl in China after death of top Chongqing Party official," Radio Free Asia, November 4, 2019.

15 Victor Mallet, "Interpol 'complicit' in arrest of its chief in China," *Financial Times*, July 7, 2019.

16 "Xi Jinping Millionaire Relations Reveal Fortunes of Elite," Bloomberg News, June 29, 2012.

17 Quoted in Bougon, *Inside the Mind of Xi Jinping*, p. 39.

18 Ibid., p. 154.

19 Yuan Yang, "Inside China's Crackdown on Young Marxists," *Financial Times*, February 14, 2019.

20 Gideon Rachman, "Lunch with the FT: Eric Li," *Financial Times*, February 7, 2020.

21 Quoted in Don Weiland, "Inside Wuhan," *Financial Times*, April 25, 2020.

22 Quoted in Michael Collins, "The WHO and China: Dereliction of Duty," Council on Foreign Relations, February 27, 2020.

23 These numbers have been greeted with some skepticism in the West. An analysis of excess-death figures by *The Economist* concluded that "Covid-19 deaths in Wuhan seem far higher than the

official count" (May 30, 2021). Chinese figures had put the numbers of deaths in Wuhan, where the first outbreak took place, at 3,869. *The Economist* revised this up to 13,400 by the end of March 2020. But even if this revision is correct, the underlying point – that there were far fewer deaths in China than the West – is uncontested.

24 Quoted in "Xi confers medals for virus fight at ceremony in Great Hall of the People," Bloomberg, September 8, 2020.

25 John Sudworth, "Wuhan marks its anniversary with triumph and denial," BBC, January 23, 2020.

26 "Unfavorable views of China reach historic highs in many countries," Pew Research Center, October 6, 2020.

27 Jonathan Kaiman, "Islamist group claims responsibility for attack on China's Tiananmen Square," *The Guardian*, November 25, 2013.

28 Stephanie Nebehay, "UN says it has credible reports that China holds 1m Uighurs in secret camps," Reuters, August 10, 2018.

29 "China forces birth control on Uighur Muslims, other minorities: birth rates fall by 60% from 2015 to 2018 in Xinjiang," Associated Press, June 29, 2020.

30 James Landale, "Uighurs: Credible case, China carrying out genocide," BBC, February 8, 2021.

31 Zheping Huang, "Xi Jinping Says China's authoritarian system can be a model for the world," Quartz, March 9, 2018.

32 "The View from Bogotá – an interview with President Iván Duque Márquez," Aspen Institute, January 22, 2021.

33 Hu Xijin, "The more trouble Taiwan creates, the sooner the mainland will teach them a lesson," *Global Times*, October 6, 2020.

4. Modi – strongman politics in the world's largest democracy

1 Conversation with the author, Delhi, May 2018.

2 Quoted in Benjamin Parkin and Amy Kazmin, "Narendra Modi renames cricket stadium after himself," *Financial Times*, February 24, 2021.

3 Many of these examples are drawn from an article by Kapil Komireddi, "India, the world's largest democracy, is now powered by a cult of personality," *Washington Post*, March 18, 2021.

4   Debobrat Ghose, "1,200 years of servitude: PM Modi offers food for thought," Firstpost, June 13, 2014.

5   Interview with Subramanian Swamy, Huffington Post, April 14, 2017.

6   Ramachandra Guha, "How the RSS detested Gandhi," *The Wire*, January 30, 2020.

7   See "Why India's Hindu hardliners want to sideline Mahatma Gandhi," BBC, January 30, 2017.

8   An outline of Modi's early career and relationship with the RSS is provided in Dexter Filkins, "Blood and Soil in Narendra Modi's India," *New Yorker*, December 2, 2019.

9   There is a portrait of Singh and his reforms in my earlier book, *Zero-Sum World* (Atlantic, 2012), pp. 78–83.

10 Gideon Rachman, "India needs a jolt – and Modi is a risk worth taking," *Financial Times*, April 28, 2014.

11 Ibid.

12 Barack Obama, "Narendra Modi," *Time*, April 15, 2015.

13 Quoted in Gideon Rachman, "How India's Narendra Modi will shape the world," *Financial Times*, May 14, 2018.

14 The conversation took place in London at a lunch organized by the Indian High Commission on July 9, 2019.

15 Interview with Swamy, Huffington Post.

16 Rachman, *Financial Times*, May 14, 2018.

17 Milind Ghatwai, "Madhya Pradesh: You vote for Lotus, you are pressing trigger to kill terrorists, says PM Modi," *Indian Express*, May 18, 2019.

18 "Outrage over right-wing Euro-MPs' Kashmir visit," BBC, October 30, 2019.

19 Quoted in Isaac Chotiner, "Amartya Sen's Hopes and Fears for Indian democracy," *New Yorker*, October 6, 2019.

20 Pratap Bhanu Mehta, "Serial Authoritarianism picks out targets one by one and tires out challenges," *Indian Express*, October 10, 2019.

21 Yogita Limaye, "Amnesty International to halt India operations," BBC, September 29, 2020.

22 See Filkins, *New Yorker*.

23 Shivshankar Menon, "Rulers of Darkness," *India Today*, October 4, 2019.

24 See Jo Johnson, "Narendra Modi's culture war storms India's elite universities," *Financial Times*, January 26, 2020.

25 Shruti Kapila, "Nehru's idea of India is under attack from the nationalist right," *Financial Times*, January 12, 2020.

26 Jason Stanley, "For Trump and Modi, ethnic purity is the purpose of power," *The Guardian*, February 24, 2020.

27 "Supreme Court judge describes Modi as 'popular, vibrant and visionary leader'," *The Wire*, February 6, 2021.

28 Quoted in Amy Kazmin, "Indians maintain faith in messianic Modi," *Financial Times*, July 6, 2020.

29 Quoted in Gideon Rachman, "Narendra Modi and the perils of Covid hubris," *Financial Times*, April 26, 2021.

30 Amy Kazmin, "Narendra Modi, the style king, puts on the guru look," *Financial Times*, July 1, 2021.

5. Orbán, Kaczynski and the rise of illiberal Europe

1 Quoted in Colin Woodard, "Europe's New Dictator," *Politico*, June 17, 2015.

2 Quoted in Paul Lendvai, *Orbán: Europe's New Strongman* (Hurst, 2017), p. 195.

3 Ibid., p. 192.

4 Quoted in Krastev and Holmes, p. 68.

5 Quoted in Lendvai, p. 201.

6 Krastev and Holmes, p. 14.

7 "Trump calls for total and complete shutdown of Muslims entering US," *Politico*, December 7, 2015.

8 Quoted in Krastev and Holmes, p. 47.

9 These details are from a profile and interview with Kaczynski, carried out by my *FT* colleague, Henry Foy, "Poland's Kingmaker," *Financial Times*, February 26, 2016.

10 Quoted in Patrick Kingsley, "As the West Fears the Rise of Autocrats, Hungary Shows What's Possible," *New York Times*, February 10, 2018.

11 Viktor Orbán, State of the Nation speech, February 19, 2020. Transcript from Remix News.

12 See Paul Lendvai, "The Transformer: Orbán's Evolution and Hungary's Demise," *Foreign Affairs*, September 2019, p. 46.

13 Ibid., p. 48.

14 George Soros, "Rebuilding the asylum system," Project Syndicate, September 26, 2015.

15 Quoted in Peter Conradi, "How the billionaire George Soros became the right's favourite bogeyman," *Sunday Times*, March 10, 2019.

16 Lendvai, *Foreign Affairs*, p. 52.

17 "How Viktor Orbán hollowed out Hungary's democracy," *The Economist*, August 29, 2019.

18 Quoted in Valerie Hopkins, "How Orbán's decade in power changed Hungary," *Financial Times*, May 21, 2020.

19 Quoted in Lendvai, *Foreign Affairs*, p. 54. Original interview in *La Repubblica* in 2018.

20 Ibid.

21 Tony Barber, "Europe's patience with Viktor Orbán starts to wear thin," *Financial Times*, March 8, 2021.

22 Jan Cienski, "Poland's constitutional crisis goes international," *Politico*, December 24, 2015.

23 Jan Cienski, "New media law gives Polish government fuller control," *Politico*, December 30, 2015.

24 Quoted in Marc Santora, "After a president's shocking death, a suspicious twin reshapes a nation," *New York Times*, June 16, 2018.

25 "Half of Poles believe foreign powers deliberately spreading coronavirus," *Notes from Poland*, April 20, 2020.

26 Quoted in Anne Applebaum, *Twilight of Democracy* (Allen Lane, 2020), p. 31.

27 "Playing the Family Card," *The Economist*, June 20, 2020.

28 "Poland's draconian restrictions on abortion," *Financial Times*, November 8, 2020.

6. Boris Johnson and Brexit Britain

1 Gideon Rachman and Nick Clegg, "Is joining the euro still too big a risk for Britain?," *Prospect*, January 20, 2002. The article was a debate with Nick Clegg, who was then an MEP and later became Britain's deputy prime minister. Clegg argued in favor of Britain joining the euro.

2 Hill, p. 71.

3 Daniel Boffey and Toby Helm, "Vote Leave embroiled in race row over Turkey security threat claims," *Observer*, May 22, 2016.

4 Tim Shipman, *All Out War: The Full Story of Brexit* (William Collins, 2017), p. 299.

5 Roger Eatwell and Matthew Goodwin, *National Populism: The Revolt Against Liberal Democracy* (Pelican, 2018), pp. 35–6.

6 Ibid., p. 17.

7 Quoted in Sonia Purnell, *Just Boris* (Aurum, 2012), p. 50.

8 Boris Johnson and Nicholas Farrell, "Forza Berlusconi," *Spectator*, September 6, 2003.

9 Gideon Rachman, "Boris Johnson has failed the Churchill Test," *Financial Times*, February 22, 2016.

10 Rajeev Syal, "Cameron: Johnson said Leave campaign would lose minutes before backing it," *The Guardian*, September 16, 2019.

11 Rick Noak, "Brexit needs some of Trump's madness, Boris Johnson suggests," *Washington Post*, June 8, 2018.

12 Katie Weston, "Brexit conspiracy: Boris Johnson warns the deep state's great conspiracy will backfire," *Daily Express*, January 14, 2019.

13 Sebastian Payne, "Downing Street glee as gang of 21 expelled from the Tory party," *Financial Times*, September 4, 2019.

14 Dominic Cummings blog, "On the referendum – Actions have consequences," March 27, 2019.

15 Peter Walker, "UK poised to embrace authoritarianism, warns Hansard Society," *The Guardian*, April 8, 2019.

16 Allison Pearson, "We need you, Boris – your health is the health of the nation," *Daily Telegraph*, April 7, 2020.

17 Rush Doshi, *The Long Game: China's Grand Strategy to Displace American Order* (Oxford University Press, 2021), p. 13.

7. Donald Trump – American strongman

1 Philip Bump, "The real story behind that viral clip of Keith Ellison predicting a Donald Trump victory," *Washington Post*, February 22, 2017.

2 Gideon Rachman, "We deride chances of Marine Le Pen and Donald Trump at our peril," *Financial Times*, November 30, 2015.

3 Ibid.

4 Conversation with the author.

5 Later research by Deaton and Case showed that while there remained a gap in life expectancy between white and Black Americans, the most significant determinant was now levels of education. Blacks and whites with college degrees had similar levels of life expectancy – which were, in turn, higher than those of Blacks and whites without college degrees.

6 Gina Kolata, "Death Rates Rising For Middle-Aged White Americans, Study Finds," *New York Times*, November 2, 2015.

7 Willam H. Frey, "The US will become 'minority white' in 2045, Census projects," Brookings Institution, March 14, 2018.

8 Michael Anton (writing as Publius Decius Mus), "The Flight 93 Election," *Claremont Review of Books*, September 5, 2016.

9 Alec Tyson and Shiva Maniam, "Behind Trump's victory: Divisions by race, gender, education," Pew Research Center, November 9, 2016.

10 See John Sides, Michael Tesler and Lynn Vavreck, *Identity Crisis: The 2016 Presidential Election and the Battle for the Meaning of America* (Princeton University Press, 2018).

11 Ibid., p. 71.

12 Ibid., p. 88.

13 Quoted in Thomas Edsall, "White Riot," *New York Times*, January 13, 2021.

14 Cited in Larry M. Bartels, "Ethnic Antagonism Erodes Republicans' Commitment to Democracy," *Proceedings of the National Academy of Sciences of the United States of America*, September 15, 2020.

15 The *Playboy* interview with Donald Trump, March 1, 1990.

16 Ibid.

17 Michael Schmidt, "In a Private Dinner, Trump Demanded Loyalty: Comey demurred," *New York Times*, May 11, 2017.

18 John Wagner, "Praise for the Chief," *Washington Post*, June 12, 2017.

19 See Jonathan Rauch, "Trump's Firehose of Falsehood," *Persuasion*, November 18, 2020.

20 Alexander Griffing, "Remember when Donald Trump appeared on Alex Jones's Infowars," *Haaretz*, August 6, 2018.

21 Peter Baker, "Dishonesty Has Defined the Trump Presidency. The Consequences Could Be Lasting," *New York Times*, November 1, 2020.

22 Hill, p. 220.

23 Ibid.

24 Quoted in Franklin Foer, "Viktor Orbán's War on Intellect," *The Atlantic*, June 2019.

25 Bolton, p. 312.

26 Ibid., p. 181.

27 Ibid., p. 63.

28 Conversation with the author.

29 Axios, September 14, 2020.

30 Bolton, p. 191.

31 Gideon Rachman, "Lunch with the FT: Chris Ruddy," *Financial Times*, March 2, 2018.

32 Hill, pp. 220–1.

33 Bolton, p. 297.

34 Edward Luce, "Beware Trump's admiration for Putin, Xi and Erdoğan," *Financial Times*, January 16, 2020.

35 Hill, p. 221.

36 Aaron Blake, "What Trump said before his supporters stormed the Capitol," *Washington Post*, January 11, 2021.

37 Ibid.

8. Rodrigo Duterte and the erosion of democracy in Southeast Asia

1 Louis Nelson, "Trump praises Duterte for unbelievable job cracking down on drugs in the Philippines," *Politico*, May 24, 2017.

2 Nicola Smith, "Trump praises Kim Jong-un as 'terrific' and pledges to hold second summit," *Telegraph*, September 25, 2018.

3 "Remarks by President Trump in Press Conference," US Embassy & Consulate in Vietnam, February 28, 2019.

4 Will Worley, "Philippines president Rodrigo Duterte tells people to go ahead and kill drug addicts," *The Independent*, July 3, 2016.

5 "More than 7,000 killed in the Philippines in six months," Amnesty International, May 18, 2020.

6 Ibid.

7 Rambo Talabong, "Big funds, little transparency: How Duterte's drug list works," Rappler, February 16, 2020.

8 Patrick Symmes, "President Duterte's List," *New York Times*, January 10, 2017.

9   Jonathan Miller, *Duterte Harry: Fire and Fury in the Philippines* (Scribe, 2018), p. 86.

10 Carlos H. Conde, "Killings in Philippines Up 50 Percent During Pandemic," Human Rights Watch, September 8, 2020.

11 Davinci Maru, "CHR Chief: Drug war deaths could be as high as 27,000," ABS-CBN News, December 5, 2018.

12 Aurora Almendral, "Where 518 inmates Sleep in Space for 170 and Gangs Hold It Together," *New York Times*, January 7, 2019.

13 "The Rodrigo Duterte Interview," *Esquire Philippines*, August 25, 2016.

14 "Philippines: Duterte confirms he personally killed three men," BBC News, December 16, 2016.

15 "Philippine leader says once threw man from a helicopter, would do it again," Reuters, December 29, 2016.

16 Eleanor Ross, "Philippines President Duterte's Drug War, One Year On," *Newsweek*, June 30, 2017.

17 Sheila Coronel, "The Vigilante President," *Foreign Affairs*, September 2019.

18 Richard Heydarian, "A Revolution Betrayed: The Tragedy of Indonesia's Jokowi," Al Jazeera, November 24, 2019.

19 "Prevalence of drug use in the general population – national data," *World Drug Report,* United Nations Office on Drugs and Crime, 2018.

20 "The Dangers of Duterte Harry," *The Economist*, May 19, 2016.

21 Miller, p. 194.

22 Coronel, *Foreign Affairs*.

23 Miller, p. 44.

24 Maria Cepeda, "Arroyo thanks Duterte for helping to acquit her of plunder," Rappler, July 9, 2019.

25 There is a good account of Duterte's upbringing and career in Jonathan Miller's *Duterte Harry*. See also Michael Peel, *The Fabulists* (Oneworld, 2019).

26 Andrew R. C. Marshall and Manuel Mogato, "Philippine death squads very much in business as Duterte set for presidency," Reuters, May 25, 2016.

27 See Miller, p. 2.

28 Mike Frialde, "Murder Rate Highest in Davao City," *Philippine Star*, April 1, 2016.

29 Camille Elemia, "Photo used by Duterte camp to hit critics taken in Brazil, not PH," Rappler, August 26, 2016.

30 Alexandra Stevenson, "Soldiers in Facebook's War on Fake News Are Feeling Overrun," *New York Times*, October 9, 2018.

31 Dino-Ray Ramos, "'A Thousands Cuts' Trailer: Ramona S. Diaz's Docu About Journalist Maria Ressa and Press Freedom in Duterte's Philippines Sets Theatrical Run," Deadline, July 12, 2020.

32 Rebecca Ratcliffe, "Amal Clooney decries legal charade after journalist Maria Ressa charged again with libel," *The Guardian*, January 12, 2021.

33 Ben Blanchard, "Duterte aligns Philippines with China, says US has lost," Reuters, October 20, 2016.

9. The rise of MBS and the Netanyahu phenomenon

1 Ben Hubbard, *MBS: The Rise to Power of Mohammed bin Salman* (William Collins, 2020), p. 267.

2 See Bradley Hope and Justin Scheck, *Blood and Oil: Mohammed bin Salman's Ruthless Quest for Global Power* (John Murray, 2020), p. 54.

3 Hubbard, p. 110.

4 Jodi Kantor, "For Kushner, Israel Policy May Be Personal," *New York Times*, February 11, 2017.

5 Rachman Review podcast interview with Anshel Pfeffer, *Financial Times*, September 10, 2020.

6 Anshel Pfeffer, *Bibi: The Turbulent Life and Times of Benjamin Netanyahu* (Basic Books, 2018), p. 17.

7 Ibid., p. 45.

8 Yoram Hazony, *The Virtue of Nationalism* (Basic, 2018).

9 Quoted in Constanze Stelzenmüller, "America's policy on Europe takes a nationalist turn," *Financial Times*, January 30, 2019.

10 Gideon Rachman, "Why the new nationalists love Israel," *Financial Times*, April 1, 2019.

11 "Duterte meets Netanyahu: 'We share the same passion for human beings,'" Rappler, September 3, 2018.

12 William Galston, "What's Beijing Doing in Haifa?," *Wall Street Journal*, May 28, 2019.

13 Quoted in Robert Kagan, "Israel and the decline of the liberal order," *Washington Post*, September 12, 2019.

14 Hubbard, p. xv.

15 Ibid., p. 10.

16 Thomas L. Friedman, "Letter from Saudi Arabia," *New York Times*, November 25, 2015.

17 Thomas L. Friedman, "Saudi Arabia's Arab Spring at Last," *New York Times*, November 23, 2017.

18 See Hope and Scheck, pp. 59, 64.

19 See Hubbard, pp. 127–9.

20 Jamal Khashoggi, "Saudi Arabia wasn't always this oppressive. Now it's unbearable," *Washington Post*, September 18, 2017.

21 Julien Barnes and David Sanger, "Saudi Prince Is Held Responsible for Khashoggi Killing in US Report," *New York Times*, February 26, 2021.

22 Quoted in Hubbard, p. 272.

10. Bolsonaro, Amlo and the return of the Latin American caudillo

1 Gideon Rachman, "Brazil and the crisis of the liberal world order," *Financial Times*, August 28, 2017.

2 See Richard Lapper, *Beef, Bible and Bullets: Brazil in the Age of Bolsonaro* (Manchester University Press, 2021), p. 22.

3 Ibid., p. 29.

4 Vincent Bevins, "Where conspiracy reigns," *The Atlantic*, September 16, 2020.

5 Sam Cowie, "Brazil's culture secretary fired after echoing words of Nazi Goebbels," *The Guardian*, January 17, 2020.

6 For a sense of what happened in that period, it is worth reading Luiz Eduardo Soarses's *Rio de Janeiro, Extreme City* (Penguin, 2016), in particular chapter 2, "No Ordinary Woman." Jacobo Timerman's *Prisoner Without a Name, Cell Without a Number* (Knopf, 1981) is a classic account of imprisonment during Argentina's Dirty War.

7 Michael Reid, *Forgotten Continent: The Battle for Latin America's Soul* (Yale University Press, 2009), p. 123.

8 Ibid., p. 12.

9 Quoted in Anne Applebaum, "Venezuela's Suffering is the Eerie Endgame of Modern Politics," *The Atlantic*, February 27, 2020.

10 Tom Burgis, "Livingstone secures cheap oil from Venezuela," *Financial Times*, February 20, 2007.

11 Michael Albertus, "Chávez's Real Legacy is Disaster," *Foreign Policy*, December 6, 2018.

12 Bello, "The surprising similarities between AMLO and Jair Bolsonaro," *The Economist*, December 7, 2019.

13 "It's all about him," *The Economist*, November 30, 2019.

14 Quoted in Michael Stott, "Pandemic politics: the rebound of Latin America's populists," *Financial Times*, September 23, 2020.

15 Gideon Rachman, "Jair Bolsonaro's populism is leading Brazil to disaster," *Financial Times*, May 25, 2020.

16 "Brazil's Bolsonaro backs Trump fraud claims after unrest," France 24, January 7, 2021.

17 Alfonso Zárate, *El país de un solo hombre* (Temas de Hoy, Mexico, 2021).

18 Ibid.

19 Gideon Long, "Leftist Pedro Castillo finally confirmed as Peru's next president," *Financial Times*, July 20, 2021.

11. Abiy Ahmed and democratic disillusionment in Africa

1 David Pilling, "Why Abiy Ahmed is more popular in Norway than in Ethiopia," *Financial Times*, February 29, 2020.

2 A conversation with Abiy Ahmed, prime minister of Ethiopia, World Economic Forum, January 25, 2019.

3 Michela Wrong, "Ethiopia, Eritrea and the Perils of Reform," *Survival*, September 2018.

4 Michelle Gavin, "Ethiopian conflict erodes Abiy's credibility," Council on Foreign Relations, December 30, 2020.

5 "Will Mnangagwa go East as more sanctions come in from the West?," Africa Report, February 8, 2021.

6 The stories of some of these leaders, including Mugabe and Mobutu, are told in Paul Kenyon, *Dictatorland: The Men Who Stole Africa* (Head of Zeus, 2018).

7 "Jacob Zuma – the survivor whose nine lives ran out," BBC News, April 6, 2020.

8 Tom Wilson, "Graft under Jacob Zuma cost South Africa $34 billion says Ramaphosa," *Financial Times*, October 14, 2019.

9 "Young Africans want more democracy," *The Economist*, March 5, 2020.

10 Anjan Sundaram, "Rwanda: The Darling Tyrant," *Politico*, March/April 2020.

11 William Wallis. "Lunch with the FT: Paul Kagame," *Financial Times*, May 13, 2011.

12 David Pilling and Lionel Barber, "Interview: Kagame insists 'Rwandans understand the greater goal,'" *Financial Times*, September 27, 2020.

13 Aislinn Laing, "Rwanda's president Paul Kagame 'wishes' he had ordered death of exiled spy chief," *Daily Telegraph*, January 24, 2014.

14 Michela Wrong, *Do Not Disturb* (PublicAffairs, 2021).

15 "Uganda/Rwanda: Investigate Journalist's Murder," Human Rights Watch, December 6, 2011.

16 Jason Burke, "Rwandan government accused of abducting Paul Rusesabagina," *The Guardian*, September 1, 2020.

17 Sundaram, *Politico*.

18 William Wallis, "FT interview: Meles Zenawi, Ethiopian prime minister," *Financial Times*, February 6, 2007.

19 Armin Rosen, "A Modern Dictator: Why Ethiopia's Zenawi Mattered," *The Atlantic*, August 21, 2012.

20 Awol Allo, "Ethiopia's Meles Zenawi: Legacies, memories, histories," LSE Blogs, September 18, 2014.

21 "The man who tried to make dictatorship acceptable," *The Economist*, August 25, 2012.

22 Nic Cheeseman, *Democracy in Africa* (Cambridge University Press, 2015), pp. 138–40.

23 Ibid.

24 Yun Sun, "Political party training: China's ideological push in Africa?," Brookings Institution, July 5, 2016.

25 Lily Kuo, "Beijing is cultivating the next generation of African elites by training them in China," Quartz, December 14, 2017.

26 Amy Hawkins, "Beijing's Big Brother Tech Needs African Faces," *Foreign Policy*, July 24, 2018; Samuel Woodhams, "How China Exports Repression to Africa," *The Diplomat*, February 23, 2019.

27 Jevans Nyabiage, "How Zimbabwe's new parliament symbolises China's chequebook diplomacy approach to Africa," *South China Morning Post*, January 5, 2020.

28 Abdi Latif Dahir, "Why these African countries are defending China's mass detention of Muslims," Quartz, July 16, 2019; "Spotlight: Ambassadors from 37 countries issue joint letter to support China on its human rights achievements," Xinhua Net, July 13, 2019.

29 Judd Devermont, "Russian Theater: How to Respond to Moscow's Return to the African Stage," Lawfare, October 18, 2019. The author is a former CIA analyst.

30 Robbie Gramer and Jefcoate O'Donnell, "How Washington Got on Board with Congo's Rigged Election," *Foreign Policy*, February 1, 2019.

31 @jakejsullivan, November 25, 2020.

32 "Africa's population will double by 2050," *The Economist*, March 28, 2020.

12. Merkel, Macron and Europe's struggle against the strongmen

1 Quoted in Sophie Pedder, *Revolution Française: Emmanuel Macron and the Quest to Reinvent a Nation* (Bloomsbury, 2018), p. 73.

2 Ibid., p. 129.

3 Sunny Hundal, "Angela Merkel is now the leader of the free world, not Donald Trump," *The Independent*, February 1, 2017.

4 "What did Angela Merkel do when the Wall came down?," BBC, September 19, 2013.

5 Quoted in Lionel Barber, *The Powerful and the Damned* (WH Allen, 2020), p. 96.

6 Constanze Stelzenmüller, "The AfD wolf is at the door in eastern Germany," *Financial Times*, September 8, 2019.

7 Rachman Review podcast, "Germany's shifting foreign policy," *Financial Times*, November 20, 2019.

8 "Emmanuel Macron warns Europe: NATO is becoming brain-dead," *The Economist*, November 7, 2019.

9 "Réactions des Français à la tribune des militaires dans Valeurs Actuelles," Harris Interactive, April 29, 2021.

10 "President Macron on Trump, Brexit and Frexit," BBC, January 21, 2018.

11 Quoted in Victor Mallet, "Debate on Islamist extremism law exposes deep rifts in France," *Financial Times*, February 11, 2021.

12 Victor Mallet, "Resurgent Marine Le Pen revels in Macron's woes," *Financial Times*, January 30, 2020.

13 "[Scandale Soros] Marine Le Pen: 'Macron ne peut plus garder le silence,'" *Valeurs Actuelles*, February 20, 2020.

13. George Soros, Steve Bannon and the battle of ideas

1 Gideon Rachman, "Soros hatred is a global sickness," *Financial Times*, September 18, 2017.

2 "The Forbes 400, 2020," Forbes.com.

3 Figure cited in Emily Tamkin, *The Influence of Soros* (Harper, 2020), p. 4.

4 George Soros, foreword to Karl Popper, *The Open Society and Its Enemies* (Princeton University Press, 1994).

5 Roula Khalaf, Interview with George Soros, FT Person of the Year, *Financial Times*, December 18, 2018.

6 See Tamkin, pp. 74–5.

7 Seth Mydans, "Malaysian premier sees Jews behind nation's money crisis," *New York Times*, October 16, 1997.

8 See Robert Mackey, "The Plot against George Soros Didn't Start in Hungary, It started on Fox News," The Intercept, January 23, 2018.

9 "Fiona Hill Blasts Anti-Semitic Conspiracy Theories Against George Soros in Testimony," Huffington Post, November 22, 2019.

10 "A Conversation with Rudy Giuliani," *New York*, December 23, 2019.

11 Peter Walker, "Farage criticised for using antisemitic themes to criticise Soros," *The Guardian*, May 12, 2019.

12 "George Soros, the man who broke the Bank of England, backing secret plot to thwart Brexit," *Daily Telegraph*, February 18, 2018.

13 See Tamkin, p. 172.

14 @YairNetanyahu, April 28, 2019.

15 Osman Kavala, "710 Nights in a Turkish Prison," *New York Times*, October 11, 2019.

16 George Soros, "Remarks Delivered at the World Economic Forum," January 24, 2019.

17 Saul Friedländer, *The Years of Extermination: Nazi Germany and the Jews* (Phoenix, 2007), pp. xvii, xviii.

18 Quoted in Khalaf, *Financial Times*.

19 Quoted in Conradi, *Sunday Times*.

20 Gideon Rachman, "America is the revisionist power on trade," *Financial Times*, May 13, 2019.

21 Qiao Liang and Wang Xiangsui, *Unrestricted Warfare: China's Master Plan to Destroy America* (Filament Books, 2017).

22 Trump's speech in Warsaw, full transcript, CNN, 6 July 2017.

23 Sarah Marsh, "Steve Bannon calls for Tommy Robinson to be released from prison," *The Guardian*, July 15, 2018.

24 An account of this meeting is given in Benjamin R. Teitelbaum, *War for Eternity* (Allen Lane, 2020), pp. 153–61.

25 Jan-Werner Müller, *A Dangerous Mind: Carl Schmitt in Post-War European Thought* (Yale University Press, 2003), p. 11.

26 This section draws heavily on my own article on Schmitt. Gideon Rachman, "Liberalism's most brilliant enemy is back in vogue," *Financial Times*, January 11, 2019.

27 Quoted in Ryan Mitchell, "Chinese Receptions of Carl Schmitt since 1929," *Journal of Law and International Affairs*, May 2020.

28 Xu Jilin, *Rethinking China's Rise: A Liberal Critique* (Cambridge University Press, 2018), p. 27.

29 Ibid.

30 Ibid.

31 Quoted in Gao, *The Diplomat*.

32 Quoted in Mark Galeotti, *We Need to Talk About Putin* (Ebury, 2019), p. 68.

33 Leticia Duarte, "Meet Olavo de Carvalho," *Atlantic*, December 28, 2019.

34 See Olavo de Carvalho, "The Battle of the Monsters," *Diario de Comercio*, June 16, 2004.

35 Quoted in Duarte, *The Atlantic*.

Epilogue: Biden in the Age of the Strongman

1 David E. Sanger, "Biden Defines His Underlying Challenge with China: 'Prove Democracy Works,'" *New York Times*, April 29, 2021.

2 Ibid.

3 Thomas Edsall, "Mitch McConnell Would Like Trump to Fade Away," *New York Times*, February 24, 2021.

4 Michael Gerson, "Trump's rot has reached the GOP's roots," February 15, 2021.

5 See Edsall, *New York Times*.

6 Eliza Relman, "Mark Meadows says all the top 2024 GOP candidates have Trump as their last name," *Business Insider*, February 27, 2021.

7 Jonathan Kirshner, "Gone but not forgotten: Trump's long shadow and the end of American credibility," *Foreign Affairs*, March/April 2021.

8 Jake Sullivan et al., "Making US Foreign Policy work better for the middle class," Carnegie Endowment, September 23, 2020.

9 "Kremlin accuses Joe Biden of spreading hatred," Reuters, October 26, 2020.

10 Quoted in Henry Foy, "The Brutal Third Act of Vladimir Putin," *Financial Times*, March 11, 2021.

11 Tom Mitchell, Primrose Riordan and Nicolle Liu, "Hong Kong will sit on China's lap," *Financial Times*, March 13, 2021.

12 Quoted in Sanger, *New York Times*.

13 Demetri Sevastopulo and Tom Mitchell, "Bitter summit shows no reset in chilly US-China relations," *Financial Times*, March 20, 2021.

14 David Smith, "How Tucker Carlson and the far right embraced Hungary's authoritarian leader," *The Guardian*, August 8, 2021.

15 Martin Donai, "Political outsider prepares to take on Orban," *Financial Times*, October 19, 2021.

16 Bryan Harris and Michael Pooler, "Bolsonaro tests Brazilian democracy," *Financial Times*, September 28, 2021.

17 Laura Pitel and Funja Guler, "Turkish opposition leader helps shape unlikely alliance to challenge Erdoğan," *Financial Times*, December 5, 2021.

18 Jonathan Ames, "Boris Johnson plans to let ministers throw out legal rulings," *The Times*, December 6, 2021.

Index